An Introduction
to C. S. Peirce

Charles Sanders Peirce (1839–1914)

An Introduction
to C. S. Peirce

Philosopher, Semiotician,
and Ecstatic Naturalist

Robert S. Corrington

Rowman & Littlefield Publishers, Inc.

ROWMAN & LITTLEFIELD PUBLISHERS, INC.

Published in the United States of America
by Rowman & Littlefield Publishers, Inc.
4720 Boston Way, Lanham, Maryland 20706

Frontispiece: Charles Sanders Peirce, photo courtesy of
The Peirce Edition Project, Indiana University, Indianapolis.

British Cataloging in Publication Information Available

Library of Congress Cataloging-in-Publication Data

Corrington, Robert S., 1950–
An introduction to C.S. Peirce : philosopher, semiotician, and
ecstatic naturalist / Robert S. Corrington.
p.   cm.
Includes bibliographical references and index.
1. Peirce, Charles S. (Charles Sanders), 1839–1914. I. Title.
B945.P44C67 1993   191—dc20   92-40976   CIP

ISBN 0-8476-7813-X (cloth : alk. paper)
ISBN 0-8476-7814-8 (paper : alk. paper)

Printed in the United States of America

The paper used in this publication meets the minimum requirements of
American National Standard for Information Sciences—Permanence of
Paper for Printed Library Materials, ANSI Z39.48–1984.

Dedicated to
Carl R. Hausman
Mentor and Friend

Contents

Textual References

Throughout the text, Peirce's writings are referred to by the standardized notations. They are as follows:

The designation CP abbreviates *The Collected Papers of Charles Sanders Peirce*, Vols. I–VI, eds. Charles Hartshorne and Paul Weiss (Cambridge, Mass.: Harvard University Press, 1931–1935) and Vols. VII–VIII, ed. Arthur W. Burks (same publisher, 1958). The abbreviation followed by volume and paragraph numbers with a period between follows the standard CP reference form. For example: [CP 6.212].

The designation W followed by volume and page numbers with a period in between abbreviates the ongoing *Writings of Charles Sanders Peirce: A Chronological Edition*, Vols. I–IV, ed. Max Fisch (Bloomington: Indiana University Press, 1982–1986). For example: [W 2.232].

The designation SS followed by page numbers abbreviates *Semiotic and Significs: The Correspondence between Charles S. Peirce and Victoria Lady Welby*, ed. Charles S. Hardwick (Bloomington: Indiana University Press, 1977). For example: [SS 27].

The designation MS followed by catalogue number and page number is taken from Richard S. Robin, *Annotated Catalogue of Charles Sanders Peirce* (Amherst: University of Massachusetts Press, 1967), which is a catalogue of the microfilm edition based on the manuscripts housed at Harvard. For example: [MS 318 pp. 00205–00206].

As an aid to teachers, I have also cross-listed references whenever possible with the standard course textbook, *The Essential Peirce: Selected Philosophical Writings* (1867–1893), eds. Nathan Houser and

Christian Kloesel (Bloomington: Indiana University Press, 1992). Volume 2 (1894–1914) is forthcoming. The designation EP 1, followed by a period and page number, will be from *The Essential Peirce*. It will follow the reference from either CP or W, which will always be listed first. For example: [W 2.468 & EP 1.89].

Preface

I first encountered Peirce in an undergraduate seminar on American philosophy in 1972 at Temple University. The professor, Philip P. Wiener, author of *Evolution and the Founders of Pragmatism*, and editor of *Charles S. Peirce: Selected Writings* was tolerant of my youthful Heideggarian leanings, all the while hoping that I would see the light and find my way 'home' to the pragmatists. The subsequent journey over the past twenty years has been a complex one and any 'homecoming' must remain ambiguous. Yet I have been drawn to Peirce again and again, convinced of his sheer categorial power and his insights into the various structures of signification. While writing my dissertation on Josiah Royce, I had occasion to work through Peirce's early papers from a different angle and to reinforce my sense of his fecundity.

The most important period for my Peirce studies came during my years on the faculty of Penn State where I worked closely with Carl Hausman on Peirce's texts. Our jointly taught graduate seminar on American philosophy made it clear to me that any serious work in metaphysics and semiotics must start and end with Peirce's papers. The Semiotic Society of America has also proved to be a rich source for Peirce studies and has given me the opportunity to work with such people as the late David Savan, Vincent Colapietro, John Deely, Thomas Sebeok, John Sheriff, Michael Raposa, Ed Petry, Jr., and Mark Bandas. My colleague and Peirce scholar Peter Ochs has been a creative interlocutor during the past several years. Finally, the Society for the Advancement of American Philosophy has provided a broad context within which to wrestle with Peirce vis-à-vis the other writers of the Golden Age.

I have become persuaded that Peirce needs to be rethought from the standpoint of his pansemioticism and his initial insights into what I have elsewhere called "ecstatic naturalism." The semiotic reading of Peirce now has a firm hold on the scholarly community, and there seems to be no reason to belabor the point. However, it is not clear that his semiotic perspectives have been fully integrated into his metaphysics. Semioticians by and large are not friendly to metaphysics. Of course, they share this attitude with many philosophers who seem to be operating under a rather truncated and polemical understanding of the nature and scope of metaphysical query. Be that as it may, it is important that Peirce's semiotic structures become located under and within his more generic categorial architectonic. This is of a piece with a reappraisal of his naturalism. As will emerge in the text, Peirce's approach to nature is one that seems to vacillate between a bare descriptive naturalism that stresses habit and the growth of law, and an ecstatic naturalism that points to the self-transforming potencies within the heart of nature. I am convinced that Peirce was an important precursor of ecstatic naturalism and that he gained some fundamental insights into the elusive depth of nature. Unfortunately, contemporary understanding of nature is marred by an inability to find either the generic or the ecstatic. This has made it difficult to gauge the utter radicality of Peirce's metaphysics, and of his fragmentary conception of God.

By stressing the correlation of semiotics and metaphysics, and by showing the underlying principles of an implied ecstatic naturalism, I hope to engage in an act of emancipatory reenactment in which Peirce is allowed to speak with a new voice. This can only be done if one honors the textual material and allows *it* to speak. However, the traditional view of Peirce, which comes from earlier decades where positivism or its cousins dominated the stage, has made it difficult to hear what these texts are saying. Of course, it is all too easy to say that one's own reading is the one that truly frees the subject from hermeneutic contamination! This work is undertaken in the spirit of fallibilism, with the hope that Peirce is not compelled to say things that would be uncongenial to his nature, and that the unsaid lying at the heart of his naturalism can emerge with greater force and clarity.

Robert S. Corrington
Drew University

Introduction

Peirce's Melancholy

America's greatest philosopher and semiotician lived a complex, impulsive, and tragic life.[1] Born into the Boston and Cambridge gentry, with family roots reaching back to England and the religious dissenters, Peirce manifested a tendency toward arrogance, selfishness, and abusive behavior toward others. At the same time, he was driven in an unusual degree to create an edifice of thought that he ranked with that of Leibniz and Aristotle. His sheer intellectual and constructive power, combined with a lack of self-control and a lack of sensitivity for the needs of others, especially his two wives, conveys a vivid image of a man who was in many respects out of joint with himself and his times. There is a kind of primal restlessness in Peirce that points to an underlying melancholy, a melancholy that is manifest in his life-long quest for some form of grace and transfiguration. Peirce was aware that he was in need of self-control, and deeply felt the lack of a moral center in his life. Yet his driving ambition kept him from finding this center and consequent means of control in his dealings with others.

His upbringing was unconventional and privileged. His father, Benjamin Peirce (1809–1880), was considered by many to be the greatest applied mathematician in the country. He was one of the dominant forces on the faculty of Harvard and exerted a lasting and, in some respects, tragic influence on Charles. His mother, Sarah Hunt Mills, was the daughter of a prominent senator and her influence on Peirce is often ignored or downplayed. As we will see, there is a strong correlation between his adult behavior and aspects of his maternal relationship. The Peirce family as a whole was unconventional in that it valued independence and freedom above other values, and gener-

1

ally refused to impose any moral guidelines on its children. Peirce had an older and two younger brothers as well as a sister. His older brother, James Mills, went on to a distinguished career in mathematics at Harvard, a career that seemed to mock the younger Charles, whose relations to established universities were always tenuous and fraught with tension and eventually ended with his rejection by each institution with which he was affiliated. Charles brought much pain and embarrassment to his family, but his relatives remained loyal to him throughout his life, including during the period of his painful and highly public divorce from his first wife.

Peirce was born on September 10, 1839, in Cambridge, Massachusetts. He was the second child born to Sarah and Benjamin and quickly became his father's favorite. Because of his father's high social position and his mother's distinguished family history, Peirce was protected from poverty and from social and personal neglect. He was thoroughly indulged and spoiled as a child and quickly came to see himself in inflated terms. The root for this psychic inflation, which plagued Peirce throughout his life, seems to be in his relation to his father, who pushed him toward intellectual feats requiring physical and mental stamina of the highest order. He early on knew of his unusual abilities and fully expected others to acknowledge them. This attitude does not seem to have been discouraged by other family members.

Details of Peirce's early years are scarce. He seems to have had some health problems, probably the standard ones of his period, and to have developed his intellectual gifts at an early age. Among the privileges of his upbringing was that he was surrounded by some of the best minds in New England, and frequently encountered them in his home. Between the members of his extended family, and their circle of accomplished friends, Peirce was exposed to the cutting edges of many major disciplines. Max Fisch describes this unusual situation:

> The full range of the learned professions of law, medicine, divinity, and higher education, as well as business, engineering, politics, and diplomacy, was represented in the immediate family or by near relatives. Literature, the theater, and other arts were cherished if not represented. Benjamin Peirce, Charles's father, was a member of the Saturday Club, along with Emerson, Longfellow, Oliver Wendell Holmes, and other literary figures. The Peirces were devotees of the theater, attended plays in Boston, and entertained actors in their home. Amateur theatricals were a common form of home entertainment.[2]

Peirce retained his love of theater and continued to write and perform plays in his later years. His omnivorous intellectual appetites were first stimulated by this circle of talented people who found their way into the Peirce home. The model of the small society, meeting on a regular basis to discuss the latest advances in a field, remained a congenial one for Peirce, culminating in his activities in the Metaphysical Club of Cambridge in the 1870s. In addition to the literary Saturday Club he had observed, were the Cambridge Scientific Club and the Cambridge Astronomical Club, which usually met every two weeks. The Scientific Club met in Peirce's home and it can be assumed that the young Charles took its deliberations seriously. Much of the intellectual work in American was still done outside of the universities, which were just beginning to take on the task of advanced graduate education based on the German model. Throughout his life, especially during those periods when he was most estranged from the formal academic world, Peirce cherished the ideal of noninstitutional intellectual clubs, whose purpose would be to bring together the most eminent persons devoted to a particular task.

This overwhelming artistic and intellectual presence certainly helped Peirce define his own life task. However, out of this plenitude, one particular element emerged with some force. One of the most cited events of Peirce's youth concerns his discovery of logic. Around his twelfth birthday (1851) Peirce came upon his older brother's Harvard textbooks. One of them was Whatley's *Elements of Logic*. Peirce became so entranced with the text that he worked his way through its entire contents in a matter of days. By his own recollection, this momentous event shaped his subsequent intellectual development to such an extent that he devoted his life to explorations in logic. Almost everything that he wrote had some bearing on logic and its underlying principles. Yet he came to reshape and redefine logic in such a way that it gave birth to the more fundamental discipline of semiotics (the systematic study of all forms and means of signification).[3]

This emphasis on logic was combined with an interest in chemistry, which stemmed from youthful experiments with chemistry equipment. Later he would earn an advanced degree in chemistry, even though he never earned his living as a chemist or as a teacher of chemistry. Yet he used images and concepts from chemistry throughout his writings, and found himself drawn to chemical analogies when he was unfolding his most basic categories and his theories of method.

While he was not an outstanding student in his earlier years, perhaps because of his lack of external discipline and self-control, he was a voracious reader. In particular, he immersed himself in some of the classics of philosophy. The text that became the most important for him was Kant's *Critique of Pure Reason* (1781) which he read in the original German. Under his father's guidance, along with that of one of his young friends, he worked through Kant's deductions again and again until he had practically memorized the work. The spirit of Kant's transcendental strategy remained with Peirce in each stage of his philosophical evolution, giving him a sense of the importance of both logic and architectonic in philosophy. At the same time, Kant's critical philosophy became a model of the precision required of the philosophical researcher. What makes Peirce especially interesting in these early years is his desire to find some kind of language that would bring the worlds of chemistry, logic, and philosophy together. Peirce was determined not to let each discipline fall into some kind of private and incommensurate language game, but rather to show that each enterprise belonged to a much larger and fully coherent structure of intelligibility.

In religious terms, Peirce was brought up in a rather genteel Unitarian environment in which theological disputation played little if any role. The spirituality of his family seemed to be that of his social class; namely, a rather safe and comfortable sense of human perfectibility and evolutionary improvement that had no place for concepts of depravity and sin. Peirce's own theological evolution took him away from his family's Unitarianism toward the liturgically and theologically richer world of trinitarian Episcopalianism.

Peirce remained within the Episcopal church his entire adult life. He was an irregular communicant, but felt that the basic trinitarian structure of the broader Anglican Communion was in tune with his semiotic triads. His first marriage in 1862 to an Episcopalian, Harriet Melusina Fay, known as Zina, was preceded by his official confirmation in the Episcopal Church. His wife Zina reinforced his trinitarian speculations by her own reflections on the masculine and feminine roles within the trinity, assigning the feminine role to the Spirit.

As noted, Peirce was an indifferent student. His high school record is without distinction, finding him near the bottom or middle of his class year after year. His undergraduate years at Harvard were not much better, although he did do exemplary work in the field of chemistry. During his sophomore year he seems to have developed a problem that plagued him throughout his life, a tendency to abuse alcohol. He was frequently reprimanded by the faculty for his drunkenness and his tardy attendance at lectures. There is strong evidence from a variety of sources that his drinking problem later caused him difficulties in his personal and professional relations. This tendency was further exacerbated by his seeming inability to practice sexual fidelity to either of his wives.

Brent gives one clear reason as to the urgency of Peirce's drinking. He seems to have suffered from a disease known as facial neuralgia (now known as trigeminal neuralgia), which causes extreme pain in the nerves of the face. In Peirce's time there was no cure for this disease, which can now be treated by surgery. His father seems to have been a fellow sufferer and they both learned to administer anesthesia themselves. Peirce later developed a dependence on opium, morphine, and cocaine (all of which could be obtained legally during this period). Brent speculates that some of Peirce's violent behavior can be traced to the pain caused by this illness, combined with the effects of the various substances used to dull the pain. As we will see much later in the text, Peirce had a fascination for the effects of anesthesia on human culture and its understanding of pain and evil.

The picture that has emerged at this point is that of a brilliant but erratic young man, fully aware of his genius and totally unwilling to make compromises with the reigning bourgeois morality of his class. He also manifested many of the prejudices of his peers, especially a tendency to ignore the suffering of African Americans and the Irish immigrants who performed most of the manual labor in the Boston area. His stand on abolition was lukewarm at best, and callous at its worst. Yet this prejudice was fairly common in his immediate family.

While continuing his studies at Harvard, Peirce, like many young students of the sciences, went on a summer (1858) research expedition with the U.S. Coast and Geodetic Survey. This event proved to be momentous for Peirce's life because it was the beginning of a three-decade-long involvement with this official branch of the U.S. government. It provided him with a salary during his darkest years when academic employment was not available to him, and it also gave him the means for extensive travel throughout Europe on official Survey business. As we will see, it also became the source of deep public humiliation when he was charged by the Allison Commission with misusing Survey funds.

In 1859 Peirce, while surveying off of the coast of Louisiana, read Darwin's *Origin of Species* and quickly recognized its revolutionary implications, some of which he attempted to soften in his later (ca. 1880s) writings. He was also continuing his philosophical research. Under his father's guidance he read Hegel, Hobbes, Mill, Locke, and works in logic and moral theory. His ability to cross over the boundaries from science to technical philosophy (often reading the works in the original Greek, Latin, French, or German), proved invaluable to his later mature system in which elements from chemistry or physics would converge with elements from the history of philosophy. He developed a strong interest in medieval philosophy, with particular attention to John Duns Scotus (ca. 1265/1266–1308) and his brand of realism.

The Civil War of 1860 found Peirce unwilling to become enlisted or drafted into the Union Army. He wrote a letter to Superintendent Bache of the Survey asking if he could get a deferment from the draft. He was freed from the obligation of military service, as were many sons of the Boston Brahmin class, and avoids almost all mention of the Civil War from then on. He comments that "I should feel that I was ended and thrown away for nothing."[4] One can certainly argue that the gain for philosophy outweighed the minimal gain that would have been attained for the Union army. Yet one can also surmise that Peirce had little time or energy for the public good, however defined, and that his life focus was centered around his own intellectual projects.

Without a war to bother him, and with a new marriage to nurture, Peirce devoted his energies to his studies at Harvard, where he was doing advanced work in chemistry at the new Lawrence Scientific School. In the middle of the Civil War (1863) he graduated *summa cum laude* from Lawrence. He continued to work for the Survey while lecturing at Harvard on logic and philosophy. He was not a member of the faculty but gave these lectures (1866) in the format of a semipublic forum. It is clear that Peirce spent the late 1860s in hopes of getting a regular academic appointment at Harvard. President Eliot was exploring the possibility of creating a graduate school at Harvard, and lecture series such as these helped to pave the way. A graduate school was created in 1890. This practice of giving lecture series is one that Peirce continued throughout his career, culminating in his 1903 lectures on pragmatism at Harvard. The former set of lectures (1866) were fairly well received, which is remarkable given that Peirce was in his mid-twenties at the time. He lived with Zina, first in his family home, and later in small houses in Cambridge.

Zina, three years older than Charles, came to the marriage with strong views on women's rights and on the redistribution of house-work and domestic chores. As an early feminist, she wrote articles and founded the Cooperative Housekeeping Society of Cambridge for the betterment of the treatment of women. Her early successes may have nettled Charles and, given his somewhat backward attitude to-ward women, brought out strong tensions within the marriage. Peirce's family was sometimes less than charitable toward Zina, and took his side when the separation and subsequent divorce took place.

One of the reasons for his marital difficulties was his constant travel to Europe on Survey business. During the several month-long tours he conducted research, in particular with swinging pendulums so as to gain insight into the nature and manifestation of gravity. He also lived beyond his means and insisted on always having the best food and accommodations. He developed into a "dandy," insisting on dressing in an elegant and highly refined manner, often presenting himself as a member of the aristocracy (a tendency that continued into his declining years when he set himself up as a kind of country gentleman). His attraction to and for women, combined with his abuse of alcohol and drugs, made it impossible for him to sustain a sound marriage to someone who had strong views about the emancipation of women, both within and without marriage.

Lest this picture become too dark, it is important to remember that in spite of his moral failings, Peirce continued to work at a prodigious pace, advancing knowledge of nature and its logical and semiotic features. He could put in strenuous days at his scientific research, often taking over for his incompetent subordinates and, in effect, doing the work of several individuals. He was very well regarded in scientific circles and published many articles detailing his work. That his family remained loyal to him even during his most dismal personal and professional failures, indicates that he had some personality traits that were highly compelling to others. He was a brilliant conversationalist and storyteller, often reveling in what he referred to as a Rabelaisian sense of humor. He had a capacious appetite for the world and its gifts, if lacking in the kind of self-control necessary for shaping his desires.

As Max Fisch points out, 1867 was an important year for Peirce.[5] He was appointed to the status of "Assistant" at the Survey. His father had assumed the role of superintendent, thus paving the way for Peirce's promotion. Without the protection of his well-connected father, Peirce would have had a far more difficult time making his way in the world. During this watershed year he was also appointed to the post of assistant of the Harvard Observatory. His dual positions brought him more directly into the world of international science. He was able to travel extensively in Europe doing research on solar eclipses. He continued to publish advanced technical papers in chemistry, astronomy, logic, and mathematics, some of which he presented before learned societies.

By 1868 Peirce was ready to publish philosophical papers. His earlier work had been in science and logic and he was ready to start drawing some of the implications of his foundational reflections. The *Journal of Speculative Philosophy* was friendly to his ideas and provided him with a national forum for his work. This journal, the first of its kind in the United States, was published by the Hegelian W. T. Harris.[6] In his correspondence with Harris, Peirce discusses the issues of nominalism and realism and locates his own perspective within the history of this debate. As we will see in subsequent chapters, Peirce at that time was struggling away from nominalism toward his unique form of Scholastic realism, which affirms the full reality of general traits.

In 1872 Peirce returned from his European study of the solar eclipse. He realized that his Harvard position with the Observatory was tenuous, owing to the growing displeasure of President Eliot (who forever after blocked all attempts to get Peirce a permanent Harvard professorship). He resigned from the Observatory and devoted his professional energy to the Coast Survey. He moved to Washington with Zina and commuted back and forth to Cambridge, conducting pendulum experiments in a cave in Massachusetts. It is in this period that Peirce founded the famous Cambridge Metaphysical Club. While Peirce tended to romanticize the importance of this club in his later years, it is clear that it was an important gathering of minds during the beginning of the so-called "Golden Age" of American philosophy. The origin of pragmatism is attributed to the Metaphysical Club, who had among its members such thinkers as William James, Chauncy Wright, John Fiske, Nicholas St. John Green, and Oliver Wendell Holmes, Jr. Such clubs were quite common in the Boston area in the 1870s and Peirce's club was certainly no exception. It should also be remembered that Zina was highly active in creating societies for women's emancipation along similar lines.

The discussions of the club were free ranging, covering a variety of topics from evolutionary theory to political economy to psychology, to more traditional metaphysical issues. The participants came from several walks of life and none were what would today be called 'professional' philosophers.[7] The club had a brief tenure, from 1872 to 1875, but continues to occupy a special, if slightly inflated, place in the history of American philosophy.

Peirce left again for Europe in 1875, thus effectively ending the brief reign of the Metaphysical Club. He conducted numerous pendulum-swinging experiments, designed to measure the shape of the earth, and interacted with many of the leading scientists of the Continent. This period turned out to be especially troubling for Peirce. His wife Zina, fed up with his drinking, sensuality, and possible physical abuse, left him and returned home to the United States. He also had serious financial difficulties, stemming in some measure from his inability to understand the funding procedures of the Coast Survey. He remained out of touch with his superiors and ended up with more debts than credit.

In 1876 Peirce seems to have suffered a nervous breakdown, clearly caused in no small measure by his marital and financial difficulties. Brent paints a stark picture of Peirce during this period:

> In May 1876, Peirce suffered a serious nervous collapse, the principle symptom of which was temporary but complete paralysis. The collapse, taken together with his irresponsible performance [for the Survey], his exaggerated sensibility, and his tendency to break down under strain, indicates that Peirce had suffered an attack of conversion hysteria (also called dissociative reaction), of which the major symptom is complete paralysis. . . . In giving emotional stress as the reason for his mental collapse, Peirce underlined his own awareness of his lifelong mental instability. His family, on second thought, blamed excessive drinking for his breakdown, an accusation which Peirce himself denied categorically.[8]

Peirce was compelled to return to the United States by the end of the summer. The Survey forgave him his financial excesses, citing his experimental successes as warrant for keeping him a member of the staff. A divorce was not immediate for Peirce, and the long separation and delay in the final divorce decree caused further problems when Peirce established a new relationship before he had completely divorced Zina. While this would not be an issue for many today, in the 1870s and 1880s, such a situation could have direct professional implications.

Peirce, did, of course, have his supporters, none being more important than William James. It is often noted that James had a genius for friendship, and that he often took eccentric students and friends under his wing. His generous spirit allowed him to acknowledge and honor genius in others, and to give them room for their various complex and antisocial behaviors. He remained committed to Peirce throughout his life and tried on several occasions to soften President Eliot's heart so that he could find some place for him at Harvard. During his ill-fated 1875–1876 year in Europe, Peirce spent time with William's brother, the novelist Henry James, and, while they did not prove to be great companions, they did manage to share a number of ideas while they visited with each other in Paris. William's loyalty to Peirce extended beyond his efforts to secure him employment, and culminated in the famous "Peirce Fund," which James created to raise money for the ailing and unemployed Peirce (during his last years in Milford, Pennsylvania).

It should also be noted that Peirce was not, contrary to later legend, an obscure lonely philosopher/scientist forced to make his way in the world without recognition. During his lifetime he was quite famous and interacted with many of the prominent artistic, scientific, and political figures of his day. He established important contacts in Washington, calling upon them in times of need, and served in several of the most important scientific societies of the time. Again we are drawn to the curious fact that in spite of his crippling personal defects, Peirce's charismatic and intellectual power kept him afloat and won him many influential friends in high places. Of course, his father's position as superintendent of the Coast Survey protected him from his own folly. Yet, as his 1876 nervous breakdown attests, his own unconscious moved in powerful ways to show him the full scope and meaning of his destructive behavior. His curious inability to listen to the meaning of his own psychogenic illnesses stands in stark contrast to his scientific and philosophic insights.

In the period 1877–1878 Peirce continued his pendulum experiments, in New Jersey and New England. He also started to entertain the offer of a position with Johns Hopkins University. He was under consideration by the university because of a positive recommendation from William James. Johns Hopkins was interested in starting America's first graduate school and was looking for a distinguished faculty to staff it. It is also during this period, one year after his separation from Zina, that Peirce is seen in and around Cambridge with a mysterious woman named Madame Pourtalai. Given the mores of the time, his open relationship with another woman caused Cambridge society to ostracize him. By now his reputation was beyond repair at Harvard and the Johns Hopkins possibility must have been especially attractive.

Peirce started his teaching career at Johns Hopkins in 1879. He retained his position with the Coast Survey because of the tentative nature of his academic appointment, and because of his low salary. He needed both incomes to keep his head above water, especially given his tendency to overextend himself financially. The Hopkins appointment started with great hopes on both sides. Peirce fully expected to be given a more permanent position after a brief period establishing himself as a lecturer. Yet tensions emerged right from the start. Peirce set up his pendulum experiments in York, Pennsylvania and commuted from Baltimore on a regular basis. He often missed classes because of his other responsibilities, and complained to President Gilman of his difficulties. The result of this dual life is that Peirce suffered another nervous breakdown at the end of the fall term. He feared insanity. His relations with Juliette, who alternately went by the last names of Pourtalai or Froissy, were less than harmonious. Not only did they both endure the strain of living outside of the legalities of marriage, but Peirce seems to have been an abusive companion who may have been unfaithful to Juliette from early on in their relationship.

Johns Hopkins was in the process of establishing the first graduate program in the United States, and Gilman had the courage to bring in some of the best minds in the country. He was actually fairly tolerant of Peirce's lapses and reappointed him for several years in a row even though Peirce did not fulfill his contractual obligations with real consistency. Peirce was a difficult and often obscure lecturer, although he soon found an ardent group of followers, with whom he published a collection of logical essays. John Dewey was among his students, although Dewey was not too taken with Peirce at that time (reflecting in later years that he had learned more than he had realized at the time). Several of Peirce's students from the Hopkins years remained loyal to him throughout his life.

Little is known about Juliette. She fabricated several stories about herself, always involving royalty and intrigue. Some thought that she was little more than a courtesan. Peirce's family was less than enthusiastic about her, even while remaining strangely tolerant of Peirce's behavior. Juliette probably had French origins; whether from royalty is anyone's guess. She stayed with Peirce until his death in 1914, although she complained to Peirce's relatives that he abused her, both physically and psychologically. It is always difficult to gauge the accuracy of these stories, but the picture that emerges of Peirce's second marriage, which took place in 1883 (six days after his final divorce decree from Zina was handed down), is that of a deeply complex relationship.[9] The complexity stems from Peirce's great dependence on Juliette, combined with a callous indifference to her feelings.

The worst thing that happened to Peirce during this period was the death of his father in 1880. The implications were immediate. Peirce lost his protector in the Coast Survey, and he suffered a more attenuated, if less dramatic, mental collapse. Nathan Houser sheds light on this crucial event:

> The full impact on Charles of his father's final illness and death can only be guessed at. The emotional toll is manifested in his impulsive decision to quit logic and philosophy and sell his library, a decision he soon came to regret, and in a general malaise that settled over him. Upon returning to Baltimore after the funeral in Cambridge, Peirce

wrote his mother in late October: "I have had a fog resting on my spirit ever since I have been back, so that I have not been working very successfully but I hope it is clearing up. It has been just like a steamer forging through a fog."[10]

The 41-year-old Peirce now had to rethink his life plan and to re-evaluate his relations with both Johns Hopkins and the Coast Survey. And he had to do this in the midst of his social and professional problems associated with his open relationship to Juliette when he was technically still married to Zina. What is striking is that Peirce continued to write prodigiously during this period and to make some of his most important insights. His writing focused on issues in mathematics, the logic of relatives, his pendulum experiments, and, as always, issues in logic. He paid less attention to strictly philosophical topics, while gathering insights that would flower in some of his most important papers of the 1880s.

There has been much scholarly speculation as to why Peirce ultimately failed at Johns Hopkins (his only academic appointment). It is clear that he did something that deeply offended President Gilman. It is possible that his open relations with Juliette played some role. It is also possible that Peirce's continual relations with the Coast Survey, which often took him away from campus, alienated Gilman, who saw the role of the professor as that of a moral guide of youth. Given Peirce's lack of moral self-control, it is unlikely that anyone would have seen him in the role of moral exemplar. His brilliance was fully acknowledged by the faculty of Johns Hopkins and there is some evidence that the faculty moved very carefully in removing Peirce, even going so far as to institute structural changes that would make it appear as if Peirce was removed because of general budgetary considerations rather than moral turpitude. Be that as it may, Gilman developed an antipathy to Peirce that never abated. So by 1884, when Peirce was relieved of his duties as an instructor of logic, he had alienated two of the most powerful university presidents in the country. He had no prospects at either Harvard or Johns Hopkins. Unfortunately, his fortunes at the Coast Survey were also taking a turn for the worse.

Peirce continued to work with great intensity for the Survey. He conducted his gravity experiments up and down the east coast, from Maine to Florida, as well as setting up pendulum stations in Virginia, Pennsylvania, and at Stevens Institute in Hoboken, New Jersey. His published papers were always of the highest order and continued to win him praise from the international scientific community. All of this would seem to bode well for Peirce, giving him a professional home that would secure him against the vagaries of the more volatile and politically charged academic world. Yet the world of politics soon invaded the Survey. With the death of his father, and the subsequent death of his other supporter in the Survey, Superintendent Patterson, Peirce was left without any protection from above.

As noted by Houser, the Coast and Geodetic Survey originally had a strong research mission. It served as a kind of scientific society, living at government expense outside of the university system. Its staff members were given a fairly free reign to conduct experiments as they saw fit, always allowing for foundational and time-consuming types of research, rather than more limited and narrowly practical pursuits. By the mid-1880s, however, the Survey came under great governmental and public scrutiny and started to shift away from pure research to more immediately practical concerns. One of the reasons for this shift can be traced to the fact that subsequent superintendents were not scientists but political appointees, often bowing to pressure from a Congress with less patience for the more flamboyant attitudes (not to mention expense accounts) of the past decades. Peirce was thus caught up in political changes for which he was ill prepared.

In the summer of 1885, public attention was drawn to the Survey. The so-called "Allison Commission" started an investigation designed to see if the Survey had misused government funds. One superintendent was fired and another, from the Internal Revenue Bureau, was put in his place. Brent quotes from newspaper accounts of the period that give some indication of how serious these charges became. He cites a July 26 article by the *Washington Post* that, while humorous, gives a clue as to the emerging public sentiment:

> The Treasury officials . . . had come to regard the [Coast Survey] as a supercilious little aristocracy of scientists, who considered themselves an entirely self-contained and independent organization, accountable only to Congress, the appropriations committees of which they could always control by bringing the influence of college professors to bear on them, and representing that science would suffer if the bureau was crippled by common restrictions or [ruled by other than] its own scientific heads. The men at the head of the service are a close set of old barnacles who have always tried to have things their own way, without any checks, supervisions or interferences; and having succeeded so long they are impatient under the present movement of reform.[11]

Charges and countercharges continued to swirl in and out of the press for years. Peirce was cited as one of the worst offenders. He was never indicted or faced with imprisonment or fine, but his reputation never recovered from the combined effects of his dismissal at Johns Hopkins and the congressional investigation of the Survey. He was allowed to continue with the Survey for a few more years, but he fully realized that the writing was on the wall and that he had to look elsewhere for other prospects.

In the late 1880s Peirce continued to hope for some kind of academic appointment. In each case, his hopes were dashed because of the intervention of Eliot and/or Gilman. It should be remembered that the academic world of the late nineteenth century was much more intimate and confined than today and that the word of a university president could affect one's career throughout the country. Peirce was rejected by the very Brahmin class that had helped to create some of his most idiosyncratic personality traits. Since he was cut off from regular academic work, he was forced to work on the fringes of the academy. As noted, he gave important lecture series whenever he could. Among them were the earlier and later Lowell lectures in Boston (1865, 1892, 1903), where he was able to present some of his work in logic. During this period Peirce also developed relations with several journals, chief among them being *The Nation* where he became one of their most important book reviewers. Peirce was paid $40 per review, which gave him income and made it possible for him to build up his library. Without this important relation with *The Nation* Peirce might have been cut off from some of the major developments in his field.

In 1887 Peirce and Juliette made the momentous decision to buy some property in the rural area of Milford, Pennsylvania. They picked Milford for several reasons. It was an inexpensive place to live, yet it provided access to New York City via a two-hour train and ferry ride. Situated in the corner where New Jersey, Pennsylvania, and New York meet, Milford became the summer residence for some of the New York gentry. The Peirces quickly established relations with the Pinchot family and entered into their social life. This relation with the Pinchot family proved to be a salvific one for the Peirces because it gave them a social outlet and, in later years, provided them with some minimal social and financial protection when they were suffering from dire poverty.

Of course, Peirce continued to live beyond his means. In Juliette's name, he also purchased a house and outbuildings on the Milford property, continuing to add acreage whenever he could (his initial capital came from an inheritance). The house was a modest one, but Peirce quickly decided to expand it and to turn it into some kind of summer resort where the New York gentry would come for his projected summer philosophical salon. These plans, like so many others, never came to fruition. He contracted with local workers for numerous additions and soon ran into difficulties when they demanded payment. He named the house "Arisbe" after a Greek island (reputed to be the source of early Greek metaphysics) that he had visited during one of his Survey trips.[12] During this period, they also kept their apartment in New York City, spending a great deal of time commuting between both worlds.

Peirce's dream of creating a philosophic center in Milford ran parallel to his dream of finding a wealthy sponsor for his work. He likened himself to Aristotle in need of an Alexander to facilitate his research. Needless to say, no such Alexander emerged, even though Peirce courted several candidates during this period. He knew that his days with the Survey would soon be over and that he would be forced to find his way through writing and, if possible, lecturing. By making the move to Milford, Peirce tied himself to a house and acreage that would hang about his neck like the proverbial albatross. Yet he entered into the post–1887 period with high confidence, perhaps heightened by his use of drugs, that he would at long last find his proper place in the world as the Aristotle of the gentry.

Meanwhile, the new director of the Survey demanded from Peirce the results of his innumerable pendulum experiments. Peirce continued to delay, even after making numerous promises to comply. This final act of seeming defiance was the last straw and Peirce was forced to resign from the Survey at the end of 1891. During his just over thirty years with the Survey, he had made his international scientific reputation and had provided income for himself and both of his wives. His erratic and dandified behavior not withstanding, his contributions to gravity and photometric research are still recognized as among the most important of the nineteenth century. This final break also represented a break with his past, a past made possible by his father and the world of Cambridge gentility. The move to Milford thus represented a deep turning point in Peirce's life. On one level, he must have sensed that he would never again be part of the public arena and that he would forever be an Aristotle in exile.

In a beautifully poetic passage, Brent gives a striking portrayal of the decade now emerging for Peirce:

> The decade of Peirce's life, roughly 1890–1900, . . . is chaotic in the extreme. Its chronology is hectic and complex. I imagine him as a confidence man and prestidigitator—a frenzied juggler elegantly dressed in harlequin costume, on a flimsy but deceptively substantial stage of his own devising, gambling everything on keeping too many improb-

ably seductive objects in flight, while trying to decide which one to snare. At the end, he stands there in tatters, surrounded by the melancholy debris of his life, contrite and apologetic, asking our—and especially his dearest friend William James'—indulgence. But all the while, this poor fool, behind the scenes and between the acts, has been building piece by piece the armature of a most marvelously intricate universe, so beautiful it transfigures him amidst the wreck of his afflictions, and we gratefully see the signs around us with new eyes.[13]

This combination of melancholy trickster and architectonic genius remains the dominant one for the rest of Peirce's life. His perennial optimism forbade him to see himself and his life in realistic terms, thus fueling one absurd speculative financial or publishing scheme after another. He continued to reach out to a world that had grown impatient or disgusted with him, always hoping that he could find the right avenue for the expression of his unique vision. His interests shifted more and more to cosmology and general philosophy as he probed into the most basic features of the world.

Some have argued that by the 1890s Peirce had lost his critical and logical edge, a situation exacerbated by his use of drugs. I am persuaded that these judgments are too harsh and that some of Peirce's finest and most evocative work lay ahead of him. In his book-lined study on the first floor of his Milford home, Peirce wrote thousands of pages in foundational philosophy that have become normative for much subsequent work on the structure of law, chance, creativity, and the nature of the self. He continued to find friendly journal editors, who were more than willing to overlook his immense personal flaws in order to give him his well-deserved platform. The picture that emerges is that of an intellectual ferocity that remains unabated, manifest in an almost manic writing that, in spite of illness, poverty, and legal problems, sustained Peirce through his darkest hours.

As noted, the Peirces kept their apartment in New York City (at 109 East Fifteenth Street). During this last decade of the nineteenth century they commuted back and forth, spending long months in the city. Peirce was a member of the elitist Century Club, where he would go to hold forth on innumerable topics. He also met some of the more flamboyant members of the entrepreneurial class at the club and got talked into several bizarre financial schemes. Interestingly, Peirce invented some mechanical and chemical processes that later proved to be of value, but he always seemed to just miss out on reaping any financial reward from his speculations and inventions. Peirce continued to write reviews and to beg money from friends and editors. He was often so poor that he had to steal food from the club in order to survive.

Back in Milford, things continued to deteriorate. Peirce was often in court defending himself against liens against his property for work done that was not paid for. In addition, he was sued more than once by his servants or staff for physical abuse. While he was often charming and genial, he had a tendency to explode at those people who were financially dependent upon him. Brent cites several such cases:

> . . . Peirce's servant Laura Walters charged him with committing aggravated assault and battery two months earlier and sued him for damages. He was freed on $300 bail. This was not the first such case in which Peirce had been involved. His lifelong proclivity toward violent behavior was greatly intensified by the repeated defeats and ignominies of his life and by the constant and inescapable burden of Juliette's illnesses. The miseries and afflictions he endured sometimes caused him to explode in violent fury, especially toward his servants and workmen. Fortunately, such eruptions were usually limited to sarcasm and other verbal attacks. On some occasions, however, he became physically violent. In July 1889, he had pleaded guilty to one count of assault upon his servant Marie Blanc. Five years before that, in Baltimore, Peirce had been involved with a battle with his cook.[14]

Juliette was in continual poor health, often requiring treatment that Peirce could not afford. She underwent surgery and improved somewhat, but remained in a fragile state for the rest of her life. Peirce must have felt an enormous burden of guilt for his many personal and professional failures. If his psychic inflation pushed this guilt into the background, it certainly surfaced in his nervous breakdowns and other psychogenic illnesses. Of course, Peirce's poverty continued to grind away at his physical well being so that his physical stamina became undermined.

The legal battles in Milford became so bad that the Peirces had to flee to New York to be out of the jurisdiction of the Pennsylvania police authorities. He was subject to arrest should he appear in Milford. This situation forced him to return incognito from New York. The house almost fell to ruin during this period of abandonment. It would have been sold by the bank had there been any buyers. A softening of the legal situation made it possible for the Peirces to return to Milford in 1898 after an absence of several years.

The New York period was marked by extreme poverty. The Peirces lost their brownstone on East Fifteenth Street and Charles was often forced to wander the streets in search of food and proper housing. They found much smaller rooms and accommodations, but these were often only temporary. Given the general psychic law of compensation, it is easy to seen why Peirce was drawn to get-rich-quick schemes and why he continued to hunt for his Alexander the Great who would recognize his genius and set him up in proper style. It is also easy to see Peirce's writings as forms of compensation for his physical and emotional misery. These arguments can often be taken too far, yet there is certainly an intriguing correlation between his belief in evolutionary love and his wretched life on the streets of an inhospitable New York.

As always, William James, the recipient of several heart-rending letters from Peirce during this period, came to the rescue with some funds and with the offer of a lecture series. Harvard was not yet ready for him so that he had to give these lectures (1898) in a private home in Cambridge. It is also during this period that James is making the concept of pragmatism widely known. Peirce must have felt a strong ambivalence at seeing his creation making its way in the world, even as his own prospects were in decline. As we will see in the next chapter, Peirce was deeply concerned with separating his version of pragmatism, termed by him "pragmaticism," from James's more dyadic and voluntaristic version. While James fully acknowledges his indebtedness to Peirce, it is clear that Peirce's contributions took a back seat in the public eye.

Brent points to an irony in the period of the 1890s. Peirce is engaged in all kinds of speculation on the stock market, etc., even while coming out in print against what he called "greed philosophy." He wanted to manipulate the capitalistic system toward his own ends, always remaining insensitive to the needs of the working classes (and races), while placing the Christian doctrine of love in conflict with social Darwinism. One could conclude that this tension manifests a profound hypocrisy in Peirce, or, being more charitable, that he came to recognize the moral bankruptcy of social Darwinism. It is clear that his ethical theory, insofar as he had one as a separate field of inquiry, shifts from a focus on self-control toward an analysis of sympathy. He even goes so far (as we will see in chapter 4) to speak of a kind of group mind that is held together by the bonds of sympathetic feeling. Is his belief in sympathetic love a hypocritical ploy to win sympathy or does it represent a breakthrough in his vision, a breakthrough made urgent by his own suffering and incomplete identification with the downtrodden? Brent points to both possibilities and I suspect that this is precisely where the issue stands. Peirce was forced to live among the poor of the city and to relinquish some of his Brahmin aspirations.

By the end of the century, Peirce could look back at his sixty years of life and see a deeply ambiguous picture. He had attained the height of international fame as a researcher and had spawned one of the most significant philosophical movements of his time. He had traveled extensively, meeting with some of the finest minds and spirits of the century. He had been married twice and had experienced great upheaval in his social and professional relations. He had been dismissed from his sole academic post and come under congressional investigation for his role in the Coast Survey. He had narrowly escaped the Civil War and had managed to confine his life to his own scholarly interests. At the same time, he had battled against the extreme pain of facial neuralgia and had resorted to drugs and alcohol to dull the pain that often paralyzed him for days. He had raged against the world and some of the people in it, even while struggling to find a center of grace that would transfigure his life once and for all. Peirce's interest in religion was deeply personal, yet he had the intellectual boldness to explore some of the implications of his religiosity in cosmology and metaphysics. The man that Brent calls the "prestidigitator" created many illusions, the most important being about his own life. Yet he also worked courageously to reshape the very fabric of thought so that a more liberating and future-oriented perspective could find its place in the world.

In many respects, the final fourteen years of Peirce's life are the saddest of all. After his final (1898) return to Arisbe in the isolated area of Pike County, Pennsylvania, Peirce knew that his public years were over. He at long last gave up on some of his more flamboyant financial ventures, even while turning his attention to some rather dramatic philosophical schemes. The Peirces were barely able to keep their house in livable condition, and were frequently helped out by neighbors and friends. Peirce's old problem of facial neuralgia returned with a vengeance, often leaving him prostrate and confused for days. On top of that, Juliette continued to have problems with her lungs, due to recurrent tuberculosis. Yet in spite of hardships that might crush the spirit, Peirce continued to write at an astonishing pace, outlining a vast cosmology and logical theory that he thought would forever transform the face of Western philosophy.

In 1902 he applied for a special fund dispensed by the Carnegie Foundation. The purpose of the fund was to help thinkers develop and publish their ideas. Peirce's application for a grant gave him an opportunity to pull together the many aspects of his vision into a coherent pattern. He made the grand proposal of producing a thirty-six volume work that would deal with such topics as the classification of the sciences, simple and advanced mathematics, the categories (i.e., firstness, secondness, and thirdness), the history of philosophy, the ethical foundations of logic and the aesthetic foundations of ethics, metaphysics, chance and uniformity, and the nature of time and space. Most of the committee members were deeply impressed with this proposal and knew a great deal about Peirce's achievements in the past. However, his reputation for failing to complete work, harking back to his days with the Coast Survey, finally persuaded the board to deny Peirce any funds. Even with the positive intervention of William James and Theodore Roosevelt, Peirce was not able to escape the stigma of his past derelictions, real or imagined.

The Carnegie application was one of several such publishing schemes that Peirce entertained during his last productive years. He was constantly on the lookout for sponsors so that he could have the financial freedom to build his great system. It must be remembered that he earned his living by writing book reviews and by translating articles for journals. A Carnegie grant, or its equivalent, would have freed him from these more mundane tasks so that he could devote his dwindling energies to the major mission of his life. What is striking is that Peirce toiled away on his general system even when the outside world rejected his proposals again and again.

As noted, Peirce gave an important lecture series in 1903 on pragmatism at Harvard. The series, which will be discussed later in the text, drew a fair amount of attention even if its style and content frustrated many listeners. James was confused by what Peirce had to say, although Santayana found some congenial things in Peirce's analysis of the three categories. Unfortunately, Royce, who probably understood what Peirce was about better than anyone at the time, was out of town during the series. It should be noted that Royce developed his own logical system (system Sigma) as a way of undergirding his own version of what he called "absolute pragmatism." In any event, this lecture series reminded some people of the sheer intellectual power and boldness of Peirce at a time when he was beginning his slow and painful fade-out from the public world.

In 1909 Peirce discovered that he had cancer. He treated himself with the same drugs that he used to deal with his facial neuralgia. His money was now being supplied by others as his long-term book-reviewing relationship with *The Nation* ended with the retirement of its editor. Winters were especially hard on the Peirces as they could scarce afford fuel for their large house. Peirce continued, when possible, to visit with friends in Cambridge. One especially poignant story involves a student of James's by the name of Henry Alsberg. Brent quotes from Alsberg's 1907 account:

One day, the landlady asked him to come into one of the rooms to see an old gentleman, who had been ill and was very likely dying. When he went in, he saw a sick, worn body of a man obviously suffering from under-nourishment and lack of care; and when he asked his name, he was told, "Charles Peirce." In a wild confusion of emotions, Alsberg and a friend went to find William James, and caught him coming out of class. James listened to their story. "Why," he said, his face changing, "I owe him everything!" and swung them into a cab to call for Peirce and take him home, to the house he had left with the few cents he had in his pocket.[15]

For the rest of his life, James (who died in 1910) continued to support Peirce in any way possible. James had health problems of his own (angina) but at least had the support of a large circle of friends, not to mention a comfortable income. Others came to the rescue and sent money to Milford on a regular basis.

During this period Peirce rethought some of the foundational issues in logic and semiotic and continued to refine his categories. The work of his last years remains of a high quality and moves forward into new aspects of semiosis. With his health declining year by year, and with his continual financial problems, Peirce still insisted that his work was destined to transform thought. He became more and more unable to do even the simplest chores around Arisbe and gradually succumbed to the cancer that had been diagnosed in 1909. On the evening of Sunday, April 19, 1914, Peirce died in his bed. His remains were cremated and remained in Juliette's possession until her death in 1934. Juliette stayed in the house, which fell into ruin and decay, corresponding with her dwindling circle of friends. After Peirce's death, she sold his papers to Harvard where, under the initial stewardship of Royce, they remained unpublished until the 1930s when some of them saw their way into print in an eight-volume edition.

By way of conclusion, we may be permitted some reflections on the inner meaning of Peirce's melancholy existence. The many tensions within his personality stem from a common root that goes back to his intimate family relations. His relationship with his father has been the focus of almost all of the biographical studies to date. Little has been said about his relationship with his mother, or more particularly, to the maternal structures of his own psyche and their correlation with the men and woman in his life. Taking some cues from the work of the French psychoanalyst Julia Kristeva, who has probed into the relation between literary creativity and the quest for the maternal, we can see that Peirce was caught in a painful dialectic that says as much about the human process as it does about his own unique trajectory.

The source of Peirce's intense creative energy lies, according to an argument of this type, in his severed but desired relationship with his mother. This is not a reiteration of the Oedipal drama, although such components are certainly present, so much as a statement about the curious dynamism and sheer energy behind the quest for a new and generic language. Peirce early on knew of his unusual linguistic and conceptual gifts. He entered into the paternal world of Cambridge culture by displaying these gifts at every possible opportunity. His facility with philosophy, science, and the various disciplines of his time quickly translated into an inflated picture of his own worth and severed him from the presemiotic and prelinguistic sources that stem, according to Kristeva, from the world of the mother. His decision for the paternal as against the maternal was never negotiated fully, and his ambivalence toward his two wives, alternating between abuse and utter dependency, manifests his bindingness to a prelinguistic realm that was forever beyond his reach.

Kristeva argues that the use of language is only possible because of a prior betrayal of the maternal. The minute we enter into the realm of public semiosis, we leave behind the ejective and creative ground of signification. For some, her correlation of the maternal with the presymbolic and the paternal with the fully symbolic, might seem like a misuse of gender designations. Even if this should turn out to be the case, the underlying and implied ontology still holds true. Peirce was a master of the art of advanced forms of signification. He could enter into several distinctive semiotic systems and codes with great ease and always find pathways for connecting them. Yet in doing so he pulled further and further away from the ground of signification, perhaps originally presented to him by his mother.

I am persuaded that Peirce remained haunted throughout his life by a sense of melancholy loss, a loss felt on the fringes of all of his daring analyses of the basic structures of the world. His attempts to delineate the domain of firstness, both phenomenologically and cosmologically, are responses to the lost realm that his paternal affiliation drove him from. His obsession with continuity in all of its guises stems, at least in part, from his concern with finding a presymbolic domain of connectedness in which the various fissures of his being could be transfigured.

Brent makes a great deal of Peirce's sense of identification with his fellow dandy Charles Baudelaire. Both figures were trapped in a world of signs and signification. Both lived beyond their means and were compelled to engage in multiple relations with women. Both dressed in the narcissistic style of the dandy, thereby drawing even further attention to themselves. Brent correlates this dandyism with Peirce's lifelong obsession with the concept of genius. The dandy, as self-styled genius, is antisocial, rather than merely asocial. He lives in the gaze of the other for whom the dandy serves as a model of inflated decadence. John Lecthe, in his book on Kristeva, comes to conclusions about dandyism that are similar to those of Brent:

> Dandyism as "punk" before the fact, then, would be a way for Baudelaire to cope with loss of identity and a wounding of narcissism. In this sense, dandyism is not simply an individual choice which could be analysed sociologically. It is also a kind of desperate assertion of independence—of social survival—against the mother. Dandyism is the symbolic appropriation of the maternal position.[16]

The surface phenomena of refined clothes and an artificially heightened aesthetic taste point toward the lost realm of the maternal. The logic here seems to be compensatory. The verbal wit and sheer semiotic and symbolic plenitude represent attempts to flee from the presymbolic. Yet, ironically, the sheer semiotic play is a mask for the deeper semiotic rhythms of the maternal that were left behind by the identification with the cultural symbolic codes of the father.

Lest this analysis seem too precious or contrived, it must be remembered that Peirce spent a good part of his life in states of altered consciousness and in search for some kind of transfiguring experience. His sexual relations were those of the dandy in the sense that they were often without depth or any sense of commitment. The tragedy of this dialectic is that Peirce wounded himself with each increase in his architectonic. The ultimate way of expressing the inner logic of his melancholy is in terms of the transition from the plenitude of the paternal architectonic to the deeper and darker rhythms of the maternal. His quest for firstness was his answer to the dilemma of the captive in the domain of signs. Kristeva expresses this logic with precision:

> A representative of the paternal function takes the place of the good maternal object that is wanting. There is language instead of the good breast. Discourse is being substituted for maternal care, and with it a fatherhood belonging more to the realm of the ideal than of the superego. . . . Contrary to hysteria, which brings about, ignores, or seduces the symbolic but does not produce it, the subject of abjection is eminently productive of culture. Its symptom is the rejection and reconstruction of languages.[17]

Peirce vacillated between the kind of conversion hysteria that paralyzes all symbolic and linguistic functions, and the abjection or melancholy denial that flies into a hypersymbolic activity as if to fill the universe with signs so that the maternal and its sensed loss is drowned. This intense dialectic between hysteria and abjection marked Peirce throughout his life. Whenever he could, he would spend hours filling up page after page of paper so that he could push the maternal, manifest in the many women in his life and in his excessive dandified behavior, into the background. However, this manic frenzy often gave way to a total symbolic and physical paralysis as the inner contradictions of his compensatory strategy bore down upon him. Peirce's pansemioticism represented his inner flight from the maternal. His preoccupation with firstness was the one place where the maternal could leave some traces in his paternal code-filled universe.

Was Peirce at all conscious of this tragic but inevitable dialectic? My sense is that he was deeply puzzled by it and that his physical symptoms were the only means he had of gaining some awareness of what was torturing him. Brent hints that Peirce came close to understanding his demons toward the end of his life, and that he found some form of acceptance for living with his fissures. His later cosmology, and its scrutiny of the greater and lesser forms of nothingness, to be discussed in chapter 4, represents a profound attempt on his part to overcome the break between the maternal and the paternal. This is not to say, in a literal reductive fashion, that Peirce sought his own mother, but that he knew that his broken and antisocial behavior pointed to an unsaid melancholy lying at the heart of his vision. His affirmation of Christianity and the spirit gave him one way of moving past his tragic split toward a transfigured life. The greatness of Peirce's melancholy is that it spawned a culture-transforming semiotics that has given later thinkers a means for moving backward toward the lost maternal that continually eluded Peirce. When we look at Peirce's analysis of firstness we will see the hidden face of the maternal, a face that continued to appear even in the most manic moments of Peirce's creative life. Behind his melancholy is an ecstatic presence that appears in a fragmented way in his naturalism. It was as a precursor of ecstatic naturalism that he came closest to finding his transfiguring center.

NOTES

1. The best biography of Peirce is that of Joseph Brent. It first appeared in 1960 as his UCLA dissertation, *A Study of the Life of Charles Sanders Peirce*. It has been revised and expanded as *Charles Sanders Peirce: A Life*

(Bloomington: Indiana University Press, 1993). Brent has brilliantly captured the dark and demonic aspects of Peirce and has shown in detail how Peirce's personality undermined many of his professional achievements. Further biographical information can be found in the introductions to each of the volumes in the ongoing *Writings of Charles S. Peirce*, under the general editorship of Max Fisch. Also of value is the anthology *Peirce, Semeiotic, and Pragmatism*, by Max Fisch, edited by Kenneth Laine Ketner and Christian J. W. Kloesel (Bloomington: Indiana University Press, 1986). In addition, there is *Charles Sanders Peirce: Leben und Werk*, by Elisabeth Walther (Baden-Baden: Agis-Verlag, 1989). For an earlier biographical account, see Paul Weiss's 1934 article in the *Dictionary of American Biography*, Vol. 14, pp. 398–403. Finally, readers will want to consult, Philip P. Wiener's *Evolution and the Founders of Pragmatism* (Cambridge: Harvard University Press, 1949).

2. From the Introduction to *Writings of Charles S. Peirce*, Vol. 1, Max H. Fisch, General Editor (Bloomington: Indiana University Press, 1982), pp. xvi–xvii.

3. Peirce preferred the spelling "semeiotic" to that of "semiotic." In all that follows, the more common spelling will be used.

4. Brent, *Charles Sanders Peirce: A Life*, p. 61.

5. See his Introduction to Vol. 2 of the *Writings of Charles S. Peirce*, pp. xxi–xxxvi.

6. This important journal was reestablished in 1987 under the title *The Journal of Speculative Philosophy: New Series*, and continues to publish articles in metaphysics, aesthetics, and pragmaticism.

7. The so-called "professionalization" of philosophy at the end of the nineteenth century is a fascinating study in its own right. Students of this period will want to read *The Rise of American Philosophy: Cambridge, Massachusetts, 1860–1930* by Bruce Kuklick (New Haven: Yale University Press, 1977).

8. Brent, *Charles Sanders Peirce: A Life*, pp. 105, 106.

9. Nathan Houser has a less critical picture of this period in Peirce's life than does Brent. See his excellent Introduction to Vol. 4 of the *Writings of Charles S. Peirce*. Houser's meticulous scholarship brings out many key details of the Peirce/Johns Hopkins relationship. My own sense is that Brent's more negative portrayal of Peirce's self-destructiveness is more on target. It should be noted that Brent's 1960 dissertation, which does not deal with Peirce's thought, is more negative in tone than his 1993 book, where an effort is made to show the heroic qualities of Peirce's struggle (both personal and philosophic).

10. From the Introduction to Vol. 4 of the *Writings of Charles S. Peirce*, p. xx.

11. Brent, *Charles Sanders Peirce: A Life*, p. 168.

12. The house has been preserved by the U.S. government under the aegis of the Delaware Water Gap National Recreation Area. Visitors are welcomed and can be given an informal tour by the government employees who

occupy the building. Most of the surrounding property was sold off by Peirce during his life time.

13. Brent, *Charles Sanders Peirce: A Life*, p. 203.

14. Brent, *Charles Sanders Peirce: A Life*, p. 244.

15. Brent, *Charles Sanders Peirce: A Life*, p. 305.

16. John Lechte, *Julia Kristeva* (London: Routledge, 1990), p. 181.

17. Julia Kristeva, *Powers of Horror: An Essay on Abjection* (New York: Columbia University Press, 1982), p. 45.

Chapter One

Pragmatism and Abduction

Throughout his career, Peirce was concerned with issues in methodology. As a logician, he sought to define the valid rules of reasoning and inference as they applied to every area of human inquiry. As a scientist, with special training and interest in chemistry, he sought a method of inquiry that would assure the successful outcome of experiment in the infinite long run. To undergird this concern, he developed a theory of community as the locus for all forms of empirical inquiry, insuring that personal and idiosyncratic perspectives would give way to the wisdom of the scientific community. As a student of religion, with a particular interest in trinitarian Christianity, he sought a method that would bring the individual closer to the divine. As a student of psychology, who conducted careful and detailed experiments on the nature of perception and perceptual judgment, he sought to find a method that would show how interpretation interacts with each sensation and emotion to build up a perceptual picture of the world. In each of these areas Peirce made striking advances that continue to compel admiration. What makes Peirce unique is that he worked toward an integrated perspective that would encompass and shape all of these areas of inquiry. His individual reflections on method all point toward a general sense of the role and scope of methods within the world as a whole.

In describing Peirce's several concepts of method one must always keep in mind that he locates method within a much larger metaphysical and evolutionary perspective that attempts to show how nature and its organisms are themselves methodic in their forms of behavior. It might jar on common sense to see nature as somehow capable of

methodic behavior, but this possibility becomes less shocking once
we have delineated the main outlines of Peirce's metaphysics where
nature itself is seen as an evolving sign system growing through forms
of self-control. All methods, whether they involve a high degree of
self-consciousness or the mere transformation of blind habit, must make
their way in an evolutionary universe that has little patience with
confused or chaotic forms of interaction. For Peirce, some form of
self-control must be manifested by any organism seeking to stabilize
its relation to the surrounding environment. As we will see, the concept of self-control becomes more and more central to Peirce as he
applies it to larger and larger areas of the world. By his last decades
he came to see the universe itself as moving toward more and more
self-control.[1]

Methods, then, involve some form of self-control in an evolutionary context that has little patience with mere random play (with the
exception of what Peirce calls "interpretive musement" in the human
order, which will be discussed later). It is important to understand
that Peirce links the right use of method with evolutionary survival.
Consequently, any analysis of method that sees it as being somehow
purely arbitrary or merely secondary misses the urgency of Peirce's
pragmatism. To understand the right use of method is to assure survival in a universe that is continually moving forward toward higher
forms of generality and reasonableness. To fail to be reasonable is to
fail to become attuned to the direction in which the universe is moving.

For persons, the right use of method involves certain moral choices
as to the proper place and function of method in building up genuine
community. While Peirce did not develop a specific ethical theory as
a separate field of inquiry, he did understand the ethical implications
of his fundamental categories and shaped them in such a way that
they helped toward the creation of an ethical human community. Persons become ethical when they transform anticommunal methods into
those that will make it possible for inquirers to share and compare
their respective conceptions of the world. Any method that works to
foreclose inquiry or to deaden genuine communal impulses must be
rejected by the pragmatist. Any method that helps to build up a genuine common consensus, but one that still remains open to self-correction and acknowledges its fallibility, is a pragmatic method. To understand what Peirce means by "pragmatism" is to understand the
larger ethical and communal aspects of methodic behavior. The concept of pragmatism has often been characterized as a mere practicalism
that denies the importance of just ends or is insensitive to some kind

of overarching good. One of the insights that will emerge from our exploration of Peirce's pragmatism is the realization that it entails a deep concern with a highest good, what he called the *summum bonum* that cannot be reduced to a mere means. The highest good becomes realized in an incomplete way in any community that uses pragmatic and scientific methods to converge on truth. Methods establish their validity insofar as they embed themselves in the subject matter of nature and make it possible for the human process to come closer to the structures and powers of an evolving universe.

In exploring Peirce's concept of method, we will trace his key essays and lectures from the 1870s though 1908. Our focus will be on the process of finding and fixing belief within an evolving universe. In particular, we will examine his conception of pragmatism, and its subaltern methods of induction, deduction, and abduction (also known as retroduction). Each of these last mentioned methods work together to support a general pragmatic methodology that emphasizes the emergence of truth in the future through collective forms of inquiry. Abduction will receive more extended treatment because it represents Peirce's most innovative and profound contribution to our understanding of method.

Fixing and Clarifying Belief

We will begin our exploration of Peirce's pragmatic method by examining six important early papers that lay out his basic understanding of the role of ideas and beliefs in communal life, and their supporting methodological and logical principles. All of these papers appeared in 1877 and 1878 in the journal *Popular Science Monthly* under the general title of *Illustrations of the Logic of Science*. In order of their appearance they are "The Fixation of Belief," "How to Make our Ideas Clear," "The Doctrine of Chances," "The Probability of Induction," "The Order of Nature," and "Deduction, Induction, and Hypothesis." Peirce meant these papers to be read together. They represent some of his more popular and accessible reflections on the nature of method and form an important entry point into his more mature and complex reflections.

For Peirce, our ability to reason well is a late addition to individual life. We start out as creatures of habit and instinct who only have a tentative grasp of the basic principles of valid inference. To learn to reason is to grow into a complex art that requires a great deal of self-control. Put in the simplest terms, good reasoning does not come easily to individuals. Peirce is fully aware that social habit and inertia work against the proper use of analysis and inference. Consequently, it is important that the individual learn how to navigate among the various methods, or pseudomethods actually employed, in order to arrive at an understanding of the most useful and appropriate method for fixing belief.

In "The Fixation of Belief," Peirce describes four methods that represent divergent ways of moving toward established beliefs. These are the methods of tenacity, authority, a priori reasoning, and science. Each of these methods has its own sphere of operation and its own efficacy. What makes Peirce's account interesting is that he acknowledges that the three nonscientific forms of method have their own evolutionary value, thus explaining their continual appeal. It does not follow, of course, that because these methods have some kind of social survival value they are therefore free from criticism. The superiority of the scientific method is obvious for Peirce, and it is this superiority that will in turn determine the role of the other forms of method.

Peirce links the advance of science with the advance of logic. Each step in scientific evolution is also a step in our understanding of the rules of inference. Peirce makes it clear that logic is not a discipline describing the habits of mental life, but a discipline describing the rules by which mental life should be governed. That is, the rules of logic are normative rather than descriptive and tell us precisely how we *ought* to examine premises and then derive necessary or probable conclusions. Peirce does not derive logic from human psychology, but sometimes appears to go in the other extreme of deriving human psychology from the principles of logic (defined most broadly as the study of signs and sign systems). Consequently, in looking at his conception of method we will be pointing toward his understanding of the self (to be detailed in the next chapter).

The basic momentum of the human process is from a state of doubt toward that of belief. Peirce links doubt to a kind of neurological or physiological irritation that causes the organism to seek means of relief. Doubts emerge whenever habits are no longer in tune with environing circumstances. We seek new beliefs that will in turn generate new habits. These new habits will overcome the irritation of doubt and enable the organism to return to a more harmonious relation to the environment. "The irritation of doubt causes a struggle to attain a state of belief. I shall term this struggle *inquiry*, though it must be admitted that this is sometimes not a very apt designation" [W 3.247 & EP 1.114]. Hence, inquiry emerges within a biological context in which the organism responds to a doubt that must be converted into new habits.

At times, Peirce sounds as if he is reducing the complexities of mental life to neurological structures. However, his conception of perception and the process of idea formation is far from reductionistic. Ideas are not bare copies of antecedent sensations, but represent interpretations and judgments that have already transformed sense-data into instruments for habit and control. To think is to engage in a plan for action that has as its goal the securing of evolutionary survival. Inquiry is the organism's best means for remaining viable.

The move from doubt to belief takes place through inquiry, which has as its object the settling of opinion. Peirce argues that philosophy should not indulge in paper doubt, or doubt for its own sake, but should aid the individual toward an understanding of real and living doubt and its possible amelioration in new, more encompassing habits of mental life.

As noted, the first method used by the self for settling opinion is that of tenacity. The method of tenacity is an individual method and does not involve the larger community. What this method enables the individual to do is to cling to a private opinion that does not admit of any counterevidence. As such, tenacity provides a kind of security and comfort to the individual that is to be envied. Mystics, for example, use the method of tenacity whenever they defend a private vision of ultimacy that they hold aloof from communal forms of inquiry and testing. Peirce fully acknowledges the attractions of this method and notes that it can preserve the individual from the shocks of negative realities.

The method of tenacity is, however, vulnerable to larger social forces and forms of control. The state, desiring to impose political and theological norms on the population, advances the method of authority. Peirce traces the method of authority back to the period before the modern state structure, but holds that its logic remains much the same. The method of authority is better than the method of tenacity because it enforces a rigid communal form of control that can produce great and lasting works. His prime example is that of massive architectural structures:

> Its success is proportionately greater [than tenacity]; and, in fact, it has over and over again worked the most majestic results. The mere structures of stone which it has caused to be put together—in Siam, for example, in Egypt, and in Europe—have many of them a sublimity hardly more than rivaled by the greatest works of Nature. [W 3.251 & EP 1.118]

The method of tenacity merely protects individual opinion from social control, while the method of authority can transform the space of both personal and social life. The method of authority is reinforced by a special priestly class that insures that no individual will question the power of the social order. Peirce argues that the method of authority is powerful because it becomes internalized in the form of individual conscience. The self becomes its own policing force whenever it roots out its own allegedly deviant opinions.

While the method of authority has great scope in history, another method emerges that settles opinion through an appeal to reason rather than social power. This third method is called the a priori method because it secures opinion through an appeal to propositions that are held to be necessary and universal. However, the appeal to opinions that are "agreeable to reason" is actually an appeal to personal taste. The individual reasoner forgets that his or her a priori proposition is arbitrary and merely an expression of individual interest. He cites the example of the distinction between monogamy and polygamy. Any given individual can appeal to a priori reason to warrant an affirmation of either perspective, but such an appeal is actually to personal preference masked behind the appeal to some kind of pure reason removed from external evaluation. There is a sense in which the a priori method is merely an elitist version of the method of tenacity insofar as it does not allow for social or external critique. Peirce advances an argument that today would go by the name of "hermeneutics of suspicion," which asserts that all fundamental knowledge claims are actually structures of personal preference or moves toward control and power that belie the surface and seemingly innocent claims of so-called 'pure' reason.

All three methods have their own role to play in personal and collective history, but they all fail to point to anything truly external to the self or the community. In this sense, these methods are intrapsychic and do not reveal anything about the structures of nature. Peirce argues that a fourth method must be developed that is open to external structures and powers. He calls this final method the method of science. "To satisfy our doubts, therefore, it is necessary that a method should be found by which our beliefs may be caused by nothing human, but by some external permanency—by something upon which our thinking has no effect" [W 3.253 & EP 1.120]. The last clause points to Peirce's realism; namely, the view that there is an independently existent real world that has traits and features that are not human products. Peirce's realism also affirms that universals are independently real and not mere products of human languages (the position of nominalism that he emphatically rejects). Thus the method of science can help us through and past purely intrapsychic perspectives toward an encounter with the real per se.

Unlike the other three methods, the method of science admits of a right and a wrong use. The method of authority, for example, can never be wrong simply because the state sets the very definition of rightness in terms of what it imposes on the sum of its citizens. The method of science, on the other hand, must distinguish between a right and wrong use insofar as external constraints impinge on its opinions. Peirce is quite clear on the status of real independent things and laws:

> . . . There are real things, whose characters are entirely independent of our opinions about them; those realities affect our senses according to regular laws, and, though our sensations are as different as our relations to the objects, yet, by taking advantage of the laws of perception, we can ascertain by reasoning how things really are, and any man, if he have sufficient experience and reason enough about it, will be led to the one true conclusion. [W 3.254 & EP 1.120]

The method of science works as well as it does because there are independently real laws and events that await their disclosure by the community of scientific inquirers. Peirce implicitly contrasts two types of community in his analysis. The community operative in the method of authority could be described as a kind of "natural" community in that it does not engage in self-reflection or allow for its basic presuppositions to be challenged. The community of scientific inquirers, on the other hand, is a kind of "interpretive" community in that it encourages a kind of cross-examination of its findings. This cross-examination is conducted by other community members and by nature itself. The dual constraints provided by nature and fellow scientists keeps the method of science from degenerating into the other three methods.

Peirce's commitment to realism, as opposed to a nominalism that denied the full independence of objects and generals, was enunciated with great clarity and force six years before the appearance of "The Fixation of Belief." In his extended review of Frazer's four-volume edition of the works of George Berkeley, he lays out the implications of his own realism. This review, published in the *North American Review* in 1871, is an important document detailing Peirce's evolution toward his more fulsome realist position.

Peirce begins by arguing that the British philosophical tradition has often shown strong nominalistic tendencies. Berkeley continues within this tradition and combines his own extreme nominalism with a

Platonism that gives an honorific status to universals, even though they are mind-dependent (at least, dependent on the divine mind for their 'existence'). Peirce firmly rejects this brand of nominalism, even though remaining appreciative of the cognitive insight that many so-called "primary qualities," e.g., space, are actually built up through inference. The real, regardless of how we approach it, is independent of what we may think or infer: "The real is that which is not whatever we happen to think it, but is unaffected by what we may think of it" [W 2.467 & EP 1.88]. Human opinions are bound by the objects and generals that obtain in their own right. Given enough time and resources, the self and its communities would converge on the independently real structures of the world.

Peircean realism rejects unknowable the thing in itself as an unnecessary fiction. In the long run, we will find the thing as it actually prevails and unveil its features to inquiry. Peirce combines his optimism with a much larger sense of both community and the time process to outflank any nominalism that wishes to deny us access to the real in itself:

> But human opinion universally tends in the long run to a definite form, which is the truth. Let any human being have enough information and exert enough thought upon any question, and the result will be that he will arrive at a certain definite conclusion, which is the same that any other mind will reach under sufficiently favorable circumstances. [W 2.468 & EP 1.89]

The final opinion is independent of any given individual, and of all individuals in consort with each other. There is thus an ideal correspondence between human forms of method, insofar as they are scientific, and the structures of the world. Peirce grafts a traditional correspondence theory of truth to a temporally extended consensus theory in which the community becomes the 'place' where knowledge is won. It is important to stress, however, that the consensus theory is measured and governed by a deeper correspondence theory that insists that there is an evolutionary convergence between thought and its object. Consensus is always validated by extracommunal means.

To return to our analysis of "The Fixation of Belief," it is clear that in terms of our long-term evolutionary prospects, the method of science is the only one of the four that can assure that the human organism remains responsive to the vast forces of nature. The other methods have their own forms of efficacy, but they prove to be problematic when examined from a broader perspective. Peirce is not simply contrasting abstract formal procedures, as if means for attaining knowledge can be detached from the ends sought, but showing how methods respond to subject matters not fully under their control. The method of science is more than a mere means toward some kind of social consensus. It is the sole method for revealing the depth structures of the objects and events that surround the human process.

As noted, Peirce did not develop a separate ethical framework, but probed into the ethical implications of his categories and methodological principles. The method of science is intrinsically ethical insofar as it entails the rejection of personal prejudice in favor of the good of the community. In choosing the method of science, the individual is making a fundamental ethical commitment to forgo personal forms of power and domination and allow the sovereign powers of nature and independent realities to determine the upshot of inquiry. Peirce gives a sacramental status to the method of science: "The genius of a man's logical method should be loved and reverenced as his bride, whom he has chosen from all the world" [W 3.257 & EP 1.123]. In choosing this method, the individual becomes sacramentally wedded to a community of inquiry that seeks to bind all selves together into a future-directed momentum that insures that the highest good will emerge in history. It should be noted that Peirce early on joined scientific/logical language with religious imagery. At the heart of his pragmatism, both early and late, is the religious vision of a transfigured community of truth seekers.

In his next article in the *Popular Science Monthly* series, "How to Make Our Ideas Clear," Peirce further clarifies his understanding of the nature of doubt and belief and lays out his basic pragmatic principles. Once we have rejected the three methods of tenacity, authority, and a priori reasoning, we are in a position to explore the implications of the scientific method vis-à-vis the history of philosophy.

Peirce notes that most logic textbooks start with accepted definitions of "clear" and "distinct" ideas and make these ideas normative for subsequent forms of logical reasoning. He is quite critical of both Descartes and Leibniz for their insistence that all inquiry start from intuitively obvious clear and distinct ideas. As we will see in detail in the next chapter, Peirce firmly rejects the concept that we can have unmediated intuitions of either the self or aspects of the world. Consequently, there can be no agreed-upon self-evident concepts from which to derive further truths. The a priori method of seventeenth century metaphysicians cannot advance new knowledge: "Nothing new can ever be learned by analyzing definitions" [W 3.260 & EP 1.126]. Only a judicious combination of general principles with external and piecemeal perceptions can advance knowledge.

Again we are reminded that the primary function of thought is the production of belief. And the purpose of belief is to secure new habits that can put thought to rest. The irony here seems to be that the goal of thought is to think itself out of existence. Of course, Peirce's framework is more subtle. Thoughts exist to transform doubts into beliefs/habits, but thought also has an independent dimension that consists in the free exploration of semiotic possibilities and actualities. Peirce's pragmatism never degenerates into an anti-intellectualism or mere vitalism. Thought is itself an action that exits to overcome threats to our established habits. Thought does not seek its own cessation but the cessation of particular confused thoughts can emerge whenever a habit is broken by a transformed environment.

Mere paper doubt—that is, doubt for its own sake without any practical purpose—is rejected as a fruitless enterprise. Yet Peirce fully acknowledges a positive role for a certain kind of floating doubt that serves to open up possibilities for inquiry:

> Feigned hesitancy, whether feigned for mere amusement or with a lofty purpose, plays a great part in the production of scientific inquiry. However the doubt may originate, it stimulates the mind to an activity which may be slight or energetic, calm or turbulent. Images pass rapidly through consciousness, one incessantly melting into another, until, at last, when all is over—it may be in a fraction of a second, in an hour, or after long years—we find ourselves decided as to how we should act under circumstances as those which occasioned our hesitation. In other words, we have attained belief. [W 3.262 & EP 1.128]

Feigned hesitancy may have a long-term value for the self insofar as it allows possibilities to play across the mind that might not otherwise be given a chance to make their appearance under the impress of more immediate concerns. This sensitivity to less urgent forms of doubt flowers into his mature conception of "interpretive musement," expressed in his 1908 paper, "A Neglected Argument for the Reality of God." In musement, as we will see, signs are allowed a free reign in the mind so that they can enter into a depth momentum that points toward the reality and existence of a divine power in nature. In the context of these earlier papers, feigned doubt keeps the human process from sinking into brute and immediate instrumentalities and holds open the possibility that more subtle and much richer forms of belief can find a place within the human process.

Thought, emergent from doubt, runs through our various perceptions holding them together into some kind of harmony. Peirce uses the analogy to music here to show how sensations and perceptions (sensations rendered intelligible through judgments) are brought into unity. Thought is the melody that holds the bare notes of sensation together. Melodies have the larger purpose of creating new habits and beliefs that will express the inner logic of the melodic configuration of sensations.

Peirce links the musical image to the logic of belief to show how we move from an incomplete and tentative structure toward a kind of harmonic closure:

> And what, then, is belief? It is the demi-cadence which closes a musical phrase in the symphony of our intellectual life. We have seen that it has just three properties: First, it is something that we are aware of; second, it appeases the irritation of doubt; and, third, it involves the establishment in our nature of a rule of action, or, say for short, a *habit*. [W 3.263 & EP 1.129]

It is important to note that Peirce links the concept of "habit" to that of "rule of action." A habit is not merely a blind behavioral event, such as a reflex response to a stimulus, but a general structure of intelligibility that can guide further forms of behavior. The correlation of habit and rule is fundamental to pragmatism. Habits that do not evoke general rules have little value to the organism. Habits that instantiate rules are capable of sustaining beliefs that give the organism or self a stable location within the world.

One of the purposes of pragmatic method is to generate and protect new rules for action. These rules are not equivalent to a priori (that is, necessary and universal) propositions, yet they have more than a personal scope and interest. Peirce's pragmatism is deeply committed to the increase of intelligibility and generality in the world. Given thoughts and habits emerge from particular irritations and doubts, but they seek to go beyond their originating conditions toward a more inclusive and generic perspective that grasps the conditions behind the specific irritations of doubt so that more pervasive and successful forms of amelioration can be created.

As should by now be clear, pragmatism moves away from antecedent conditions toward future possibilities. A priori definitions are too weighted with the past and too self-contained to have any efficacy in a perspective that constantly drives toward the open future. Peirce puts pressure on the very concept of "definition" insofar as it tends to connote a static location of a particular class or order within a genus. Further, an obsession with classification and definition can foreclose inquiry by degenerating into a mere verbal battle (or an appeal to authority) that cannot generate new habits of action or belief. For

Peirce, many of the debates within the history of philosophy (particularly during the medieval period) are merely verbal. Purely verbal distinctions are pseudodistinctions that make no practical difference.

His example of a merely verbal distinction, not a particularly felicitous one, is that of the difference between Catholic and Protestant conceptions of the Eucharist. The Catholic has a strikingly different theory of the events taking place during the consecration of the bread and wine than does the reformation Protestant. For the Catholic, the bread and wine actually become transformed into the mystical body and blood of the Christ, while for the Protestant the event on the altar merely serves to remind the community of an historical event that has become normative for its life of faith. Each position makes assertions and puts forward definitions that shape a particular conception of the Eucharist. The two communities seem to be at an impasse insofar as it is logically impossible for both of them to be right in their assertions. Peirce invokes the spirit of pragmatism (not named as such in these early papers) to provide a way past this dilemma. For the pragmatist the question becomes: Is there any practical difference between these two views in terms of the behavior of Christians? If there is no practical difference, then the debate between those who believe in transubstantiation and those who believe that the Eucharist is mere memorial event is not a real difference. It is merely a verbal difference and hence can be transcended by an appeal to practice and habit.

The example is problematic precisely because it is very difficult to separate belief from habit on such a complex issue as the ontological nature of the consecrated bread and wine. One can make a case that the belief in transubstantiation, because it plays for higher metaphysical stakes, as it were, produces different habits in the believer than a belief that one is recollecting a founding event in church history. In these early papers Peirce often engages in a kind of polemical and rhetorical debate against metaphysics and theology that does not always advance his problematic. As his thought matured, he came to recognize the need for metaphysical inquiry, even though he remained reticent about theology. These cautions aside, the general principle can survive his infelicitous use of this example. The future-directed habits are what matter to the pragmatist, not the antecedent propositional affirmations.

In what is certainly one of the most oft quoted passages in all of Peirce's writings, he makes it clear that pragmatism considers effects and practical implications in its understanding of objects: ". . . Consider what effects, which might conceivably have practical bearings, we conceive the object of our conception to have. Then, our conception of these effects is the whole of our conception of the object" [W 3.266 & EP 1.132]. It should be noted that he puts equal emphasis on "practical bearings" and on "conception." Peirce's pragmatism is fully intellectualistic, if one means by this notion that it remains committed to framing general concepts by and through which we come to understand objects. We engage in both practical and conceptual experiments in developing a sense of the overall contour of any given object of inquiry. The role of inquiry is to determine which conceived effects are pertinent to the object and which are not. The "object" (a complex reality that we will examine in more detail in the context of Peirce's semiotic theory) is always underway toward completion in the future. We propose a number of imagined concepts and practical effects that we hope will adequately delineate the object in its dynamic inner nature. The community of scientific inquiry tests these proposals to gauge their validity.

Peirce applies this pragmatic conception of definition to the concepts of hardness and weight. Rather than give an antecedent definition of hardness, for example, we engage in the act of trying to scratch the object under study. To understand the hardness of a diamond (to use his example), is to see what will or will not scratch it. When this process is completed, we will have a pragmatic definition of the hardness of not only the diamond under study, but, through induction, of all members of its class. Certain concepts, such as that of "force," might become less useful to the pragmatist because they do not lend themselves to practical tests. One of the implications of the shift to a pragmatic notion of definition is that certain long-cherished concepts may prove to be hollow. Peirce's pragmatism never degenerates into an unrestricted use of Ockham's razor, always honoring complexity and continuity where it obtains, but it does provide a means for weeding out some of the less useful concepts within both science and philosophy (cf. CP 5.416–17).

Behind the shift in focus to practical bearings and future-oriented conceived possibilities is an evolutionary optimism that assumes that the truth will indeed appear in the infinite long run. There is a 'fit' between the human mind and nature, a fit produced by millions of years of evolution, that guarantees the eventual convergence of thought and reality. Throughout his writings, Peirce evidences this optimistic belief, even going so far as to argue that all great thinkers in the Western tradition have been optimists. In the context of these 1877–1878 papers, the optimism appears in the claim that we are somehow fated to come to the right opinion: "The opinion which is fated to be ultimately agreed to by all who investigate, is what we mean by the truth, and the object represented in this opinion is the real" [W 3.273 & EP 1.139].

As noted, Peirce links each major advance in science with an advance in logical theory. This is especially evident in the rise of theories of probability as they correlate to classes of things in the world. As a chemist, he was of course aware of how the statistical theory of gases advanced our implied understanding of the particular molecules under study. Probability theory could at least show us what a given molecule is likely to do under certain conditions of heat and pressure. Peirce was aware by 1859, when he read Darwin's just-published *The Origin of Species* while working off of the coast of Louisiana, that probability theory as applied to population studies had made it possible to frame general principles of biological evolution. Consequently, probability theory emerges as basic for recent advances in science.

In the third paper in this *Popular Science Monthly* series, entitled "The Doctrine of Chances," Peirce probed into the logic of probability as it correlated to scientific inquiry and to more practical problems of human living. He initiates the discussion by arguing that exactness came into science through quantification. But this use of mathematical reasoning is not confined to counting or bare enumeration, but has its higher expression in the doctrine of continuous quantity. Throughout his career, Peirce was deeply concerned with the logical and metaphysical aspects of continuity within nature and its semiotic systems. In this early paper, he ties the concept of continuity to that of the framing of species designations in biology.

The Naturalist, for example, is confronted with a variety of samples that must be classified in some way. He or she must find some regional features that demarcate these living systems and make them unique. However, there will be no perfect replication of features from case to case. Some deviation, however slight, will always occur. Consequently, the Naturalist must think along a continuum so that there will be poles within which the various samples fall. Mathematics has developed various ways for dealing with the continua in nature and these can be employed by the Naturalist. Difference can be broken down into "differences of degree" [W 3.278 & EP 1.144], without threatening the integrity of the species under investigation. Throughout nature, then, are continuous quantities that allow for extremes of variation within a given genus or species.

Peirce ties the concept of "continuity" to that of "probability" to show how all probabilities exist within a continuum that can be plotted and defined. Probability is thus a continuous quantity that can be grasped through a series of inferences. To make an inference is to work within a probabilistic framework that governs the outcome of a class of inferences. Peirce makes it clear that probability theory does not apply to a single case, but involves class notions. Probabilistic inferences, like all logical inferences, have as their goal the production of truth. That is, probability theory is concerned with what will or will not be successful in the long run. It is easy to see how Peirce can link probability theory to his general pragmatic principles in that all probability claims have the pragmatic goal of securing positive outcomes for the individual or group.

Peirce makes an interesting inference from science to human living when he insists that in neither case does probability apply most adequately to the individual instance. Just as probability theory tells us about a quantity of gas as a whole, so too it must tell us about larger human groupings. His argument here is that probabilities can work against a given individual when considered in isolation, but that they can work for an individual when he or she is placed within a larger communal setting. The argument hinges, as one might suspect, on the concept of continuity.

An individual has a finite life span within which to enact certain probabilities. Peirce argues that this finite life span can actually be a blessing in that an infinite (or at least a very long) span would certainly bring about a collapse of human purposes. If we lived long enough, all of our positive attainments would be undermined, this according to the laws of probability. He uses the example of a gambler who may win in the short run, but who is destined to lose in the long run because of the nature of the controlled probabilities involved. All living things are analogous to the gambler who must pull out at the right time in order to preserve any winnings. By the same probabilistic argument, insurance companies are doomed to fail given enough time and the probable course of human and natural catastrophes. Hence, finitude works in our favor and against the inevitable processes of decay.

The way past our dilemma is not to attain more longevity but to move horizontally, as it were, into larger orders of communal interaction where the laws of probability work toward a much more favorable outcome. Here we see a clever link between general pragmatic principles, always emphasizing the role of practical bearings and future-leading conceptions, and the mathematics of continuity and probability, always emphasizing the correlation between classes or species and future consequences. Peirce links logic to the social impulse:

It seems to me that we are driven to this, that logicality inexorably requires that our interests shall not be limited. They must not stop at our own fate, but must embrace the whole community. This community, again, must not be limited, but must extend to all races of beings with whom we can come into immediate or mediate intellectual relation. It must reach, however vaguely, beyond this geological epoch, beyond all bounds. He who would not sacrifice his own soul to save the whole world, is, as it seems to me, illogical in all his inferences, collectively. Logic is rooted in the social principle. [W 3.284 & EP 1.149]

Logic, as the formalized study of inquiry (equivalent in scope to semiotics), has a salvific function for the community because it insures that merely individual interests become governed by the deeper needs of the social order. Peirce advances an argument akin to more recent theories in sociobiology that assume something like a benevolent or group interest in living systems. To think logically is to think ethically, which in turn means to think in terms of an unending human community that preserves the values and goods of its members, even if individual members must fall by the wayside.

As noted, Peirce's attitude toward Christianity is a complex one. He affirms its basic trinitarian principles and has deep respect for its social impulse. On the other hand, he is highly critical of its tendency to thwart inquiry because of an obsession with a priori principles, or a commitment to the method of authority. One place where he finds a congenial relationship to the tradition is in his recognition that the three cardinal theological virtues of faith, hope, and charity, as enunciated by St. Paul, have their parallel in the pragmatic principles of the unlimited community and its values. The pragmatist displays hope in truth in the long run, is faithful to the principles of inquiry, and has charity to other members of the community, especially insofar as they need the corrective of method to advance their own legitimate survival needs.

The fourth and fifth papers in this series explore the implications of probability theory and their correlation to our sense of the order of nature. In "The Probability of Induction" (1878), Peirce examines the psychological and material bases of probabilistic inferences and distinguishes between the two basic classes of reasoning, namely, the explicative/deductive and the amplicative/synthetic. In "The Order of Nature" (1878), Peirce probes into the issue of whether or not we can characterize the universe as a whole, and if so, whether we have just grounds for calling it orderly. He hedges his bets in some of his conclusions, but makes some important points about induction and the correlation of the human mind and nature that are worth examining.

In "The Probability of Induction," Peirce reminds us of one of the conclusions of the previous paper, namely, that probability deals with a class of inferences pertaining to a genus or class of objects. He relates the logic of probability to traditional medieval logical systems that contrast the antecedent and foundational principle with its consequences. Deductive schemes use a logic of implication that can be transformed to illuminate inductive and probabilistic arguments. A probabilistic argument correlates consequents to antecedents in terms of the number of times a given consequent will appear vis-à-vis a given antecedent. The various logical possibilities of antecedent to consequent can be plotted, thereby illuminating the nature of all probabilistic arguments.

Peirce makes it clear that there is an element of chance involved in probabilistic reasoning. However, this chance element is also part of the world of nature outside of our various argumentative schemes. Chance is a real ontological event and is not confined to our arguments, where we could always assume that the element of chance only appears because we have an inadequate grasp of antecedent propositions. The universe functions along probabilistic and statistical lines and this fact is manifest in the structure of human arguments. Peirce shies away from the notion that our sense of chance is based on inadequate knowledge. Probabilities and chances are real in themselves and cannot be reduced to human feelings of ignorance or surprise.

The first type of reasoning is, as mentioned, explicative or deductive. In this type of reasoning, no new knowledge is produced. That is, there is nothing in the consequent that is not implied or given in the antecedent. In the second type of reasoning, that of the amplicative or synthetic form, new knowledge is indeed gained through the mechanism of induction, which itself functions according to the logic of probability. While explicative knowledge is useful, only amplicative reasoning produces real gain for the community. Induction, an important but not the sole form of synthetic reasoning, works by taking a random sampling of a class of things so that some classwide conclusions can be drawn about respects held in common by all members of the class.

Of course, induction does not enter into a realm of pure observation in which antecedent facts come to it all lined up in neat and tidy configurations. Peirce advances an argument that is fundamental to his epistemology and theory of the self, namely, that all so-called observation contains an element of reason right from the start. In other words, we do not somehow add a reasoning process onto a pure given, but actively shape the very givenness of what comes to the mind: ". . . there is no judgment of pure observation without reasoning" [W 3.300 & EP 1.164]. The term "judgment" is crucial here. Observation is always tied to judgment, which is in turn tied to reasoning. While perceptual judgments are not conscious, they do relate to more deliberate and conscious processes of reasoning. As we will see in this and in the next chapter, Peirce traces the process of judgment and reasoning from the most simple forms of sensation to the most elaborate forms of semiotic musement. To interact with the world in any way is to make judgments that have a deductive, inductive, or hypothetical status.

Induction will hold good in the long run because the world is constituted in such a way as to be disclosable to the human mind. The correlation of the structure of the human mind with that of an evolving universe is presupposed in Peirce's argument, and he can find no solid grounds for challenging it. The correlation is manifest in every successful belief or habit that makes it possible for an organism or human self to remain viable.

Of more philosophical interest is the essay "The Order of Nature," where Peirce combines bold affirmations about the nature of mental activity with an agnosticism about the ultimate 'shape' or character of the universe. The essay leaves the reader with a slightly uneasy feeling because it does not really answer the question it sets out to analyze; namely, as to whether or not we have logical grounds for assuming that the universe per se is orderly and whether, once this is established, we can assume a divine orderer. Is the concept of "order" one that applies to the universe as a 'totality' or is it of only regional import?

Peirce clearly affirms that the universe is not ". . . a mere chance-medley" [W 3.308 & EP 1.172], and that some sense of order is a given for experience. Yet he makes a surprising move by connecting the sense of order to the level of intelligence of the creature involved in looking for order. His straightforward equation is: the higher the intelligence, the greater the sense of order in the surrounding world:

> We may, therefore, say that a world of chance is simply our actual world viewed from the standpoint of an animal at the very vanishing-point of intelligence. The actual world is almost a chance-medley to the mind of a polyp. The interest which the uniformities of Nature have for an animal measures his place in the scale of intelligence. [W 3.312 & EP 1.176]

After making this correlation of intelligence and order he drops a tantalizing hint that there is an incremental ratio of order that is manifest in the relation between a finite and an infinite mind. The infinite mind of God must have an unlimited sense of the order of the universe, while the finite human mind remains limited in its understanding of the scope of order within the world. God could make the claim that the universe as a whole is orderly, but the human mind must confine itself to the recognition of regions of order *within* the universe. On a deeper level, Peirce correlates order with intelligence in an evolutionary context that sees all of creation as underway toward more intelligence and hence more order. The reasoning processes of the self work themselves down into the most basic dimensions of experience. There is a sense in which Peirce gives a physiological reading to the Kantian claim that our knowledge of the fundamental structures of space and time is innate to the self.

But Peirce does not see space and time as a priori orders of intuition (*Anschauung*) as did Kant. Rather, our sense of space and time is a biological product of evolution. Invoking the spirit of Bishop Berkeley, Peirce argues that our awareness of the third dimension of space is based on an unconscious inference. Depth perception is made possible by an internal but evolutionary process that builds up depth through a series of logical inferences from previous material of sensation. The physiological aspect of this argument relates to the structure of the retina of the eye that has a different spatial configuration than its intentional objects. To move from the excitations of certain nerve points in the eye to complex three-dimensional space is possible only because of inferences that weave a new fabric out of minimal electrochemical materials.

In the end, our experience of three-dimensional space and three-dimensional time is the result of extended processes of natural selection. All animals carve out, via unconscious inferences, their own relations to space and time. In a sense, each animal uses something like pragmatic criteria in framing its immediate environment. The push and pull of body mass and energy give shape to the sphere of efficacy:

> The great utility and indispensableness of the conceptions of time, space, and force, even to the lowest intelligence, are such as to suggest that they are the results of natural selection. Without something like geometrical, kinetical, and mechanical conceptions, no animal could seize his food or do anything which might be necessary for the preservation of the species. [W 3.318 & EP 1.181]

These "conceptions" are preconscious, yet they have very clear manifestations that can be consciously appraised by the scientific observer. In later chapters we will explore Peirce's commitment to the doctrine of "panpsychism"; namely, the idea that all so-called

material realities are actually muted forms of mental life. At this point
it is important to note that Peirce's evolutionary perspective, with its
emphasis on the material conditions of spatial and temporal awareness, points in the direction of a transformed conception of mentality
that can work downward into the 'lower' orders of creation. Here
Peirce takes the human category of "inference" and locates it in unconscious processes and animal forms. It will not be a great leap to
argue that the structure of mentality, which gets tied to feeling, also
works its way into all of the organic orders. The relation between
mentality and the inorganic orders is much more complex and will be
addressed in the context of our discussion of Peirce's semiotics.

In the final paper in the *Popular Science Monthly* series, "Deduction, Induction, and Hypothesis" (1878), Peirce moves beyond his
analyses of induction and adds one more form of reasoning to his list.
In "The Order of Nature," Peirce had come to an agnostic conclusion
concerning the issue of the order of nature as a whole. Because we
can assume no extranatural uniformity for nature as a whole, it is
impossible to found a belief in induction on a belief in the uniformity
of nature. Induction must make its own way through its ability to
produce pragmatically testable conclusions about classes of things. Its
inferences are validated by reference to future samplings, rather than
by references to antecedent uniformities (or a kind of grand uniformity).

Yet induction proves to be an insufficient guide to the creation of
new knowledge (amplicative knowledge) insofar as it remains tied to
cases and respects (traits) that belong to observed and homogenous
classes. Peirce argues that a third type of reasoning be confirmed that
has the power to go beyond observed cases into unexplored territory.
This third type of reasoning is that of "hypothesis" (later Peirce will
call this type of reasoning "abduction" or "retroduction").[2] Unlike an
inductive inference, which moves from random samples toward a
conclusion about a class of objects, hypothesis goes in the opposite
direction, proceeding from a general rule or theory toward a given
particular case. The rule of the hypothetical inference has a less secure status than the conclusion of an induction. After all, inductive
inferences move among familiar cases, while hypothesis must strike
out from the observed toward a rule that will explain the occurrence
of the observed. While these rules may themselves be the products of
previous samplings, they also hover over the case under study and
attempt to deliver an explanation that will be compelling. Hypothetical reasoning thus takes ". . . a bolder and more perilous step . . ."
[W 3.330 & EP 1.192] than inductive reasoning does.

Synthetic or amplicative reasoning divides into induction and hypothesis, even though any given synthetic argument may use both forms of inference in ways that make it very difficult to tell them apart. Peirce urges us to separate these two types of synthetic inference so that we can gain a certain kind of freedom to frame hypotheses that go beyond the more obvious strategies of induction. His definition of these two forms is quite precise:

> By induction, we conclude that facts, similar to observed facts, are true in cases not examined. By hypothesis, we conclude the existence of a fact quite different from anything observed, from which, according to known laws, something observed would necessarily result. The former, is reasoning from particulars to the general law; the latter, from effect to cause. The former classifies, the latter explains. [W 3.332 & EP 1.194]

The inductive move from similar facts to further similar facts does not advance any explanation as to the causes involved in the formation of the objects under analysis. The hypothetical inference explains the contour of the object through a posited cause. Insofar as the hypothesis helps to explain the origin of a particular, it will have some kind of validation within inquiry. Peirce gives a simple example of one of his own hypothetical inferences. Upon arriving at a seaport in Turkey, he sees a man on horseback surrounded by four other men on horseback holding a canopy over him. He inferred that this man must be the governor of the province. The assertion "He is the governor of the province" is a general rule applied to explain a given case. The inference moves backward from a hidden but plausible cause to a given case. In this example, the inference is not especially bold or problematic, but it follows the logic of all hypothetical inferences.

While this distinction between an inductive and a hypothetical inference has become quite commonplace, Peirce will derive further implications from it that open up some dramatic possibilities for the advance of knowledge. As we will see at the end of this chapter, the concept of "hypothesis" becomes deepened into that of "abduction," which in turn opens up the possibility of "interpretive musement." In this final dimension of reasoning, the possibility emerges for an existential encounter with the divine. There exists a continuity between Peirce's conception of scientific inquiry and his implied philosophical theology. Both the scientist and the theologian rely on a common body of inferential strategies in coming to conclusions about the ultimate explanations of things. Peirce's mature theological reflections are nothing if not eminently rational, even though they hint of a darker background.

Peirce concludes this final essay in the series with some psychological observations about the three forms of inference. While Peirce never reduces logic to psychology, he is committed to showing how each type of reasoning carries with it certain psychological corollaries. Induction has as its corollary the production of new habits. A habit is a belief enacted. Therefore, induction creates new beliefs and new rules that instantiate physiological habits. Hypothetical reasoning, on the other hand, takes a tangle of sensations and thoughts and weaves them into one dominant emotion and sensation. In Peirce's example of the horsemen, the hypothesis weaves together the sights and sounds of the five figures and creates a single unified thought/feeling. As such, Peirce refers to hypothetical reasoning as a sensuous form. Finally, deduction, which is analytic and does not add new knowledge, has the psychological aspect of focusing attention on a sequence. As such, deduction is correlated to the volitional aspect of the self.

These three psychological and physiological corollaries—habit, sensual unification, and volition—embody inference in an ongoing human process. Peirce walks a fine line between the reduction of logic to mere passing mental processes and an extreme formalism that would ignore or deny any embodied correlations to inferential procedures. His pragmatism insists that whatever logic is, it is fully part of the social and biological processes of the self, even while transcending them and giving them shape.

In examining the particular sciences, Peirce categorizes them according to the type of reasoning most pertinent to their form of inquiry. The inductive sciences are: systematic botany, zoology, mineralogy, and chemistry. The sciences of hypothesis are: geology and biology. The theoretical sciences, namely, those that mix induction and hypothesis, are: astronomy and pure physics. Since each science is concerned with advancing knowledge, i.e., with using amplicative inferences, none of them can be purely deductive. Peirce lavished great care on the varieties of deduction, induction, and hypothesis, insisting that each of the three forms of reasoning stem from common logical principles.

Several conceptions have by now become clarified from our examination of these six early papers. Throughout, Peirce is concerned with showing how the human process, as but one process within nature, works in an evolutionary context to secure knowledge and to render its future more secure. There is a biological urgency behind the quest for knowledge. One of the most fundamental presuppositions in these essays is that there is a fit between the mechanisms of the human mind and an evolving and changing universe.

Knowledge does not float over the world in a spectatorial gaze, but enters into its own struggles with natural selection. All inferential processes have psychological and physiological corollaries and collectively work together to make future prospects available to the self in process. The history of science is but one aspect of the history of the self-disclosure of the inner nature of logic. Consequently, the reflection on method is basic to the configuration of all forms of empirical inquiry. No logical method is purely private. Each points toward the larger social order and works to secure that order against a kind of semiotic entropy that would erode the products and deliberations of inquiry. Logic is itself founded on ethics because it is primarily concerned with both how we *ought* to think and with the good of the community (a good grasped through aesthetics that points toward the *summum bonum* or highest good).

The picture we get from these 1877–1878 papers is that of a steady growth of amplicative knowledge through a deepened self-understanding of the basic principles of all inference. Peirce brings us into a new world in which hypothetical reasoning can leap beyond the bounds of the given or familiar to create rules applicable to difficult cases. The freedom gained through a use of hypothetical reasoning actually serves our sheer survival needs as each hypothetical inference promises to bring us closer to the hidden causes and explanations of things. This gain in explanatory power gives the human process its most powerful weapon against the natural forces of decay and chaos. Peirce shows that order and intelligence are almost equivalent terms and that an increase in one entails an increase in the other.

Pragmaticism and Synechism

Peirce continued to explore the implications of his pragmatic method. The term "pragmatism" became increasingly popular and entered into public debate by the end of the century. Peirce had not yet used the term in print, even though he was commonly associated with it and was its acknowledged creator. By 1905 Peirce felt that it was time to enter into the public debate and to defend pragmatism from its more popular expositors like William James and F.C.S. Schiller. In order to make his own claim to priority clear, and to show how his conception of pragmatism differed from that of others, Peirce published three articles in *The Monist* in 1905 and 1906 where he uses the term in print for the first time and defines its scope.[3] He specifically mentions the enunciation of the pragmatic maxim in the first of the series of papers from 1877–1878 that we have just discussed.

In 1903 he gave a series of seven lectures at Harvard University that delineated the main features of his pragmatism (he gave an eighth lecture in mathematics). These lectures left many members of the audience confused, chief among them William James, but they are indispensable to anyone wishing to understand the full scope of pragmatic method and its metaphysical underpinnings. In this chapter we will discuss the final lecture. The first six lectures will be dealt with in chapter 3.

Finally, Peirce pushed his concept of method to a new boundary when he made "interpretive musement" central to his understanding of religious life. We will conclude this chapter with a brief analysis of his 1908 article, "A Neglected Argument for the Reality of God." Together, these essays display Peirce's mature reflections on pragmatism and its potential role in the reconstruction of philosophy. Where appropriate, other manuscripts will be briefly mentioned and dealt with.

The three articles in the 1905–1906 *Monist* series represent more technical reflections on the logic behind pragmatism. In these essays Peirce publically introduces his term "pragmatism" only to replace it with the term "pragmaticism" that will mark his version off from other competing varieties. The essays, "What Pragmatism Is," "Issues of Pragmaticism," and "Prolegomena to an Apology for Pragmaticism," probe into the nature of continuity, generality, and the corollary semiotic aspects of pragmatism. At the same time, they refine the early reflections from the 1870s to show how pragmatism can enter more fully into the transformation of philosophy and its foundational discipline of metaphysics.

Peirce begins the 1905 essay, "What Pragmatism Is" by emphasizing the importance of the experimentalist mind set. He points out that he has spent most of his life working with fellow experimentalists and that he has himself been active in experiments since the age of six. Consequently, the habits of the laboratory become normative for the life of philosophy. Yet Peirce is clear that the experimental method has the most general implications and that it is not tied to piecemeal analyses of individual problems. Pragmatism is always underway toward general categories and classwide implications. As in the papers from the 1870s, Peirce stresses the correlation of concepts and practical bearings: ". . . the rational purport of a word or other expression, lies exclusively in its conceivable bearing upon the conduct of life; . . ." [CP 5.412]. And this bearing is general in nature; that is, it pertains to the whole group of habits/beliefs that govern and shape an individual's existence.

Terms must always be used with care. Peirce was long concerned with what he called the "ethics of terminology." The philosopher, especially because he or she uses terms of the broadest possible generality, must always be careful to shape a term so that its integrity and scope are truly commensurate with its subject matter. While Peirce denies that philosophy is primarily an analysis of terms and language, he does affirm that it must always probe into the full connotations and denotations of any technical term. This sensitivity to terminology frames his decision to reject the term "pragmatism" for the more precise term "pragmaticism":

> So, then, the writer, finding his bantling "pragmatism" so promoted, feels that it is time to kiss his child good-by and relinquish it to its higher destiny; while to serve the precise purpose of expressing the original definition, he begs to announce the birth of the word "pragmaticism," which is ugly enough to be safe from kidnappers. [CP 5.414]

His proposed name change has more than a mere personal interest. He is concerned with the rise of competing uses of the word "pragmatism" because they fail to emphasize the priority of generality and what he calls "synechism." The term "synechism" denotes the connectedness or continuity between and among elements in the world. The highly public pragmatism of William James lacks a sensitivity for synechistic structures within the world and tends to emphasize binary oppositions, thus ignoring deeper triadic structures of mediation.

Pragmaticism, then, accepts the basic principles of pragmatism—namely, an emphasis on the future, on practical bearings, on experimental method, on communal forms of inquiry, on habit, and on self-control—but adds the key recognition that all of reality moves toward forms of connectedness that give evidence to general laws and principles within an evolving universe. Pragmaticism is superior to the more public and popular forms of pragmatism because it starts and ends with a recognition of continuity.

Pointing back to his discussion in the 1870s, Peirce denies that philosophy can start with some kind of universal Cartesian doubt. Rather, we always start where we are; that is, with ". . . an immense mass of cognition already formed, . . ." [CP 5.416]. It is mistaken to assume that we can start with a clean slate and then hope to generate apodictic knowledge. We inherit a set of beliefs and habits that have proved their value over the long run. Allied to this is the principle of "critical common-sensism" that affirms our immersion in communal forms of practical wisdom that need not be questioned. Pragmaticism is committed to common-sensism and to the awareness of general principles of both knowledge and reality.

A further refinement takes place when Peirce ties habit and belief to the unconscious. As we will see in the next chapter, Peirce came to recognize something like a species-wide unconscious at the base of the sign-using self. In the context of his pragmaticism, the unconscious is the domain where our most basic beliefs are located:

> Belief is not a momentary mode of consciousness; it is a habit of mind essentially enduring for some time, and mostly (at least) unconscious; and like other habits, it is (until it meets with some surprise that begins its dissolution) perfectly self-satisfied. Doubt is of an altogether contrary genus. It is not a habit, but the privation of habit. Now a privation of a habit, in order to be anything at all, must be a condition of erratic activity that in some way must get superseded by a habit. [CP 5.417]

Habits have a deep evolutionary basis that makes it unnecessary for them to enter into conscious forms of awareness. To say that a belief is "self-satisfied" is to say that it has no need to defend itself or to form into a moment within a conscious idea. Our phylogenetic beliefs are unconscious and efficacious. Only a shock, evidenced in erratic behavior, brings a belief into awareness. For the pragmaticist, we always start *in medias res* and only encounter our beliefs *as* beliefs when they fail to secure the self against a transformed environment.

Habit becomes conscious when it breaks down. At that point, self-control becomes necessary as the self moves toward more generic habits that encompass and transform the situation that disrupted the self. Peirce links the self-control found in logical analysis with the self-control found in ethics. Peirce grounds logic in ethics because ethics expresses the deeper form of self-control in the context of the various *oughts* of our life. Deeper still than ethics is the aesthetic domain where we encounter the highest good, a good that is pursued whenever self-control establishes new habits that in turn secure truer beliefs.

The ultimate goal of self-control is to produce perfect knowledge. Pragmaticism is the only reliable method for helping the self and its community toward perfect knowledge, even though this ideal remains in the conditional case; namely, perfect knowledge is what "would be" the case in the infinite long run. The universe and the sign-using pragmaticist both exhibit self-control when there is an increase in the scope of generality in the world.

In addition to affirming the epistemological priority of our instinctive beliefs (which remain unconscious until challenged), pragmaticism affirms what Peirce calls a "scholastic realism"; that is, a realism harking back to the ontology of the medieval philosopher and theologian John Duns Scotus. Peirce is a realist in at least two senses. In the first sense, he is a realist because he insists that truth consists in what is the case regardless of what any individual may believe. Facts and objective realities are independently real. In the second sense, he is a realist because he insists that general categories and classes exist independently of our nomenclature. That is, classes are real in themselves and are not mere products of human language and its internal classificatory schemes. Peirce's pragmaticism is antinominalist throughout and always seeks generals and universals in the semiotic realms outside of language.

Put in even stronger language, Peirce argues that the alternative to his special kind of scholastic realism is chaos. Hence, "Generality is, indeed, an indispensable ingredient of reality; for mere individual existence or actuality without any regularity whatever is a nullity" [CP 5.431]. This is one of the implications of his principle of synechism. It is almost as if he is equating degrees of reality with degrees of generality. We will see that the issue is far more complex than this when we examine his three fundamental categories in some detail in chapter 3. Yet the tendency is often evident in Peirce to privilege generality over any of its instances.

Sensitive to the charge that pragmatism is nothing more than a simplistic philosophy of action for its own sake, Peirce boldly lays out the main features of his mature pragmaticism:

> Accordingly, the pragmaticist does not make the *summum bonum* to consist in action, but makes it to consist in that process of evolution whereby the existent comes more and more to embody those generals which were just now said to be *destined*, which is what we strive to express in calling them *reasonable*. In its higher stages, evolution takes place more and more largely through self-control, and this gives the pragmaticist a sort of justification for making the rational purport to be general. [CP 5.433]

Generals are destined to become more and more reasonable in an evolutionary universe. The pragmaticist enters into the evolution and growth of continuity in the world and, in a sense, feeds off of the energies of natural self-control that guarantee to move the universe

toward an ideal state in which the reasonable will be the real. This
emphasis on the growth of the reasonable per se becomes central to
Peirce's later reflections on method. While he was aware of the nature of continuity in the 1870s, and had already made it central to his
logic, he moves continuity into the center of his metaphysics and
cosmology and is thus in a position to provide a more sophisticated
base for his pragmaticism. The stress on the *metaphysical* aspects of
continuity sharpened in the 1890s in a series of papers that we will
examine in chapter 4.

The second paper in this *Monist* series, "Issues of Pragmaticism,"
also published in 1905, details the implications of critical common-
sensism. The theme of common-sensism goes back to the Scottish
philosophers of the eighteenth century who sought the indubitable
foundation for moral norms in some kind of species-wide innate ideas.
Peirce takes their formulations seriously, but insists that these basic
ideas must be understood from an evolutionary perspective that assumes a growth and transformation of our basic presuppositions.

Critical common-sensism, then, applies evolutionary thinking to the
unconscious and foundational propositions of our moral and scientific
life. In the previous series, Peirce argued that all animals relate to the
basic structures of their environments through kinetic and bodily
motions that shape and stabilize space and time. In this series, Peirce
brings out some of the logical and ethical implications of our original
shaping activity. Once again rejecting the Cartesian perspective of
universal doubt, Peirce affirms that we not only have indubitable propositions, but that we live through a process of indubitable inferences.
As we saw in our examination of the earlier set of papers from 1877–
1878, Peirce correlated scientific inquiry with methods in logic, all
tied to the structures of inference. In the current series of papers, Peirce
strengthens his sense of the ubiquity of inference by showing how we
move through the world with a whole cluster of unconscious and indubitable inferences that do not come under critical scrutiny.

Our most basic and general beliefs are of the nature of instincts
and are acritical. It does not follow from this that these primal beliefs
are arbitrary. They have a deep rootedness in our phylogenetic history
and would not exist at all were they not efficacious. Peirce has a basic
trust in the underlying structures of the mind, even while insisting
that these very structures are adaptable to changing circumstances.
No fundamental belief occurs in isolation from other fundamental
beliefs. Invoking the psychological law of association, Peirce insists
that such primal beliefs are tied together through a web of associational suggestions. Together, these beliefs form a consistent and coherent network of presuppositions.

The concern of the pragmaticist is to honor critical common-sensism while moving toward a deepening sense of the possibilities of self-controlled conduct. Insofar as our conduct is deliberate, it is therefore self-controlled and capable of further growth in reasonableness. He repeats his oft-stated belief that logical self-control is a species of ethical self-control. Consequently, all of our inferences have some kind of moral value, if only in the minimal sense that they struggle against random forms of inference toward a controlled outcome in which the consequent enhances the antecedent.

From our most primitive sensations to our most complex forms of inquiry, we actively shape what we encounter. Only in the most mature forms of deliberation, produced by highly complex outside shocks, is the process conscious and under deliberate self-control. The foundations of our practical life are unconscious and instinctual. We have perceptual judgments and "indubitable acritical inferences" [CP 5.442], supporting our trajectory through time and space. To doubt these structures is to invite chaos and to expose ourselves to those forces that can destroy human need and desire. Radical global doubt is not only unnecessary, it is dangerous.

Yet these indubitable propositions/beliefs are not to be confused with the clear and distinct ideas of the seventeenth-century Rationalists. The basic unconscious beliefs of the self are vague and cannot be quickly rendered into precise and definite terms. Our logical systems have not adequately dealt with vagueness because of an almost imperial sense that all vague structures must be overcome so that clear antecedents and clear consequents can emerge to guide inferences. Here we can see how Peirce turns the argument. If our most basic beliefs are unconscious and are part of the general nature of instincts, and if instincts are themselves somewhat vague in terms of their specific issue in a given case, then it follows that our primitive and indubitable beliefs are vague. In fact, if these beliefs were anything *but* vague, they would make it difficult for the self to function in a variety of situations, each with its own complex variables. Vagueness thus has a deep evolutionary value.

This commitment to critical common-sensism gives Peirce's theory of the self a strong naturalistic cast. The term "naturalistic" is certainly far from clear in its own right. In this context, the term is held to mean that the self is what it is because it finds itself within a vast nature that it neither created nor brought under complete control. Further, the naturalistic self is continuous with all other natural structures and powers and secures its own existence by shaping antecedent structures that come to it from a variety of sources. Pointing ahead to the third chapter, we see Peirce making one of his boldest affirmations about the status of the sign-using self within the world. Signs are themselves incomplete and call for further interpretations (interpretants) to render them more and more reasonable:

> It seems a strange thing, when one comes to ponder over it, that a sign should leave its interpreter to supply a part of its meaning; but the explanation of the phenomenon lies in the fact that the entire universe— not merely the universe of existents, but all that wider universe, embracing the universe of existents as a part, the universe which we are all accustomed to refer to as "the truth"—that all this universe is perfused with signs, if it is not composed exclusively of signs. [CP 5.448n]

The naturally located self is a sign-user who must enter into the infinitely complex realms of signification that surround it. The individual lives at the point of intersection where innumerable sign series deposit their incomplete semiotic charges. To survive within a universe "perfused with signs" is to rely on the depth structures of indubitable vague beliefs that have their own internal semiotic structures. These structures are, of course, reasonable in the sense that they participate in the growth of self-controlled generality within the world as a whole.

Critical common-sensism is tied to a pansemioticism that insists that whatever is in whatever way is at least virtually semiotic. The metaphysical commitment of critical common-sensism is to a scholastic realism that honors real vagueness and real possibilities. Peirce is concerned lest the concept of "possibility" lose its force. For many, the idea of possibility is a difficult one and has only a private or subjective status. That is, many affirm what Peirce called a "necessitarian" position that denied that possibilities are real in themselves. Instead, for the necessitarian, possibilities are merely intrapsychic products that disappear whenever a future event becomes actualized. The future is held to be as determined as the past and thus not open to real possibilities.

For the scholastic realist and critical common-sensist, possibilities are modally real; that is, they prevail in the objective order. Consequently, to speak of possibility is not to speak of human subjective ignorance, which assumes that we only speak of possibilities whenever we have insufficient data as to the laws governing a region of the world and its future prospects. To speak of possibility is to speak of a genuinely open future in which there is real novelty. For Peirce, the future is open, even if the past is not. Vagueness is real and possibilities are real. To attempt to eliminate either or both through an appeal to so-called necessary laws is to violate the basic structures of an evolving universe in which novelty remains as fully real as do statistical regularities.

Peirce concludes his reflections in this paper by insisting that pragmaticism has a distinctive view of time. He argues that the three modes of past, present, and future all function differently and that they have different modal properties. This reconstruction of the three modes of time makes it possible for Peirce to show how there are qualitative breaks within the flow of time (even though time is a continuum; that is, modal differences do not break the more basic ontological continuity of the modes of time). Put differently, each mode of time has its own logical structure and will differ from the others in terms of the scope of possibility and necessity.

Peirce refers to the past as the "existential mode of time" [CP 5.459], in that it acts on us in the present as if it were a brute existent. The past is closed and is constituted by the sum of its *faits accomplis*. Consequently, we cannot alter the past or envision it as the realm of possibility. The future is constituted by genuine possibility (which is objective) and is intimately tied to human conduct. As always, the pragmatist/pragmaticist privileges the future because it is amenable to self-control:

> It cannot be denied that acritical inferences may refer to the Past in its capacity as past; but according to Pragmaticism, the conclusion of a Reasoning power must refer to the Future. For its meaning refers to conduct, and since it is a reasoned conclusion must refer to deliberate conduct, which is controllable conduct. But the only controllable conduct is Future conduct. [CP 5.461]

Peirce ties the concept of self-control to that of novelty. Self-control has as its 'object' the increase of itself and its instances. This increase takes place in a future that allows for genuine novelty. It is as if self-control needs a 'space' within which to move past antecedent beliefs and their manifest habits.

The present has a more curious ontological status. It is obvious to most people that the past and the future are modally distinct. The future is open in a way that is forever closed to the past. But what of the present? Is its ontological and modal structure a blend of that of past and future? Our sense of the present is indeed a blending of the two other time senses. The future is available in the present through a feeling of "struggle over what shall be" [CP 5.462]. The present is thus the "Nascent State of the Actual" [CP 5.462]; that is, the locus where reality becomes actualized and moves toward the determined status of the past. But what is the object of present experience? Do we, as living in the passing present, have a present or given experience of the self? On this question, Peirce remains an agnostic. We do not have true introspective knowledge of a present self. Rather, we infer that there is a self:

> Introspection is wholly a matter of inference. One is immediately conscious of his Feelings, no doubt; but not that they are feelings of an *ego*. The self is only inferred. There is no time in the Present for any inference at all, least of all for inference concerning that very instant. [CP 5.462]

Once again, the pragmaticist moves the question of identity into the future. The present, like the past, seems to involve unconscious inferences that do not admit of genuine self-control. Consequently, all that we can get from the present are predetermined inferences that assure us that a self is present even if it cannot be known. Peirce transforms Hume's skepticism by pushing the problem of self-identity into a different mode of time. The self does obtain but it can only be generated and understood through the means of self-control operating out of a partially open future. In other words, the self is in the domain of the "not yet" even if it leaves some kind of trace in the present and past. Identity theory seems to be a species of the concept of self-control. This is clearly the case if one remembers that self-control is a concept that applies to all elements of nature, even if it reaches its penultimate expression in the human process. Its ultimate expression, as we will see in chapter 4, is in the divine itself as it emerges within an evolutionary cosmos.

The structure of time mirrors the structure of truth when understood pragmatically. The future is the domain of real possibility, generality, and vagueness. The past is constituted by those necessities that impinge on the inferences of the present. The present is constituted by a series of inferences whose whence and whither are shrouded in mist. Truth belongs to the domain of the future where genuine novelty interacts dialectically with generality. To speak of the counterfactual conditional, i.e., of what "would be" the case in the infinite long run, is to recognize that the future and the truth emergent from it belong to the same structure of reality. This future is held open by the divine who is itself underway toward increased generality and inclusiveness. Hence the future is the most ontologically interesting of the known modes of time. The interpretive community, using abduction to deepen deduction and induction, lives out of the opening power of the future and provides a place for the appearance of truth.

In the final paper in this *Monist* series, "Prolegomena to an Apology for Pragmaticism" (1906), Peirce introduces the reader to his own conception of "Existential Graphs" that are designed to give the reasoner an iconic (pictorial) representation of the reasoning processes found in pragmaticism. Briefly put, these graphs and drawings convert such logical categories as necessity, possibility, affirmation, negation, and intention into pictures that can be layered with several elements to show how a proposition or argument is structured. In introducing his unique system of graphs, Peirce says some important things about semiotics and the nature of abduction and mind. Our focus will be on the elements relevant for our understanding of pragmaticism.

As noted, Peirce denies that the pragmaticist starts with some kind of bare given within experience. The "percept," that is, the unitary element at the base of experience, is a vague something that is immediately given shape by a perceptual judgment. It is important to note that perceptual judgments are not amenable to self-control. They are unconscious and instinctual in their mode of operation, even if they have consequences that can be brought into awareness. Yet even though perceptual judgments are automatic, they belong to the species of inference known as abduction. We saw that Peirce defined abduction as the inference from a given case to a hypothesized general rule. The hypothesis is in the domain of the unknown or not yet known, while the case is known to the reasoner. The case has a kind of compulsive givenness for the self. That is, it comes from an external source and presents itself to the sign-using organism with a certain insistence. This "givenness" is not that of a specific and defined content but a kind of brute presentness that announces itself to the individual. Our percepts function in the same way as given cases, namely, they present themselves to us compulsively:

> Suffice it to say that the perceiver is aware of being compelled to perceive what he perceives. Now existence means precisely the exercise of compulsion. Consequently, whatever feature of the percept is brought into relief by some association and thus attains a logical position like that of the observational premiss of an explaining Abduction, the attribution of Existence to it in the Perceptual Judgment is virtually and in an extended sense, a logical Abductive Inference nearly approximating to necessary inference. [CP 4.541]

Existence, represented by the category of secondness (dyadic interaction) breaks in upon the perceiver and compels a series of judgments/inferences that have a modal status approaching necessity. This abductive inference takes two forms. Initially it attributes existence to the percept. As a secondary act (not secondary in a temporal sense) it places the percept under a predicate. Thus, for example, I can respond abductively to a percept by saying, "There is a yellow object." I attribute both existence and the predicate "yellowness" to the percept. In this sense, a perceptual judgment applies a rule to a case. Of course, induction also enters into abduction in terms of its suggestiveness for making a general claim based on past enumerations. The important point is that a perceptual judgment, while unconscious and automatic, functions as a kind of primitive abduction. Peirce actually opens up a small crack in the door by saying that this type of abductive inference approximates a necessary inference. I take this to mean that there are some other inferential possibilities available to a given perceptual judgment, possibilities held open by the laws of evolution. That is, the necessity found in perceptual judgment is only approximate and allows for alternative predicates.

Abduction remains provisional, especially in its more complex forms: "Abduction, in the sense I give the word, is any reasoning of a large class of which the provisional adoption of an explanatory hypothesis is the type" [CP 4.541n]. The testing of a hypothesis involves forms of inquiry open to the future and to the larger community of scientists. Peirce makes the scientific community normative for all morally sensitive communities. Yet his conception of science is broad enough to allow for great interpretive play within the various worlds of abduction.

In the context of his extended discussion of existential graphs, Peirce drops an aside that is quite striking in its implications. His pansemioticism, briefly mentioned above, comes forward in his linkage between signs, thoughts, and generals:

> Thought is not necessarily connected with a brain. It appears in the work of bees, of crystals, and throughout the purely physical world; and one can no more deny that it is really there, than that the colors, the shapes, etc., of objects are really there. Consistently adhere to that unwarrantable denial, and you will be driven to some form of idealistic nominalism akin to Fichte's. Not only is thought in the organic world, but it develops there. But as there cannot be a General without instances embodying it, so there cannot be thought without Signs. [CP 4.551]

Fichte's idealistic nominalism denies the full independent existence of objects and their general categorial structures. Peirce's own objective idealism affirms that ideas and thoughts are part of the world as a whole, both in the organic and inorganic orders. This issue will become problematic when we explore his semiotic theory where the mentality of each interpreting sign (interpretant) is brought into tension with his naturalistic sense of how ideas function.[4] His theory of the self presupposes that thoughts and ideas, always embodied in signs, are not *in* the self as if the self were a static container, but that the self is in some sense *in* thought. Thought is found throughout the universe and pragmaticism lives within and among thoughts that come from all of the innumerable orders of the world.

We can see how some of these conceptions now come together. The self finds itself in an evolutionary cosmos that is perfused with signs, as embodied thoughts. Each act of awareness is a form of abduction in which the compulsive and given material of the world is shaped into general categories. The momentum of the sign-using organism, whether human or not, is toward an increase in its habits so that they correspond to the general and habitual structures of the world. From our simplest automatic perceptual judgments to the most sophisticated theorems of science and metaphysics, we use abduction to get into step with the depth-rhythms of nature. Under the aegis of self-control, the habits of the universe become our habits. The self and its world grow more and more reasonable with the passage of time.

The *Monist* series of 1905–1906 helped Peirce to move into the public debate and to defend his version of pragmaticism from misunderstandings. Two years prior to publishing this series, he gave a series of eight lectures at Harvard University. The first seven lectures were given under the auspices of the Philosophy Department while the eighth was given under the auspices of the Mathematics Department. The seventh lecture in the series is the most pertinent to our concerns in this chaper. It is entitled "Pragmatism and Abduction."

In this lecture Peirce reminds the audience of the three conclusions previously enunciated in the earlier lectures:

1. Nothing is in the intellect that is not first in the senses.
2. Perceptual judgments contain general elements from which one can deduce universal propositions.
3. Abductive inference shades into perceptual judgment without any sharp line of demarcation between them.

The pragmaticist starts with the facts of immediate perception and derives all knowledge from percepts. Percepts call forth perceptual judgments, which in turn function as antecedents for necessary deductive conclusions. Abduction is the genus of which perceptual judgment is the species. It is clear that the pragmatic correlation of thought with perception is a more dynamic model than that of orthodox British empiricism. Kant early on convinced Peirce that the function of thought is to give shape to present immediacies. The percept has its own inner momentum and suggestive power, but it is incomplete until an unconscious abduction renders it into species terms. Particularity hungers for generality. Like Hegel, whom he often criticizes, Peirce insisted that generality belongs to particularity and cannot form a separate ontological realm. Put in theological terms, generals, however disclosed, manifest a desire to become fully incarnate in individuals. There is a teleological dimension to the categories in that any given individual remains incomplete until it manifests (participates in) generality (thirdness). Of course, many individuals remain incomplete and, as we will see, the categories of secondness and thirdness can be manifest in degenerate forms (which is not the case for firstness).

The abductive inferences of perceptual judgment are beyond criticism and come to us "like a flash" [CP 5.181]. Yet Peirce goes on to say that these primitive abductions are also interpretations. Perception involves interpretation. How can we combine the sense that perceptual judgments are automatic and unconscious with the sense that they are also interpretations? The answer is not as vexing as one might assume at first glance. Unconscious processes are semiotic through and through. Consciousness is neither a sufficient nor a necessary condition for semiosis or abduction. Consciousness is a necessary condition for certain higher forms of self-control, but it need not be present in each case of interpretation. Insofar as any given abduction generates an interpretant (sign interpreting a previous sign) there is interpretation. Consequently, it follows that a perceptual judgment generates an interpretant that enriches the sign of the percept. Any transition from sign to interpretant is an interpretation of the meaning and power of the original sign.

It is customary to interpret Peirce as if he privileged consciousness in his semiotics, thus making him akin to some structuralist readings of language and sign function. In fact, Peirce was fully aware of the unconscious and located some of our most basic abductive and semiotic activities below the threshold of conscious awareness. His deep concern with the edges of perception, e.g., with issues in optical illusion and liminal forms of awareness, shows his sensitivity to the preconscious realms of signification. As we will see, Peirce's semiotics is firmly rooted in a conception of natural semiosis.[5] Nature is a self-recording semiotic system that has its own methodic forms of interaction. The unconscious penetrates down into the heart of nature creating a link between the most sophisticated of known sign users and the vast domain of the semiotic universe. Consequently, it should not be too difficult to see how perceptual judgment can be interpretive and hence semiotic.

The continuity between perceptual judgment and abduction proper does allow for a difference between them. All genuine abductions allow for questioning: "An Abductive suggestion, however, is something whose truth *can* be questioned or even denied" [CP 5.186]. A perceptual judgment cannot be questioned; that is, one cannot conceive of it being wrong. However, Peirce insists that perceptual judgments are subject to evolutionary pressures and can be compelled to change. This process is a slow one however, and the individual will not be aware of any change in his or her lifetime.

Pragmaticism is primarily the study of the logic of abduction. Induction and deduction enter into abductive processes as auxiliary modes of reasoning, yet they can stand on their own outside of a pragmaticist framework. Abduction cannot function other than in a pragmatic way. What, then, is the goal or purpose of abductive and hypothetical reasoning?

> Its end is, through subjection to the test of experiment, to lead to the avoidance of all surprise and to the establishment of a habit of positive expectation that shall not be disappointed. Any hypothesis, therefore, may be admissible, in the absence of any special reasons to the contrary, provided it be capable of experimental verification, and only insofar as it is capable of such verification. This is approximately the doctrine of pragmatism. [CP 5.197]

It must be remembered that Peirce has a sophisticated understanding of "experimental verification." He allows for a broad spectrum of such experiments from laboratory tests to imaginative construction. While his language may occasionally sound like that of a simplistic scientism, his conception of what is involved in verification is rich and multilayered. As a prime example, his own affirmation of an unconscious dimension to the self is a highly complex abduction that generates a hypothesis to explain the given case of human mental functioning. The evidence for the abduction is cumulative, derived from a variety of sources and comparative methods. By the same token, the postulation of the existence of perceptual judgments is *itself* an abduction insofar as such judgments are not immediate objects of perception. We know of their existence by indirection.

Peirce gives a straightforward example of a perceptual judgment. He has a clock in his study that strikes on every half hour. Normally, he does not notice the clock striking. Suppose, however, that the clock misstrikes the hour and gives the wrong time. Suddenly, he notices the clock and attends to the error. In all of the previous strikes, he had made the unconscious perceptual judgment that the clock was telling the right time. Only a broken sequence informed him that a new judgment, this time conscious, was called for. The broken clock is a perfect metaphor for the pragmatic method. Doubts emerge from external disruptions that call forth more conscious and deliberate abductions to explain their appearance. To fix the clock is to once again let perceptual judgments take over from conscious, and time-consuming, deliberations.

Peirce concludes this seventh lecture (the final one for his philosophical audience) with a beautifully succinct statement of the nature of concepts (which manifest thirdness, i.e., generality, law, and reasonableness): "The elements of every concept enter into logical thought at the gate of perception and make their exit at the gate of purposive action; and whatever cannot show its passports at both those two gates is to be arrested as unauthorized by reason" [CP 5.212]. Thirdness is found at both sides of the border. All perception is funded with those general judgments that render percepts usable and intelligible. When a given perceptual judgment delivers itself to the 'higher' realm of conscious and self-controlled deliberation, it issues in purposive action. The goal of purposive action, if we may speak of the purpose of purposes, is to increase the scope and depth of thirdness in the world. Peirce's pragmaticism is fully committed to reason and its offspring. This is not to deny the eternal presence of novelty and chance in the universe, but to argue that they too serve the growth of concrete reasonableness.

Before bringing our study of pragmatism and abduction to completion with an analysis of interpretive musement, a few further clarifications of the basic categories of habit, self-control, and reasonableness are in order. As noted, the concept of "habit" is not limited in its application to the human order. In a late manuscript (ca. 1910) Peirce expresses the cosmic scope of habit:

> If we now revert to the psychological assumption originally made, we shall see that it is already largely eliminated by the consideration that habit is by no means exclusively a mental fact. Empirically, we find that some plants take habits. The stream of water that wears a bed for itself is forming a habit. [CP 5.492]

Both the organic and inorganic orders "take habits" and thereby stabilize their relationships with the environing fields of interaction. Each instance of thirdness is a habit. By definition, habits can grow in scope and complexity and manifest a variety of subhabits. Not all habits are under the power of self-control, although Peirce sometimes affirms that lawlike generality is itself an instance of self-control. The concept of self-control is not limited to the human order, even though, in many of the above-cited passages, Peirce seems to correlate self-control with conscious deliberation. The tension between these two views is partly ameliorated by his panpsychism, which would allow all forms of matter to be funded with enough mentality to at least point toward forms of self-control. Self-control does not require a conscious self but does seem to entail consciousness in the human order. The difference seems to be that humans have the extra dimension of control of self-control; namely, the metacontrol that brings out the thematic principles of all forms of self-control that are otherwise manifest but not thematically transformed.

Of course, the relation between our unconscious perceptual judgments and beliefs on the one hand, and our conscious and refined abductions on the other, is a dialectical one. Peirce insists that we can grow past our instinctive self toward one that takes some measure of control over the preconscious structures of life. In a ca. 1905 manuscript, he makes this dialectic clear:

Namely, he [the critical common-sensist] opines that the indubitable beliefs refer to a somewhat primitive mode of life, and that, while they never become dubitable in so far as our mode of life remains that of somewhat primitive man, yet as we develop *degrees of self-control* unknown to that man, occasions of action arise in relation to which the original beliefs, if stretched to cover them, have no sufficient authority. In other words, we outgrow the applicability of instinct—not altogether, by any manner of means, but in our highest activities. The famous Scotch philosophers lived and died out before this could be duly appreciated. [CP 5.511]

Critical common-sensism goes beyond Scottish common-sensism by adding two elements to the acritical presuppositions of instinctual life: self-control and evolution (which is itself an exercise in cosmic self-control). Peirce here evidences what could be called a kind of heroic conception of the self, a self that pulls itself up from the "primitive man" within who wars against the pragmaticist principle of enlightened rational self-control. It is as if our primitive self remains on the level of secondness (or degenerate thirdness) and fails to rise up into the lucidity of thirdness proper. It should be clear that Peirce linked his pragmaticism, with its corollary abduction, to human emancipation from antecedent causal conditions. His framework is deeply teleological, although modified, as we will see, by a developmental teleology that remains open to novel goals and purposes. I have argued throughout that Peirce was committed to showing the parallel structures connecting religious imagery with the method of pragmatism. Readers often miss this point because of Peirce's caustic remarks about the practices associated with Christianity (or religion in general). But it is the very sharpness of these remarks that point to a much deeper sense of the possibilities of religion, possibilities that are betrayed by the method of authority, or by a misuse of the a priori method.

In this same ca. 1905 manuscript, Peirce brings these religious images and concepts to the fore to show their intimate connection with pragmaticism. I am persuaded that these images are taken seriously by Peirce and that they do not represent some kind of exoteric covering masking an agnostic intent. Instead, they represent the culmination of pragmatic method:

> On the contrary what he [the pragmaticist] adores, if he is a good pragmaticist, is *power*; not the sham power of brute force, which, even in its own specialty of spoiling things, secures such slight results; but the creative power of reasonableness, which subdues all other powers, and rules over them with its sceptre, knowledge, and its globe, love. It is as one of the chief lieutenants of reasonableness that he highly esteems doubt, although it is not amiable. [CP 5.520]

Doubt is overcome through the persuasive power of abduction, which in turn serves the growth of reasonableness in the world. In examining Peirce's mature metaphysics, we will see how he ties love, evolution, continuity, and creative advance together in a cosmology that stresses developmental teleology in a goal directed universe. Each sign-using organism is goal directed, and uses some form of abduction to render the world more favorable to its needs. Yet Peirce makes the bold claim that the universe as a whole (if such a phrase be allowed) is abductive in its inner being, always seeking more generals under which to subsume and explain cases. It need not follow that the universe is some kind of mind (the perspective adopted by personalists). What must minimally be the case is that the universe is committed to the creation and preservation of innumerable centers of mentality.

Such a conception—namely, that the universe has its own purposes—

seems hopelessly anthropocentric and anthropomorphic. Surprisingly, Peirce will agree with these charges and even go so far as to affirm that anthropomorphism is the very heart of pragmaticist metaphysics. In a 1903 manuscript (originally part of his Harvard lectures on pragmatism) Peirce states his commitment to anthropomorphism:

> . . . every scientific explanation of a natural phenomenon is a hypothesis that there is something in nature to which the human reason is analogous; and that it really is so all the successes of science in its applications to human convenience are witnesses. They proclaim that truth over the length and breadth of the modern world. In the light of the successes of science to my mind there is a degree of baseness in denying our birthright as children of God and in shamefacedly slinking away from anthropomorphic conceptions of the universe. [CP 1.316]

We have a kind of 'light of nature' within us that makes it possible to probe into the basic rational structures of the universe. This light does not come to us by a kind of primal intuition, a possibility rejected by Peirce, but through our evolutionary heritage. Any argument will derive its efficacy from its willingness, among other things, to move through analogies that point toward known human features. Abduction, which we have seen moves from a known case to an unknown hypothesis that is creatively generated to explain the case, works only insofar as its hypotheses are part of a web of anthropomorphic analogy.

The creation of an ideal hypothesis is a creative act. Abduction involves creation and application. In the second phase of abductive reasoning, the created hypothesis, which may come to us "in a flash" or through an extended process of fantasy, is applied to the case at hand. But this hypothesis must compete with others. Peirce argues that we must pick hypotheses in terms of a principle of simplicity. By the same token, the simplest hypothesis must also be consistent with other accepted hypotheses about the world in general and the particular field under study. Creativity is combined with economy so that our hypotheses remain faithful to the accumulated wisdom of critical common sense and the deliberations of the sciences.

The dialectic between experience and abduction is unending. An outside event impinges upon the self, forcing a breakup of an established habit or belief. This calls for a process of inference and reasoning in which the original condition of habit can be reestablished. All three forms of inference, deduction, induction, and abduction (retroduction) come to the aid of the doubting self. Abduction finds and tests an economic and consistent hypothesis that can establish a cause for the disruptive event. Once a cause has been isolated, means of control can be applied to transform the situation into a favorable one. This process is something like an expanding dialectical circle or spiral: "Thus it is that inquiry of every type, fully carried out, has the vital power of self-correction and growth" [CP 5.582]. From our simplest instinctive and unconscious perceptual judgments to our most elaborate abductions concerning the basic categories of the world, we apply self-correction to antecedent structures. In this dialectic we move inevitably to the most profound abductive inferences concerning the basic 'why' of the world. This final stage is that of "interpretive musement" that brings us into communion with an evolving God.

In 1908 Peirce published his defense of a kind of pragmaticist conception of God. As always, he approaches the metaphysical issue through an analysis of methodology. Relying explicitly on his earlier publications (both the 1877–1878 and 1905–1906 series of papers), Peirce moves his analysis of abduction one further step into the consummatory phase of interpretive musement. The essay "A Neglected Argument for the Reality of God," published in the *Hibbert Journal*, is a remarkable meditative piece on the ultimate metaphysical upshot of pragmaticism. Politically, the essay gave Peirce yet another outlet through which he could distance himself from William James. One of the primary issues dividing these two thinkers is the status of continuity within the world. James, always the finitist and voluntarist, downplays ontological continuity in favor of dyadic forms of interaction and conflict. Peirce, moving toward generality and thirdness (the category of lawlike generality and reasonableness), stresses the mediating aspect of pragmaticism as it struggles to overcome the dyadic tensions that punctuate life.

A more obvious point of conflict between them pertains to the respective status each gives to psychology. When James writes about religious or theological issues, he does so from the standpoint of his analysis of the stream of consciousness and the human will. When Peirce writes about the metaphysical issues pertinent to the divine, he does so from the standpoint of synechism and the logic of continuity. As noted, Peirce never denies the psychological aspects of logic, even correlating specific methods with aspects of the human psyche, but he is very careful to show how logic (as general semiotic) is a normative structure for the various forms of consciousness. These respective tensions come to the surface in this essay and give Peirce the opportunity to show how pragmaticism, as opposed to James's pragmatism, advances our understanding of the powers of the creator.

Throughout, we have been making occasional references to Peirce's three metaphysical categories of firstness, secondness, and thirdness. These categories will receive an extended treatment in the third chapter, where they will be correlated to Peirce's semiotic theory, but a few further words about them are necessary at this juncture in the exposition. Peirce ties his special argument for the reality of God to the three primal categories. He is asking us to meditate on the question of the origin of the worlds depicted in these categories. Consequently, we must gain some clarity as to what these categories delineate and what kind of explanatory scope they have. Peirce lays out the categories (which actually had their preliminary formulation in the 1860s) in terms of the realms of human experience:

> Of the three Universes of Experience familiar to us all, the first comprises all mere Ideas, those airy nothings to which the mind of poet, pure mathematician, or another *might* give local habitation and a name within that mind. Their very airy-nothingness, the fact that their Being consists in mere capability of getting thought, not in anybody's Actually thinking them, saves their Reality. The second Universe is that of Brute Actuality of things and facts. I am confident that their Being consists in reactions against Brute forces, notwithstanding objections redoubtable until they are closely and fairly examined. The third Universe comprises everything whose being consists in active power to establish connections between different objects, especially between objects in different Universes. [CP 6.455]

The first universe is the domain of firstness, constituted by possibility that is dynamic and self-othering. The second universe is the domain of secondness, constituted by actual (actualized) "things and facts" that interact dyadically. The third universe is the domain of thirdness, constituted by mediating general laws that serve, among other things, to connect the first and second worlds together. It should be emphasized that thirdness is dynamic and restless. It works tirelessly to weave the fabric of concrete reasonableness in and through the world.

The three universes are found within human experience *and* within the world of nature. The order of experience is but one order among innumerable other orders that manifest the three universes/categories. It is important for the current argument that we start with the order of human experience and move outward toward an encounter with God. For Peirce, appealing to critical common-sensism, we already have a vague understanding of God to begin with. Interpretive musement merely frees up potencies that are already there. To enter into musement is thus to respond to a vague presence that can be found at both the center and the circumference of experience.

Once we have gained a preliminary grasp of the three universes of firstness, secondness, and thirdness, we must probe into that state of mind that makes it possible to explore their inner dynamics, and their interconnections. The relevant passage is quoted at length because it is so rich in its suggestiveness:

> There is a certain agreeable occupation of mind which, from its having no distinctive name, I infer is not as commonly practiced as it deserves to be; for indulged in moderately—say through some five to six per cent of one's waking time, perhaps during a stroll—it is refreshing enough more than to repay the expenditure. Because it involves no purpose save that of casting aside all serious purpose, I have sometimes been half-inclined to call it reverie with some qualification; but for a frame of mind so antipodal to vacancy and dreaminess such a designation would be too excruciating a misfit. In fact, it is Pure Play. Now, Play, we all know, is a lively exercise of one's powers. Pure Play has no rules, except this very law of liberty. It bloweth where it listeth. It has no purpose, unless recreation. The particular occupation I mean— a *petite bouchée* ["little kiss"] with the Universes—may take either the form of aesthetic contemplation, or that of distant castle-building (whether in Spain or within one's own moral training), or that of considering some wonder in one of the Universes, or some connection between two of the three, with speculation concerning its cause. It is this last kind—I will call it "Musement" on the whole—that I particularly recommend, because it will in time flower into the N.A. [neglected argument]. [CP 6.458]

Several things are of note in this passage. The process of musement is one found on the fringes of our normal activity. Once we have stabilized the struggle between doubt and belief, we have a kind of surplus semiotic energy that can be devoted to the pure play of signification. Entering into this play actually works against entropy by enhancing the amount of energy available to the self. Ordinary teleological structures are left behind so that we can enter into a kind of metapurpose that is willing to delay immediate pragmatic gratification. What is most important is the freedom to explore the interconnection and origin of the three universes. Abduction can create and apply hypotheses that explain particular cases through a quest for their causes. Interpretive musement, as a species of abduction, perhaps its culmination, goes beyond other forms of abduction to seek the cause for all three universes/categories. What is interesting is that musement does not rely on the normal argumentative and inferential strategies for finding its object. The free space opened up by musement makes it possible to listen to those vague forces and powers that animate the heart of experience.

There is a kind of inner logic to musement in that it progresses from an attentive state toward a state of pure play, which in turn gives way to a communion with God. It is very important to note that Peirce does not envision the goal of musement as the contemplation of the divine, but as the intimate encounter with a present power. God becomes very real and very near. This sense of communion, a kind of Platonic erotic connection with the ground of the world, facilitates an enhanced understanding of the nature of the three universes and their connections. As we will see in chapter 4, the divine nature participates in all three universes and serves to bind them together according to the principles of developmental teleology. More importantly, although this is a problematic issue, God lives as the creative source for the three universes of experience. God and the three universes grow together in concrete reasonableness.

Musement is, of course, a type of thinking, and, like all types of thinking, it involves the use of signs and a kind of internal dialogue. Put simply, musement invokes an internal semiotic dialogue that brings the self into communion with God. All thought involves at the very least a thinker thinking to him- or herself. Internal dialogue is communal. Musement is the most important kind of internal semiotic dialogue because it participates in the moving spirit of God. Put in theological terms, terms that Peirce would shy away from, the self comes into its own depth by participating in the spirit that secures it against semiotic entropy. The satisfaction attained by the self is not a passing one, a mistake made by James, but the ultimate satisfaction that comes from entering into the life of the divine muser.

Once again, Peirce reiterates his commitment to the full reality of habits, generals, and possibility. The God encountered in musement does not cancel our possibilities or impose a predetermined structure on the self. The issue of divine freedom—that is, whether or not God can genuinely change and grow—is a difficult one in Peirce. I will argue that Peirce's philosophical theology is deeply divided on this and other issues, but that he moves, almost in spite of himself, toward a kind of process perspective that acknowledges divine growth within the context of a larger universe of possibility. These issues are only hinted at in this essay but come to full flower elsewhere.

God is knowable to the self. On this issue, Peirce is decidedly not an agnostic. He takes issue with any concept of the "unknowable": "The Unknowable is a nominalistic heresy" [CP 6.492]. We can come to know God through the use of musement (which makes possible the "humble" argument for God's existence). We can know God in terms of the God/world correlation and in terms of how God participates in the three universes. That is, God is deeply wedded to the world and lives in all three domains. As we will see, God participates in firstness in terms of cosmogenesis, manifests secondness in terms of eschatology, and empowers thirdness in terms of the emergence of the *summum bonum* both within and at the consummated end of history. In some senses Peirce remains close to orthodox Christian trinitarian doctrine, while in other senses he moves toward contemporary forms of panentheism (that is, the doctrine that God is in the world while yet transcending it).

Interpretive musement fulfills the drive of abduction to find the causes of things. The cause of the world cannot be found by induction (which does not really advance our foundational knowledge) nor through deduction (hence Peirce distances himself from the ontological argument). Musement moves toward a sense of the cause of the world by invoking a transformed sense of the argument from design. In this case, the three universes manifest a grand semiotic design that could not be the result of pure chance. The creator is manifest throughout the created orders. Musement merely brings our vague sense of this into some kind of thematic focus. If we are honest, we cannot avoid communion with God. The ultimate goal of pragmaticism is thus religious. We study the logic of abduction so that we can enter into communion with God. This consequence gives Peirce's pragmaticism a unique flavor. The principle of synechism returns here, manifest in the religious sensibility that becomes open to the origin and connectedness among the three universes of experience. We have come a long way from the earlier essays on method, but the inner logic of this journey should be clear. The sign-using organism moves from a state of doubt to belief so as to secure new habits. Particular irritations and irruptions are dealt with by specific inductive, deductive, and abductive strategies. The ultimate irritation, the ultimate doubt, pertains to the 'why' of the three universes of experiences. Musement provides a direct answer to this doubt by bringing us into communion with the God who is the source of all reasonable habits, be they cosmic or personal.

Notes

1. For an exhaustive analysis of this issue, see *Self-Control in the Philosophy of Charles S. Peirce* by Edward Petry, Jr. (Ph.D. Dissertation: Pennsylvania State University, 1990).

2. There is a clear progression in Peirce's conception of abduction. Prior

to 1900, he tended to conflate abduction with induction, while after the turn of the century he strictly separated them. On this issue see "The Evolution of Peirce's Concept of Abduction" by Douglas R. Anderson, *Transactions of the Charles S. Peirce Society*, Vol. XXII, No. 2, Spring 1986, pp. 145–164, and "In What Way is Abductive Inference Creative?" by Tomis Kapitan, *Transactions of the Charles S. Peirce Society*, Vol. XXVI, No. 4, Fall 1990, pp. 499–512.

3. Peirce notes that he used the term in a piece published toward the end of 1890 in *Baldwin's Dictionary*. It is clear that he considers the 1905 appearance of the term "pragmatism" to be his first significant public one. He notes that he has used the term in conversation since the mid-1870s. William James started using the term "pragmatism" in print in 1897 in his *The Will to Believe and Other Essays in Popular Philosophy* (London: Longmans, Green, and Co.). In 1907 James published *Pragmatism: A New Name for Some Old Ways of Thinking* (London: Longmans, Green, and Co.).

4. For an interesting essay that shows the tension between Peirce's pragmatism and his idealism, see "Can Peirce be a Pragmatist and an Idealist" by John Peterson, *Transactions of the Charles S. Peirce Society*, Vol. XXVI, No. 2, Spring 1991, pp. 221–235.

5. On this issue see *The Scope of Semiosis in Peirce's Philosophy* by Felicia E. Kruse (Ph.D. Dissertation: Pennsylvania State University, 1989).

Chapter Two

The Sign-Using Self
and Its Communities

At the conclusion of the last chapter, it became clear that Peirce adopts an anthropocentric and anthropomorphic conception of the universe. His earliest reflections (ca. 1861) center on the nature of the self and its relation to its other. As he frames his three primal categories of firstness, secondness, and thirdness, he uses images and structures pertinent to the human order to illuminate the basic features of the world. This anthropocentric bias is fundamental to all that Peirce articulates in his metaphysics and theory of method. There is a very clear sense in which his development of pragmatism has a direct correlation to a deep need to find a transforming structure for the human process. This is not to say that he reduces pragmaticism to human need, but that he insists that no method would be of value in the long run if it did not directly shape the self so that it could let go of its more "primitive" aspects and enter into the reasonableness of the universe. Put in even stronger terms, the function of all philosophical methods and all metaphysical categories is to transform the self so that it can become a microcosmic analogue to a self-controlled universe that is moving toward its ideal consummation in the *summum bonum*. Consequently, it should come as no surprise that Peirce devotes some of his sharpest analytic energies to probing into the nature of the self.

The philosophical background against which Peirce is framing his own distinctive view of the self is that of Cartesianism. His attacks against a priorism are of a piece with his attacks against intuitionism and its belief in self-evident premises. For Peirce, the Cartesian spirit is best expressed in a belief in a static thinking substance that has immediate intuitive knowledge of itself and its internal reflections. From this alleged self-evident and nonmediated structure comes an epistemological edifice that can ground all of the empirical forms of inquiry. Needless to say, Peirce sees this as a pernicious structure, precisely because it cuts the self off from the much more pervasive natural and semiotic forces that actually contribute to its internal and external relations.

Largely because of his many years as a student and critic of Kant's *Critique of Pure Reason*, Peirce was able to frame a conception of the self that emphasized its dynamic and inferential powers to shape not only spatial and temporal structures, but the basic semiotic categories of nature and thought. From early on Peirce was convinced that the self is basically a sign-using organism deeply wedded to natural processes that are themselves semiotic through and through. Unfortunately, Peirce's language often mutes the fact that he is committed to a pansemioticism that correlates causal and teleological events to semiotic events. The danger of his anthropocentric strategy is that it often seems to privilege the human over its natural enabling conditions. However, a careful reading of Peirce indicates that he understands that the self could not take the form it does without a fully semiotic evolutionary world.

The centrality of methodological reflections is as evident in Peirce's theory of the self as it is elsewhere. There is a direct correlation between the pragmatic structures of inference and the fundamental structures of the human process. Cartesianism has an inadequate view of the self because it has an inadequate logical theory. As noted, Peirce radically redefines the scope of logic so that it is coextensive with semiotic. The semiotic reconfiguration of methods of inference has direct implications for philosophical anthropology. Logic is a normative structure that shapes the self and gives it its structures of intelligibility. The self is thus what it is because of semiotic powers that eclipse it in scope and richness. Put in even stronger terms, we can almost derive our anthropology from semiotics. There are some limits as to how far this derivation can go, but it is clear that the semiotic regrounding of logic makes it possible to break free from the Cartesian anthropology that is presemiotic.

Faculties and Incapacities of the Self

In his late twenties Peirce published a series of three papers in *The Journal of Speculative Philosophy*. This journal was the first American journal devoted to technical philosophy and played an important role in the early stages of classical American philosophy. Its editor, W. T. Harris, a Hegelian, provided an important forum for some of the most seminal papers in the early history of pragmatism. In its pages, Peirce made public his crucial arguments against earlier a prioristic philosophy and laid the foundations for both his later pragmaticism and his semiotic theory. The three papers are "Questions Concerning Certain Faculties Claimed for Man" (1868), "Some Consequences of Four Incapacities" (1868), and "Grounds of Validity of the Laws of Logic: Further Consequences of Four Incapacities" (1869). These papers are generally considered to be among the most important that Peirce ever wrote, precisely because they represent daring reconstructions of semiotics and anthropology that bore such dramatic fruits in the subsequent decades. We will begin our analysis of Peirce's semiotic theory of the self with these papers. This will prepare the way for subsequent analysis of his more mature reflections on the unconscious and its pertinence to nature's most sophisticated sign-user.

The first paper in this 1868–1869 series, "Questions Concerning Certain Faculties Claimed for Man," poses seven questions that put pressure on accepted conceptions of the self and its specific epistemological strategies. The overall upshot of these questions is to show how the self actually functions in the world with its particular physical and mental faculties. The force of the respective arguments is to show how each aspect of the self/world correlation involves rather complex forms of inference and interpretation. The concept of unmediated knowledge is severely undermined, precisely because it fails to show how the self builds up its knowledge world through a series of complex inferences that have neither a pure beginning nor a predetermined end.

The first question is concerned with whether or not the self can have an unmediated cognition of an object that is not mediated by a previous cognition. The Cartesian perspective insists that we can have immediate intuitions of objects that are directly present to the thinking self. The external reality is given to the self without an intervening previous cognition that would somehow determine or at least influence how the self cognized the object. Peirce opens the attack by doubling the levels of alleged intuitions. We not only have an intuition, but must have an immediate intuition that the previous intuition *is* an intuition. And we must do this intuitively, i.e., without any comparison of intuitions that come before or after. Put differently, we are asked to distinguish between an intuition and a cognition (which is mediated) by using an intuition. It soon becomes clear that we have already entered into a comparative process that involves interpretation and mediation. A pure intuition, one that is not mediated in any way (determined by a previous cognition), is logically equivalent to a "premise not itself a conclusion" [W 2.193 & EP 1.12]. How do we arrive at a pure premise? Do we have an intuitive faculty that tells us, without any other forms of comparison, that it has arrived at a nonderived premise?

Peirce is skeptical that the self has such a faculty. Put in terms of perception rather than in the commensurate terms of logic, we are asked to find some kind of perception that is purely given without any admixture of interpretation. Peirce reminds us that "Every lawyer knows how difficult it is for witnesses to distinguish between what they have seen and what they have inferred" [W 2.195 & EP 1.13]. Every act of perception (and perception is never passive for Peirce) is an act of interpretation. By the same token, every logical premise is also a conclusion of some previous argument. In the 1868 manuscript "Questions on Reality," Peirce links logic to history: "Indeed it may be said generally that each age pushes back the boundary of reasoning and shows that what had been taken to be premises were in reality conclusions" [W 2.166]. There is no more a first pure perception than there is a pure premise that has not been produced by some previous inferences.

As we saw in the first chapter, Peirce took Bishop Berkeley's derivation of the third dimension of space seriously. To see the depth dimension of things is to make a complex series of inferences that serve to construct space from material that is itself prevalent in only two dimensions. Of course, Peirce grafts an evolutionary and physiological argument onto Berkeley's to show how the sign-using organism takes certain basic materials and weaves them into an intelligible fabric. To bring this point home, Peirce asks us to conduct a visual experiment. We are told to take two pennies and to place them on the table in front of us. Put one on the left side of our visual field and the other on the right. Cover the left eye while looking at the left penny with the right eye. Slide the right penny toward the left while still looking at the left one. At a point several inches away from the left penny, the right one will disappear from the visual field. As it is moved further to the left, it reappears. Peirce argues that the blind spot in the retina must be filled in by a series of unconscious inferences so that we do not go around with holes in our perception. We never allow the objects in our visual field to go missing as they may chance to enter into the blind spot of the retina. As creatures dedicated to survival, we instantly fill in the missing components of all of our sensual fields. Visual perception in particular is not so much a continuous oval as it is a partially empty ring that needs to be filled in by the organism.

Turning to the other senses, Peirce advances the same argument that every perception of a so-called discrete sensum is already an interpretation that takes place in a context shaped by antecedent sensations. In moving our fingers over a cloth we must build up a complex set of sensations before we can say with any certainty that the cloth is of such and such a type. With acoustical phenomena we are always in the position of having to locate a sound in a sequence of previous cognitions that determine the experienced value of the given sound. There can be no direct intuited cognition of the given materials of any of the human senses. All sensations are mediated right from the beginning. There is a psychological aspect to the logical theory of continuity that insists that all human faculties and all sensations prevail within a set of continua that do not allow for absolute breaks or pure unmediated beginnings.

Space and time are constructed from sensations that obtain within a continuum that is generated through a series of largely unconscious inferences. Peirce insists that his own theory of spatio-temporal structures of awareness is consistent with that of Kant, especially since Kant did emphasize that the transcendental synthesis of space and time is a *process*. This is the case even though Kant uses the language of intuition (*Anschauung*) to frame his discussion of the derivation of the infinite given magnitude of space and time. Peirce notes that Kant is using the concept of "intuition" in two senses: on the one hand it refers to an "individual representation," while on the other hand it refers to the total transcendental field within which any given intuition must take place. It is the second meaning of the term that Peirce appeals to in stressing the mental process of developing a sense of absolute space and time [cf. W 2.199 & EP 1.17].

This compilation of facts from human perception shows that there can be no pure unmediated intuition of an object external to the self. In more recent terminology, Peirce attacks the "myth of the given" and provides a hermeneutic reading of the self/world transaction. To perceive is to judge and to interpret. When we do so consciously, we are in a position to advance inquiry. When we do so unconsciously, we have already secured an evolutionary niche that can secure our survival for at least the immediate future (barring a change in the environment). The conclusion is clear: ". . . we have no intuitive faculty of distinguishing intuitive from mediate cognitions" [W 2.200 & EP 1.18].

The second question in this paper moves us more directly into an analysis of the structure and dynamics of the self. Peirce asks whether or not we have an intuitive self-consciousness; that is, whether we have direct access to a private self that comes to us without mediation or acts of comparison. The skeptical conclusion reached on the issue of *external* perception carries over into the domain of self-knowledge. Peirce's arguments are similar here, but he adds some crucial nuances to his analysis that shed light on the semiotic nature of self-consciousness.

Peirce notes that young children do not have self-consciousness, but do manifest the powers of thought. This obvious fact has striking implications. For the Cartesian, there is a direct correlation of thought with self-consciousness. Thought is in fact grounded in self-consciousness and receives its confirmation and seal from the self. Peirce reverses this relationship and gives the priority to thought. Self-consciousness is a product of thought and has a more tenuous status in the world than does its originating source. In fact, Peirce goes further and undermines the privileged position of lucid thought-filled self-consciousness by arguing that our sense of self actually comes from ignorance and error. The child touches a hot stove, for example, and quickly learns that there is a gap between belief and fact. This gap opens up the possibility of error, which in turn prepares the way for a recognition that there is a self capable of error—that is, of being out of phase with the immediate environment. Without error we would have an ahistorical and ineffective ego: "Ignorance and error are all that distinguish our private selves from the absolute *ego* of pure apperception" [W 2.203 & EP 1.20].

Kant's "transcendental unity of apperception"—namely, the nonsubstantive functional unity of self-consciousness—proves to be an empty abstraction when contrasted with the flesh-and-blood ego emerging from the trials of ignorance and error. Peirce, who remained within the Kantian orbit in many respects, transforms the Kantian problematic to show how the finite and private ego receives its contour out of the shocks of error. The mechanism of self-creation comes from the series of contrasts and comparisons that show the self just what the external world involves. To be in error is to be a self with beliefs that could (and should) be otherwise. Peirce does not fall back on a transcendental argument that posits a nonobserved transcendental ego, but moves forward into the future to show how a purposive self emerges in time and place. While his general framework remains friendly to Kant's, it adds crucial natural, social, and temporal features that transfigure the critical perspective so that it can better serve a perspective that is evolutionary and semiotic.

We now know that we have made a set of inferences that point to a self that is fallible. From this it does not follow that we have disclosed a unique thinking substance that is intuitively available. Rather, it seems as if we must draw the opposite conclusion, that ". . . self-consciousness may easily be the result of inference" [W 2.204 & EP 1.21]. The status of introspective knowledge is identical to that of external knowledge. We come to know the self and external objects through a series of mediated interpretations and inferences that collectively build up a fairly reliable contour through the mechanism of error and its amelioration via established belief.

The third question in this paper asks the more subtle question as to whether or not we can intuitively distinguish between subjective and objective elements of different kinds of cognition. The example cited is that of dreams. Do we intuitively know the difference between a dream and reality? In the background to this discussion is Hume's distinction between more and less vivid impressions of sense. A present color is more vivid and intense in its mode of appearance than an imagined or remembered one. For Hume, we have an immediate sense of vividness that tells us if something is given to sensation or merely remembered. Peirce rejects this idea and insists that we are still in the position of using external acts of inference and comparison that make it possible to judge the objective status of a sensum. Put differently, there are no purely internal and intuitive (nonmediated) means by which to distinguish the origin of one color from another, or a dream from reality. Such comparisons must be done 'after the fact.' In this sense, Peirce shifts the focus to external and publicly available criteria.

The move to external and public criteria is deepened when Peirce asks a fourth question. Do we have a power of introspection or is our knowledge of the self derived from external reality? The Cartesian perspective would, of course, insist that there is an independent power of introspection that is ontologically tied to the nature of the thinking substance. As is to be expected, Peirce denies that we have a special and isolated introspective faculty that can probe into the structures of the ego (whether transcendental or empirical). In the context of this argument, Peirce advances what could be called an "intentional" theory of emotion. Such a theory denies that emotions are purely internal states of affairs that merely serve to color the surface of self-consciousness. Rather, emotions are outward-directed intentions that predicate qualities of objects. To have an emotion is to project (intend) a feeling-state outward onto an objective field. To be angry, for example, is to be angry at some thing or person. Without an external and intentional referent, the emotion could not emerge in the first place.

If emotions have external referents, it seems to follow that other mental states do as well. Peirce accepts this inference and insists that human volition moves outward into the objective world to have a proper field of operation. All aspects of the self are other directed. There is a very clear sense, then, that we learn about the self by reading its features off of the projected space of public interaction. We do not introspect in the sense of turning toward an isolated realm of purely inner signs and states, but move outward into public and natural structures that show the self what its internal and external contours are. Hence, ". . . the only way of investigating a psychological question is by inference from external facts" [W 2.207 & EP 1.23]. The reader should remember, however, that this move toward the external structures of meaning and signification does not make Peirce into a cryptobehaviorist. His underlying anthropomorphism protects him from a mindless physicalism insofar as it insists on a depth structure of mentality that supports both the internal and external semiotic realms. The so-called 'external' realities are actually funded with their own forms of intelligibility and reasonableness.

The fifth question in this paper is one that opens up some of the most dramatic possibilities for Peirce's overall project. He asks simply, "Whether we can think without signs" [W 2.207 & EP 1.23]. He has already denied a special faculty of introspection, thereby insisting that all thought is of and through external realities. External facts are always mediated to us through signs; therefore it follows that all thought must be in signs. The premise that all external thoughts are semiotic was established when Peirce showed in his analysis of the first question that all thoughts are mediated (that is, that all premises are conclusions in another order of analysis). To think is to think in signs, to acknowledge that any given thought is by definition an interpretation of a previous thought. If all thought is mediated, it follows that all thought is comparative. To compare one thought with another is to add new semiotic material to previous cognitions.

To deepen this semiotic understanding, Peirce points out its crucial temporal dimension. If Kant tended to conflate temporality with the static table of logical judgments, Peirce opens up a more dynamic conception of the flow of time. In the first chapter we noted that he combines a modal analysis of time with a stress on continuity. That is, each mode of time is distinct in its correlation of possibility and necessity, yet all three modes are linked together by continuity. Time is asymmetrical in the sense that it has a nonreversible flow. To think in signs is to think in a temporal continuum. "To say, therefore, that thought cannot happen in an instant, but requires a time, is but another way of saying that every thought must be interpreted in another, or that all thought is in signs" [W 2.207-208 & EP 1.24].

Any given sign will be an interpretation (interpretant) of a previous sign. Time and semiosis are both asymmetrical. The present, which combines possibility and necessity, moves into the past that eliminates all possibility. So too, a present sign adds to the wealth of a previous sign and leaves that sign forever changed. A sign interpreted is a sign forever augmented in some respect. We cannot reverse the flow of time or of semiosis. It follows that the universe of signs is getting richer with each passing moment. This semiotic plenitude is part of the universe's growth in concrete reasonableness. Peirce is very clear that semiosis is fully temporal and that enhanced generality lies in the future. There is a sense in which signs hunger for an increase in thirdness.

The self finds itself located within vast semiotic fields that shape it. It comes to know these external signs through the trials of ignorance and error. Self-consciousness represents but one pocket within a semiotic universe. To privilege this particular manifestation of semiosis, or to see it as the originating source of all others, is profoundly to misunderstand the structures of nature.

In his sixth question, Peirce asks us to analyze the status of the absolutely uncognizable. That is, is there some reality that the self cannot come to cognize in some way? Peirce did not insist that cognition must be free of vagueness. Consequently, he is not asking us if some cognitions remain too vague to be of direct use, but whether or not there exists something that can never be cognized in *any* respect. In answering this question, Peirce tips the scales toward his objective idealism; namely, the belief that the world is both real and part of some experience. He insists that ". . . *cognizability* (in its widest sense) and *being* are not merely metaphysically the same, but are synonymous terms" [W 2.208 & EP 1.25]. Hence to be, is to be the object of some experience. Remember that Peirce does not confine the concept of "experience" to the human process. Hence, other semiotic orders, not to mention the divine (not directly invoked in these 1868–1869 papers), experience the world in their respective ways. From this equation of cognition and being it follows that nothing can exist that is not cognized in some respect (elsewhere, Peirce distinguishes between "existence," which he correlates with secondness, and "being," which he correlates with firstness, but this distinction is not pertinent in this context).

Even infinite structures are somehow known to experience. We may not have a direct grasp of an infinite set per se, but we do cognize it through the mechanism of induction. Hence, universal and hypothetical propositions are cognizable, if indirectly. There seems to be a normative reason behind Peirce's denial that there can exist something absolutely uncognizable. If there exists something beyond human methodic powers, that reality would function as a kind of semiotic black hole absorbing the light of inquiry. It is almost as if Peirce finds the possibility of something beyond our awareness a threat to the well being of the self. This attitude could easily be interpreted as a kind of hubristic denial of the full independence of key aspects of nature. Pragmatism has a militant drive to render all of reality intelligible. Peirce's intolerance for the unknowable may have some more troubling implications in that it denies a presemiotic or preintelligible realm, a realm, as I argued in the introduction, that points to the neglected and denied aspects of the maternal.

The seventh and final question in this essay asks if there can be any cognition not determined by a previous cognition. The answer is obvious. Any given cognition will be the result of an inference from previous cognitions. These previous cognitions need not be directly known or available to the self. Every cognition ". . . arises by a process of beginning, as any other change comes to pass" [W 2.211 & EP 1.27]. There is no such thing as an absolute origin that is somehow free from its own antecedents. To be in any respect is to be part of a semiotic sequence whose beginning is shrouded in mist. We cannot find a premiss of all premisses or a cognition prior to all cognitions.

The conclusions drawn by this essay point toward a transformed conception of the self. There is no soul or thinking substance behind our cognitive acts. The unity of the self is not derived from some kind of transcendental ego, but comes from the external thought processes that are concresced into signs. There can be no pure beginning for self-consciousness in an introspective act, nor can there be a final outer boundary for the self. All mental acts, be they cognitive or emotional or volitional, are intentional in that they point outward into semiotic orders larger than the self. Consequently, it makes no sense to see the self as some kind of self-contained realm of awareness. To be a self is to be part of ancient and vast semiotic networks that permeate the universe.

In the second article in *The Journal of Speculative Philosophy* series, "Some Consequences of Four Incapacities" (1868), Peirce advances his semiotic analysis of the self and probes more thoroughly into the structure of the sign. Since we will analyze the nature of signification in the next chapter, our concern here will be with those elements pertinent to his semiotic anthropology. Peirce specifically states four presuppositions of Cartesianism that need to be further undermined. The first is the belief that philosophy must begin with universal doubt. The second is the belief that the ultimate test of certainty lies in the individual consciousness. The third is the belief that all inference belongs to a single logical chain. The fourth is the belief that we have regions of reality that remain inexplicable. These four false beliefs are dispatched in short order. The first belief is rejected on pragmatic grounds; namely, that we cannot ". . . pretend to doubt in philosophy what we do not doubt in our hearts" [W 2.212 & EP 1.29]. The second belief is rejected on the grounds that all knowledge claims are validated by a community, if only because the scope of the problems dealt with in philosophy eclipses the power of any given individual. The third belief is rejected on the grounds that argument is a highly complex logical structure more akin to a cable with many intertwined fibers than to a chain with one simple principle of connectedness. The fourth belief is rejected on the grounds that any claim about a so-called unknowable sphere is already a claim using signs and thought. Any explanation from the grounds of inexplicability is not an explanation. Therefore the concept of the inexplicable can never be used in an argument because it has no argumentative status.

By way of reminding the reader of the results of the previous article in this series, Peirce lists the four main conclusions of his anti-Cartesian argument:

1. We have no power of Introspection, but all knowledge of the internal world is derived by hypothetical reasoning from our knowledge of external facts.
2. We have no power of Intuition, but every cognition is determined logically by previous cognitions.
3. We have no power of thinking without signs.
4. We have no conception of the absolutely incognizable. [W 2.213 & EP 1.30]

Reality, then, is constituted by known or knowable external signs that live in the domain of thought. The self intersects with these semiotic chains and becomes open to the rational structures of the universe. Insofar as the self attains what might be called "self-knowledge," it must do so through acts of comparison that work their way through the series of external signs and their fields of meaning. These external signs are then internalized and self-consciousness is given a texture and shape.

The mind functions according to the structure of the syllogism. Insofar as we are prepared to act, we have already derived some conclusions from premises within the mind. There is a direct link between our willingness to act and an unconscious process of inference that manifests certain conclusions. "Something, therefore, takes place within the organism which is equivalent to the syllogistic process" [W 2.214 & EP 1.31]. Thus all mental acts take on the formula of valid reasoning and inference. The mind conforms to logical rules, yet these very same rules remain viable because of their 'fit' with the larger universe of signs and powers. Peirce works through his distinction between induction and hypothesis and applies these forms of inference to mental processes.

More relevant for our concern here is his temporal and semiotic reconstruction of the self. He lays bare the three basic functions of the sign in terms of its relation to objective referents. While this discussion points ahead to the next chapter, a preliminary analysis of his early semiotic theory is pertinent in the context of his anthropology. The three functional aspects of the sign are defined as follows:

> When we think, then, we ourselves, as we are at that moment, appear as a sign. Now a sign has, as such, three references; 1st, it is a sign *to* some thought which interprets it; 2nd, it is a sign *for* some object to which in that thought it is equivalent; 3rd, it is a sign, *in* some respect or quality, which brings it into connection with its object. [W 2.223 & EP 1.38]

Any given sign will push outward into a relational network in which it will become more and more efficacious. Initially, a sign points to an emerging thought that is its interpretation. By the same token, and at the same time (since these are not temporally distinct stages), the sign will point to an object, even though that object may remain partially veiled from view. Finally, the sign will refer to its object in particular finite ways. Signs may be somewhat vague, but they will always have some value or quality in terms of which they support the predication of a trait to an object. When we apply this threefold analysis of the sign to the self, we get the first glimpse of the sophistications found in a semiotic anthropology.

We appear to ourselves as a sign, or, more precisely, as an intersection of various sign series. Each given sign helps to establish the contour of the self through its threefold structure. First, the sign generates a subsequent thought/sign that is an enhanced expression of the outward involvements of the self (dimension of the future). Second, that same sign points toward the object that is the self in its previous state (dimension of the past). Finally, the sign points to a quality of the previous self that is still pertinent in the present (dimension of the present). The self is an asymmetrical sign series that is continually being built up and, in different respects, torn down and reconfigured. This process is fully temporal and involves, as noted in the first chapter, a kind of internal dialogue. The present self is constituted by signs of the past self, which in turn point toward an emergent future self. The self and its signs are temporally extended. No natural beginning nor ending can be seen for this extended process of signification.

Signs link together through associational patterns that suggest and determine natural and appropriate linkages. Peirce makes it clear that sign linkage is not necessarily the product of conscious forms of deliberation. Each sign seems to coax subsequent signs into its orbit so that it can attain a kind of objective immortality through unlimited semiosis. The law of association is the shaping force of this expanding series:

> But if a train of thought ceases by gradually dying out, it freely follows its own law of association as long as it lasts, and there is no moment at which there is a thought belonging to this series, subsequently to which there is not a thought which interprets or repeats it. There is no exception, therefore, to the law that every thought-sign is translated or interpreted in a subsequent one, unless it be that all thought comes to an abrupt and final end in death. [W 2.224 & EP 1.39]

This process of unending association is teleological in the sense that signs seem to seek a fullness and completion in and through their attendant series. It is as if signs hunger for an increase in semiotic density and scope and convey their restlessness to the sign-using organism. The three temporal aspects of the self are fully embedded in this restless process. The past self continues to offer its semiotic wealth to the present self in process, while the future self, operating through an ideal limit, goads the present self into transformations that promise to produce semiotic wholeness. As we will see, self-control is at the center of the quest for self-identity.

Peirce, looking directly at the sign-vehicle itself, distinguishes between its "material" aspect and its "demonstrative application." Its material aspect is that property of the sign that is not identified with the thing signified. It is the actual embodied essence of the sign itself. The word "man," to use his example, can refer to a genus within the animal kingdom. Yet the three English letters—m, a, and n—are material properties that make the sign-vehicle what it is. Every sign will have some material property, even if the material property is not composed of matter in the more conventional sense. The demonstrative property of the sign is its direct relational structure, tying it closely to its object. The demonstrative application can be either natural or conventional. A natural demonstrative connection would be one that occurs outside of human forms of language, such as a weather vane pointing to (participating in) the direction of the wind. A conventional demonstrative relation is one that is created by human language communities to secure communication among their members. These connections (between sign and object) are arbitrary and have no direct rootedness in the extralinguistic orders of the world.

The semiotic self is surrounded with natural and conventional signs, each with material and demonstrative properties that were not created by the individual self. To use more contemporary language, the self survives by learning to decode the innumerable encoded messages of a fully semiotic universe. All internal knowledge is derived from external codes. The contour built up by the semiotic self is one that emerges from conflict and semiotic contrast. Self-control is absolutely crucial to the self as it weaves the wealth of natural and conventional semiosis into an integrity that promises to move the self toward an ideal transfiguration in the future. The self is the conscious locus for the vast semiotic series of the world.

How does the semiotic view of the self reshape our understanding of metaphysics and its general categories? If the world and the human process are both fundamentally semiotic through and through, does it follow that all general categories, e.g., the category of "Being," refer to signs? Peirce answers in the affirmative:

> The conception of being is, therefore, a conception about a sign—a thought, or word;—and since it is not applicable to every sign, it is not primarily universal, although it is so in its mediate application to things. Being, therefore, may be defined; it may be defined, for example, as that which is common to the objects included in any class. But it is nothing new to say that metaphysical conceptions are primarily and at bottom thoughts about words, or thoughts about thoughts; it is the doctrine both of Aristotle (whose categories are parts of speech) and of Kant (whose categories are the characters of different kinds of propositions). [W 2.231 & EP 1.45-46]

Passages such as this have a much more nominalistic cast than similar analyses in the later writings. Some scholars see Peirce as gradually abandoning an alleged nominalism after this 1868–1869 set of papers (e.g., in his 1871 review of Frazer's edition of the writings of Berkeley, discussed in the previous chapter). In the later writings he will affirm that categories such as "Being," or "existence," refer to something outside of human speech and its conventions. However, the situation is somewhat more complex in that Peirce, even in these early writings, affirms that the semiotic self belongs to a larger order of interaction that is not, strictly speaking, a human artifact. My sense is that his growing pansemioticism required some maturing before it could be integrated into a more robust metaphysical structure. Further, the influence of Kant here is stronger than it will be later (although it never disappears). One must, of course, be wary of reading the later Peirce into the earlier, yet it is also pertinent to note tensions within the early texts that point toward his mature, and more realistic, metaphysics. I would argue that Peirce is an objective idealist throughout, but that he emphasized either the realism or the idealism differently in different orders of discourse, each having a different pragmatic purpose.

Be that as it may, metaphysics is primarily about how signs are used and shaped by the self. The correlation of semiotics and metaphysics occurred early on to Peirce and he never wavered from the sense that the two enterprises require each other. Again, it must be stressed that Peirce's rhetorical blasts against metaphysics and theology never apply to his *own* metaphysical and theological commitments, but to those prepragmatic formulations that fail to honor thirdness, continuity, novelty, and the evolutionary God.

From one extreme of cognition to the other, the semiotic self lives in the realm of signs. On the most generic level of reflection, that pertinent to the foundational principles of ontology, the self uses signs to articulate its sense of the world. On the most particular level of individual sensations, the self uses signs to interpret each and every sensum so that a perceptual field can be generated. It is important to note that there is an absolute continuity connecting perceptual judgment and the most generic products of philosophy. Peirce may or may not have been a nominalist (a controversial point), but he remained committed, early and late, to the notion that this continuity must be semiotic.

The semiotic self forms habits, which generate further signs (interpretants). This process of habit formation is an induction. Particular actual and possible habits are correlated so that a general conclusion/inference can be put forward. The successful habits represent successful inductions from antecedent material. Self-control guides habits and inductions so that the semiotic self does not squander its precious energy on provincial or self-defeating purposes.

Each sense abstracts and selects from the environment. The self could not survive if each sense failed to be selective and interpretive right from the start. The shift to a semiotic redefinition of the self is also a shift to a finite and time-bound sense of the self. To interact with the world of signs and interpretants is to make innumerable and often unconscious selections as to which signs and powers are pertinent to the self in process. "Moreover, that perceptions are not absolutely determinate and singular is obvious from the fact that each sense is an abstracting mechanism" [W 2.236 & EP 1.50]. To perceive is to judge and to interpret in such a way as to free the precarious self from an overload of irrelevant semiotic material.

As we saw in the previous chapter, reality is promised to us in the future, in the "would be" or the not yet. The semiotic self cannot hope to find reality on its own or solely from antecedent signs. Consequently, the sign-using self must arise within a community if it is to participate in the depth semiotic structures of the world:

> The real, then, is that which, sooner or later, information and reasoning would finally result in, and which is therefore independent of the vagaries of me and you. Thus, the very origin of the conception of reality shows that this conception essentially involves the notion of a COMMUNITY, without definite limits, and capable of an indefinite increase of knowledge. And so those two series of cognitions—the real and the unreal—consist of those which, at a time sufficiently future, the community will always continue to affirm; and of those which, under the same conditions, will ever after be denied. [W 2.239 & EP 1.52]

Peirce does not adopt a mere consensus theory of truth, namely, one that asserts that truth is little more than what a given hermeneutic community will establish by agreement or tradition. Rather, the community serves an evolutionary reality within which it is embedded and uses the methods of pragmatism (not enunciated as such in these papers) to arrive at the general features of the world. The self finds both itself (insofar as it can read backward from external signs to internal signs) and the generic features of the world only insofar as it fully participates in the community.

The community of inquiry is not a mere inherited community, but looks forward toward those liberating signs that promise to bring its members into conformity with nature's forms of semiosis. The metaphysical commitment here, in spite of the nominalistic language concerning the correlation of categories and signs, is still realistic: ". . . generals must have a real existence" [W 2.239 & EP 1.53]. More importantly, the correlation of signs and words to the human process is a dialectical one (although Peirce does not use the word "dialectic" in this context). "In fact, therefore, men and words reciprocally educate each other; each increase of a man's information involves and is involved by, a corresponding increase of a word's information" [W 2.241 & EP 1.54]. Words have a sphere of meaning that can be augmented; that is, any word can grow through adding interpretants to its scope and integrity. By the same token, and through the same process, the self can add interpretants to its being when it lets words and signs shape its self-consciousness.

It does not follow from this, contra neopragmatist misreadings of Peirce, that the self is little more than a text that can add any meaning it wishes to its evolving contour. Rather, the self must select those interpretants that reinforce its survival value and power in a naturalistic context. Even in the play of musement, in which the self drifts through the worlds of semiosis, there remains a kind of vector directionality that guides the self toward its own transfigured future. Self-control insures that each interpretant encountered must pass muster according to criteria that derive from the depths of the self. Peirce avoids the two extremes of, on the one hand, positing an atemporal substantive self, and, on the other hand, positing a purely arbitrary self that can manipulate signs at will. Put differently, the self not only manipulates semiotic possibilities, but assimilates the tendencies and leadings of natural and communal sign systems.

Peirce brings this second essay in the series to a philosophical crescendo when he equates the sign with the self. This bold ontological move makes it absolutely clear that the human process is part of a much larger process that locates and shapes it:

> . . . the word or sign which man uses *is* the man himself. For, as the fact that every thought is a sign, taken in conjunction with the fact that life is a train of thought, proves that man is a sign; so, that every thought is an *external* sign, proves that man is an external sign. That is to say, the man and the external sign are identical, in the same sense in which the words *homo* and *man* are identical. Thus my language is the sum total of myself; for the man is the thought. [W 2.241 & EP 1.54]

The self is an external sign—more properly, sign series—that can internalize and transform the world of language to create and sustain an internal self. Where does language come from? For Peirce, it must come from the community, which has the responsibility for using words to point to objects, interpretants, and specific traits. Language cannot be purely arbitrary if only because it consists of signs. These signs are what they are because of the threefold structure of interpretation that moves the sign into temporal and rational structures. The sign evokes an interpretant, helps to unveil an object, and points to specific features that belong to the significant field of meaning of the object. The community enters into this threefold momentum of signification and provides a rational framework for the self-controlled unfolding of further interpretants.

Outside of the semiotic community, we are as nothing. The self is born into ignorance and error and would remain in this state without the interpretive community that surrounds it. Through the community, the sign-using self finds its future self, and a means for transforming and purifying its past self. Peirce remains adamant that pure or unmediated self-knowledge is a proud delusion. He finishes this seminal essay with a quote from Shakespeare's *Measure for Measure*:

> proud man,
> Most ignorant of what he's most assured,
> His glassy essence.

Our true essence is not an opaque substance with a static identity through time and place, but a transparent lens through which plays the infinite semiosis of the world. The individual (if this notion is not itself ruled out logically) represents a clearing into which pours the wealth of social and natural existence. The contours of the self are large, for they reach out into all of the orders of signification. Yet the actual shape of the self is finite and limited because the wealth of external signs must be refracted through a particular lens that can reach far, but can only see in a certain way. The tensions between our "glassy essence" and our finite locatedness become even more pronounced as Peirce's anthropology evolves.

Before moving on to later writings, a few brief words are in order concerning the third essay in *The Journal of Speculative Philosophy* series. The final essay, "Grounds of Validity of the Laws of Logic: Further Consequences of Four Incapacities" (1869), is more directly concerned with logical than anthropological issues, yet we can mine a few items from it that advance our study of the human process. In particular, Peirce sheds further light on the nature of self-control and the centrality of the community for securing self-identity.

Peirce devotes his energies to demonstrating the correlation between deduction and induction, in turn showing how the formal principles of inference relate to the structures of the mind. He advances further arguments for his thesis that there can be nothing that is not cognizable. In the context of this extended argument, he reinforces his commitment to the principle of continuity within mental life: ". . . the action of the mind is, as it were, a continuous movement" [W 2.250 & EP 1.63]. Deductive and inductive forms of inference work because there is a continuous momentum linking antecedent to consequent. The human mind follows this logical procedure and does not make absolute or discontinuous leaps from one domain to another. This belief in mental continuity is of a piece with his Kantianism, which insists that the mind is a synthesizing agent bringing heterogenous material together under a series of synthetic judgments (which, as we saw, are largely unconscious).

Mental continuity has two dimensions. On one level it is a kind of ontological given. That is, the mind must work continuously to shape and order the materials of sensation (via perceptual judgments and more sophisticated and attenuated forms of abduction). The mind is also ontologically continuous in terms of its innate temporal structures, which are both continuous and asymmetrical. On a second level, the mind is continuous because of the moral energy of self-control. As noted in the previous chapter, moral self-control derives its power and momentum from the self-control manifest in an evolutionary universe. In the context of this 1869 essay, self-control is correlated to freedom and an open future. In an extended footnote attacking the necessitarians, Peirce adds crucial elements to his anthropology:

> Self-control seems to be the capacity for rising to an extended view of a practical subject instead of seeing only temporary urgency. This is the only freedom of which man has any reason to be proud; and it is because love of what is good for all on the whole, which is the widest possible consideration, is the essence of Christianity, that it is said that the service of Christ is perfect freedom. [W 2.261n & EP 1.72]

What is occurring here is a melding of the two dimensions of self-control, namely, the ontological and the ethical. Ontologically, self-control opens the self to an expansive future in which possibility may eclipse necessity (the modal view of time). Ethically, self-control supports both the social and the religious impulse. The social aspect is clear in that the self can seek the good of the whole, against personal short-term interests. The religious aspect is clear in that true freedom can only come from service to Christ. In his many reflections on Christianity, Peirce returns again and again to the theme that the essence of his chosen religion is love, rather than doctrine or a particular sense of a given confessional community. Some commentators, because of a positivistic bias, have overlooked or even questioned Peirce's statements on religion, thereby generating difficulties concerning Peirce's alleged "transcendentalism" in his later writings.[1] It should by now be clear that Peirce has what can be called a "theonomous" conception of the self, namely, a belief that the self is only fulfilled when it participates in the depth dimension of the world, which is religious. Put differently, Peirce's anthropology is fulfilled by eschatology, the religious expression of radical hope.

The moral aspect of self-control (with its social and religious dimensions) overcomes mere self-interest or the pursuit of pleasure. Peirce is very clear that psychological egoism is false, assuming instead that persons act out of the principle of self-sacrifice rather than selfishness. This self-sacrifice is manifest whenever the individual manifests the centrality of scientific method over more short-term strategies. We must transform our interests and ". . . subordinate them to the interests of the community" [W 2.271 & EP 1.81]. Peirce even goes so far as to challenge some of his own beliefs in the infinite long run. He never assumes a straightforward linear progress, but prefers to speak in the condition of what "would be" the case. Yet he often surges past this conditional language to invoke something far more radical. Against the rational belief in progress, which can always admit of counter-arguments, is our true hope:

> This infinite hope which we all have (for even the atheist will constantly betray his calm expectation that what is Best will come about) is something so august and momentous, that all reasoning in reference to it is a trifling impertinence. [W 2.272 & EP 1.82]

The very heart of the self and its communities is the presence of a hope that cannot be reduced to a projection or prediction about the tendencies of the long run. This eschatological language is not added at the end of the article as a kind of exoteric coda that can reassure readers of the writer's orthodoxy, but a profound and logically compelling move, fully consistent with the commitment to self-control and a transforming community. Without this hope, which can never be verified by induction or abduction (remembering that Peirce conflates these two strategies in his earlier writings), the self cannot survive in a universe that seems without an overarching order.

In his superb work on Peirce's theory of the self, Vincent Colapietro argues that the semiotic self remains bound to higher values (values that are religious), and that self-identity comes from the self's ability to become permeable to larger realities outside of itself:

> The self can only realize itself by exerting control over itself; and it can only exert control over itself by committing itself to ideals, since

"self-control depends upon comparison of what is done with an ideal admirable *per se*, without any ulterior reason" [MS 1939]. However, since ideals can conflict, a commitment to one ideal frequently requires an abandonment of another ideal. Moreover, our commitments to ideals are, especially with regard to loftier ideals, more like acts of surrender than acts of acquisition: The higher ideals take possession of us rather than we of them. In fact, Peirce maintained the realization of the self demanded a series of acts by with the self surrenders itself to ever more inclusive ideals.[2]

The sign-using self, in what can best be described as a religious act, lets go of its internal plenitude and lets the more powerful and generic structures of the semiotic universe enter into and shape its self-consciousness. When it is remembered that self-control is both a human and a cosmic fact, it follows that the real power behind the self-control of the individual self is rooted in the self-control of an evolving universe. Colapietro stresses the centrality of agency and the quest for reasonable autonomy in Peirce's philosophical anthropology.

It is important to note that Peirce grounds logic and method in hope rather than on some principle of the alleged uniformity of nature. As we saw in the previous chapter when we examined his 1878 paper "The Order of Nature," Peirce denies that nature as a whole can be an order of orders, or be exclusively orderly. In this 1869 paper, Peirce makes the same claim, that "Nature is not regular" [W 2.264 & EP 1.75]. There are areas of order and areas or regions of disorder. Relations among orders are often fortuitous rather than rational. He gives this example of a fortuitous relation: "A man in China bought a cow three days and five minutes after a Greenlander had sneezed" [W 2.264 & EP 1.75]. Anyone calling this a rational or internal relation is profoundly misguided about the structure of nature. The most that can be said is that we have two discontinuous orders that have no real relation to each other.

Logic, in particular the method of induction, cannot be grounded on the uniformity of nature. Therefore it follows that induction must be grounded on smaller uniformities or realities. Peirce argues that induction is partially grounded on the fact that there is some reality at all. Insofar as any reality obtains outside of the individual self, induction has a place to hang its hat. But the more basic structure is that of hope. There is a striking sense, not often noticed by scholars, that Peirce grounds logic and method in the eschatological principle. To live in hope is to participate in those structures of emerging rationality (thirdness) that promise to secure the sign-using self and its communities against annihilation. Hope comes to the self from a domain that is prerational, but it will manifest itself in and through the structures of rationality. In terms of his anthropology, the self comes into its depth structures by living within hope that connects it to both the prerational and the rational realms.

What can we conclude, then, from our study of these three crucial early papers? For Peirce, the self is a finite and temporally extended organism that uses a variety of logical strategies to survive in a world that only has pockets of order. The self is funded with innumerable habits, each of which is tied to the structure of induction and involves an inference from similar cases. The sign-using self has little tolerance for the irritation of doubt and will use personal and social means to overcome any actuality that stands in the way of successful habits and beliefs. This self must come into self-consciousness by the indirect route of external signs and social contrasts. Language, signs, and logical structures are all external to the self. Thought is actually a cosmic reality that is of greater scope and density than the 'sum' of all sign-using selves. We enter into these external and ancient semiotic series in order to find a reliable contour for self-knowledge.

On the preconscious level, we make a series of rational inferences that render each sensum intelligible. Yet this process of perceptual judgment is hermeneutic through and through. There is no such thing as a passive sensation or idea. The self actively shapes the material of the senses, each one of which has already been fully selective in its own right, in order to generate a larger perspective. From the simplest and most automatic perceptual judgment to the most complex form of abduction, we interpret signs and their portents.

The self is temporal in its self-constitution. The present self lives in the referential aspects of its signs, where the given sign refers to its object in particular respects. The past self lives as the object that exerts a kind of inertial pressure on the present self. The future self, which is the most important of the three, lives in the hoped-for interpretants that provide an ideal limit for personal and social existence. Hope in the long run is actually a hope in the unseen realm that promises to transform the community.

The move against Cartesianism has already born very rich and complex fruit. Peirce shifts to an external and community-centered anthropology that locates the self in sign series that eclipse it in power and scope. In this process of overcoming substance ontology, Peirce probes into the unconscious and its specific semiotic mechanisms. The next major step forward in his philosophical anthropology brings him to an increased awareness of the role of the unconscious, which is more than personal, in shaping the semiotic self.

Association, Purpose, and the Unconscious

Peirce's post-1869 reflections on the nature of the self are scattered in a variety of places. We will examine manuscripts, letters, and his review of James's 1890 work *The Principles of Psychology* in order to flesh out his mature conception of the human process and its communal dimensions. Some of the insights emerging from this later period are quite dramatic in their implications for our conception of the sign-using self. In particular, Peirce continues to deflate the Cartesian claims of an ego (whether transcendental or empirical) and even goes so far as to hint that the individual ego is a fiction. We are left with the prospect that the self is a mere place holder for cosmic forms of semiosis. In a conceptual move foreshadowing more recent explorations of the collective unconscious, Peirce argues that the individual self is riding on the back of an immense unconscious that may be directly linked to the depth dimension of nature and the divine life.

We will begin our explorations of Peirce's mature anthropology with his 1891 review of James's *Principles of Psychology*, which appeared in *The Nation* in two parts. This will be augmented by examining his correspondence with James in the following years. One special note is Peirce's deep interest in empirical psychology and the emerging field of perceptual studies. His review of James evidences a deep acquaintance with both German and British psychological studies and theories and he brings this material to bear in his rather arch critique of James.

After accusing James of an almost willful misuse of key terms (remembering that Peirce is deeply concerned with what he calls the "ethics of terminology"), Peirce further accuses him of falling into both a crude materialism and a dualism concerning the correlation of mind and body. Behind the scenes, of course, is Peirce's own commitment to a pragmatic idealism that deemphasizes matter and gives a privileged place to mentality, both within and without the shifting contours of the human process. He is particularly keen to accuse James of some logical confusions regarding the actual nature of unconscious perceptual judgments. He augments his own detailed reflections on perceptual judgment by showing how the conclusion appears: "In perception, the conclusion has the peculiarity of not being abstractly thought, but actually seen, so that it is not exactly a judgment, though it is tantamount to one" [CP 8.65]. Thus, the conclusion is given directly to perception even though it actually emerged through something akin to a reasoning process.

Perception entails judgment and therefore follows the basic laws of inference: ". . . perception attains a virtual judgment, it subsumes something under a class, and not only so, but virtually attaches to the proposition the seal of assent—two strong resemblances to inference which are wanting in ordinary suggestions" [CP 8.66]. Any perceptual judgment will make a classwide designation (i.e., assign a predicate to a sensum) and make a logical affirmation that the class designation is the case. James mutes or misunderstands the sheer logicality of this process because of his preference for a certain kind of physiological and associational language derived more from the British empirical tradition than from the more rigorous logic of true pragmatism. Consequently, James's approach, in spite of a certain richness and suggestiveness, removes psychology too much from logic and general semiotic. Put differently, James fails to understand that the self is not so much a consciousness as it is a sign user.

In an unpublished analysis of *The Principles of Psychology*, also written in 1891, Peirce makes his startling claim that the individual self is an illusion. This passage will link up with other reflections showing how we are indeed a "glassy essence":

> Everybody will admit a personal self exists in the same sense in which a snark exists; that is there is a phenomenon to which that name is given. It is an illusory phenomenon; but still it is a phenomenon. It is not quite *purely* illusory, but only *mainly* so. It is true, for instance, that men are *selfish*, that is, that they are really deluded into supposing themselves to have some isolated existence; and in so far, they *have* it. To deny the reality of personality is not anti-spiritualistic; it is only anti-nominalistic. [CP 8.82]

Hence, the true realist, as an objective idealist, will deny the full reality of the individual ego and recognize that the self is but one part of a thought-filled semiotic universe. The nominalist can assume an individual self because of the blandishments of language (an argument also used by Nietzsche) that posit an independent and autonomous ego lying somehow beneath experience. Peirce links his antinominalism to his idealism when he argues that the reality of the self is located in the larger social and cosmic mind that is embodied in signs (which must have some kind of material aspect). Realism and objective idealism entail each other. The true realism affirms real facts and real generals, existing independently of the self. Objective idealism affirms that all mental structures are objectively real and part of an evolutionary universe that is basically mental/semiotic. Once the nominalistic view of the self is overcome, it is possible to stretch the boundaries of the so-called "ego" to the social self.

In this same manuscript Peirce makes the interesting claim that the tongue is actually the seat of the so-called self. While the tone in these passages borders on the ironic, the conceptual import remains important. The tongue is that muscle which, in essence, talks the self into being. Without this muscle, there would be little chance for creating the illusion of a purely private self. Personality is thus not lodged in the brain but in the tongue, which has a certain autonomy. Since the primary product of the tongue is language, and since Peirce has rejected the nominalistic view of the ego, it follows that the tongue is not a proper realist! Put differently, the tongue is guilty of a nominalistic fallacy; that is, it assumes that there must be something mental or mind dependent corresponding to its products.

This curious view notwithstanding, Peirce distances himself from James's perceived nominalism and affirms a social and external view of the self. However, he does not confine himself to negative critique, but advances an alternative theory to James's dyadic one. In a letter written to James on September 28, 1904, Peirce argues that the self is both public and future in its nature. This follows from general pragmatic principles: "While the true idealism, the pragmatistic idealism, is that reality consists in the *future*" [CP 8.284]. It should be remembered that Peirce is about to appear in print (in the following year) with his rejection of the term "pragmatism" in favor of the term "pragmaticism." His distance from James is thus manifest in several ways. Of equal importance is the social dimension of the self: "Therefore to say that it is the world of thought that is real is, when properly understood, to assert emphatically the reality of the public world of the indefinite future as against our past opinions of what it was to be" [CP 8.284]. Thought is social and emergent from the future. Since thought is the genus of which self-consciousness is the species (as argued by Peirce in 1868), it should be clear that the individual is of secondary importance.

In a letter written on October 3, 1904, Peirce makes clear his triadic conception of the self and offers it to James as an alternative to the dualistic and nominalistic views that Peirce finds not only in James's *Principles* but in essays like the 1904 "Does 'Consciousness' Exist?" The triadic view involves the modes of time and the three primal categories of firstness, secondness, and thirdness:

More or less explicitly, some writers, namely the Thomists, the Hegelians, and other Intellectualists, together with some scientific thinkers not too much sophisticated by reading philosophy, recognize with me (until I shall have studied your views, which I don't believe will carry me entirely away from this anchorage) three modes of conscious-

*ness, that of feeling, that of EXPERIENCE (experience meaning pre-
cisely that which the history of my life has FORCED me to think; so
that the idea of struggle, of not mere twoness but active oppugnancy is
in it), and thirdly the consciousness of the future (whether veridical or
not is aside from the question) in expectation which enters into all
general ideas according to my variety of pragmatism.* [CP 8.291]

Feeling is correlated to firstness, the category denoting possibility, unqualified generality, and monadic reality. Experience is correlated with secondness, the category denoting brute existence, duality, opposition, and conflict. The consciousness of the future is correlated with thirdness, the category denoting mediation, qualified generality, habit, and continuity. The dyadic view of consciousness, emphasizing a stream of awareness punctuated by "flights" and "perchings," fails to understand the basic forms of embeddedness that surround the self. The self emerges from the presemiotic realm of pure feeling and becomes entangled in binary oppositions that emerge from the realm outside of consciousness. The drive toward the open future gives the self some general habits and social norms that can help control the multiple impactions coming from the domain of experience.

Feeling is intentional and points outward to objects. Hence firstness moves by its own inner momentum toward secondness. Any oppositional structure within experience/secondness will have *its* inner momentum moving toward forms of mediation and enhanced generality. Peirce thus develops a more dynamic model of experience and consciousness than does James. The self is located at the place where the three categories (read as structures of being) become most intensely instantiated. The self is the clearing within which we can witness the actual, if elusive, transmigration from firstness to secondness to thirdness. Feeling is central to this process because it forms a background within which other cognitive acts can obtain.

For James, feelings follow from physiological states and do not have an intrinsic revelatory power. For Peirce, on the contrary, feelings open the self out into the world of dyadic interaction and triadic mediation. Feeling thus functions as a kind of prethematic but essential background: "I have been inclined to think that there is a certain tinge or tone of feeling connected with living and being awake, though we cannot *attend* to it, for want of a background" [CP 8.294]. That is, feeling is itself the "background" of cognition and cannot be seen directly because there is no larger background against which it can be seen. Peirce mentions his own interest in phenomenology (elsewhere termed "phaneroscopy") as a primal field of study underlying psychology. Phenomenology in his reconstruction is concerned with the most basic features of what he calls the "phaneron"; namely, the total field of awareness prior to its subdivisions into capacities or layers. He implies that James remains caught on the level of psychology and is thus unable to understand the logical and phenomenological features underlying all aspects of the self.

Peirce's criticisms of James's theory of the self run parallel to his criticisms of Jamesian pragmatism. Neither framework understands the roles of inference, continuity, thirdness, or feeling in shaping a general picture of the world. More importantly, James fails to grasp the true nature of the semiotic aspects of the self/world transaction. James does not have any structure analogous to the sign/object/interpretant triad nor does he fully grasp the correlation between the asymmetrical view of time and the three primal ontological categories. Thus what he says in his psychology is profoundly limited in philosophical scope and depth. Another profound difference between both thinkers (although not mentioned as such in the above material) is that James (at least in 1890) denies any role for the unconscious, while Peirce sees it as integral to the momentum of the sign-using self. Of course, James came to affirm the existence of what he called the "subconscious" after the turn of the century (sometimes using the term "the more" to denote the field of awareness outside of the focus of consciousness).

We have seen how Peirce undermines the private and individual ego as a mere illusion (which is real in the sense that illusions have some kind of being). This is augmented by the contrast between the individual ego and the social self that is the true locus of self-identity. Underlying this second move is Peirce's unwavering commitment to continuity, expressed in his category of synechism. The principle of synechism is manifest in all areas of inquiry: from mathematics, to logic (as semiotic), to perception, to emotion, to the structure of matter, to evolutionary laws, to habits, and to the structure of the community. Peirce's anthropology relies on continuity to tie together the various aspects of cognition and emotion, as they in turn relate to the larger social self.

The principle of continuity/synechism denies that there can be an isolated substrate for the self and its experiences. In a ca. 1892 manuscript with the evocative title "Immortality in the Light of Synechism," Peirce argues against the notion that the self has discrete layers, even though he fully acknowledges that the self is not always aware of all of the activities taking place 'within' it. He insists that there is a continuous transition from matter to mind and that the self is a continuum involving both aspects. The continuity between matter and mind makes it possible for purposes to emerge to shape the self. As we will see in chapter 4, the concept of purpose is a complex one, especially in the light of the Darwinian conception of natural selection and random variation, but Peirce transforms it in creative ways. In the present context, purpose is seen to emerge from beings funded with mentality. There is a direct link between the principle of synechism and the concept of purpose:

> In particular, the synechist will not admit that physical and psychical phenomena are entirely distinct,—whether as belonging to different categories of substance, or as entirely separate sides of one shield,— but will insist that all phenomena are of one character, though some are more mental and spontaneous, others more material and regular. Still, all alike present that mixture of freedom and constraint, which allows them to be, nay, makes them to be teleological, or purposive. [CP 7.570]

There is a continuum moving up from so-called inert matter to the higher forms of consciousness. With each step upward, there is an increase in the amount of freedom, spontaneity, and purposive activity, which in turn is guided by self-control ("constraint"). Peirce writes purpose large on the face of the world, even while acknowledging that it manifests degrees within a continuum. The self is purposive because the universe tolerates purpose within the general laws/habits of evolution. As we will see, Peirce distances himself from Darwin in some key respects, thus providing a space for mind-funded purposes within the world.

The principle of continuity thus denies that there is a break between matter and mind (the anti-Cartesian perspective). Peirce applies the principle to the correlation between the individual and the social order, by insisting that there is no break between selves. Each self fully participates in the larger social self and can only separate itself from this pregiven continuum through ignorance. There is thus an unbroken connection between matter and mind, and personal and social selves. The continuity principle also applies to the transition between waking and sleeping. Sleep does not break the continuity of the self, but represents a mere diminution of purpose and conscious mentality.

The final manifestation of continuity in this context is the most dramatic of all. The social self might seem to be the most primal and extended, but Peirce pushes on to yet one more dimension. This final dimension is what he calls "spiritual consciousness." This pervasive consciousness is always part of self-awareness, even if it is often drowned out by the semiotic noise of the personal and social self. Just as there is no absolute break in self-identity between sleep and waking, so too there is no break between life and death. In death we fully enter into the spiritual consciousness that is only dimly sensed in life. What is important here is the belief that we have this sense of immortality here and now. It is not an inference or a hope, but a present experience lying on the fringes of awareness. "In the same manner, when the carnal consciousness passes away in death, we shall at once perceive that we have had all along a lively spiritual consciousness which we have been confusing with something different" [CP 7.577].

The continuity between social and spiritual consciousness must be rescued from oblivion. We live in forgetfulness of our attained immortality. Peirce's argument for immortality from the principle of continuity is bold and compelling. The self has a sense that its finite consciousness is floating on a vast awareness that is vague and general. We ignore this spiritual consciousness precisely because of its vagueness, but Peirce gives vagueness the highest ontological status. Insofar as the vague is the general, and insofar as the general is the real, it follows that the vague is the most real. Of course, it makes no sense to talk of "degrees of reality," but such language can be of value in a pragmatic context in which we are concerned with rescuing ignored or undervalued orders from premature oblivion.

The ladder of continuity should now be clear. We start with the simplest unconscious perceptual judgments, moving on to associational structures among judgments, moving on to the illusory private (yet fully semiotic) self, moving on to the social self, and finally moving on to the spiritual consciousness that is the hidden presence and goal of all psychic life. Once again we are reminded that Peirce's anthropology is theonomous at its heart.

The larger domain of the self, ofttimes hidden yet always operative, is not a mere oceanic realm of immortality and feeling. This unconscious domain is actually active in forming gestalts of association that manifest themselves in our native tendency to form patterns of awareness. In his ca. 1893 manuscript, "Grand Logic," in the section on the association of ideas, Peirce links traditional associational theories to his pragmatic conception of habit. Thus, the law of the succession and association of ideas is actually the law of habit. The mind works through the Humean principles of "contiguity" and "resemblance" to link together sensations into patterns. Contrast is actually a subspecies of resemblance and functions according to the same momentum. Peirce refers to these forms of the mind as "sets." The mind thus forms set clusters that shape and govern the material of the senses. It is important to remember that these patterns are formed automatically. For example, if we see a partial pattern, one that is recognizable, we automatically fill in the missing facets so that we can identify the shape as belonging to such and such a class or set of shapes.

Mental actions do not leap from domain to domain, but move more gradually and gently across and through a continuum. The sensations dealt with by the mind are general and more or less vague. Consequently it follows that we cannot make a clear distinction between an intuition and a symbolic transformation. Sensations come to us already loaded with symbolic content and meaning. Memories are vague aggregates that have an interpretive value. Hence neither present nor remembered experiences can be grasped through alleged intuitions.

Peirce hammers again at the notion that we can have some kind of introspective knowledge. His growing skepticism about the reality of the individual self emerges even more sharply here: "We cannot directly observe even so much as that there is such a thing as present consciousness" [CP 7.420]. Introspection can only reveal ". . . what seems to have been present from the standpoint of subsequent reflection" [CP 7.420]. All self-knowledge is a construct from vague or temporally modified semiotic material. What we find when we engage in introspection are our previous interpretations of the felt past self. The hoped-for future self provides the horizon within which we reconstruct the meaning and value of the past self.

Underneath conscious awareness are a cluster of what Peirce called "skeleton-sets" that shape the associational chains of awareness. These sets are skeletal because they lie beneath the skin and muscle structures of habit. They represent the true supporting mechanisms of mental life. Sets have an innate tendency to combine with other sets to form vast and highly complex linkages. These uncountable linkages form the background of the self:

> An immense number of associations are formed, and remain as long as they endure, in the background of consciousness, that is, in subjective obscurity. But as soon as a cerebromotor suggestion is made,—that is a suggestion of the idea of voluntarily exercising thought,—the whole set brightens up. [CP 7.434]

It is interesting to note that Peirce sees an inner dynamism to the structure of these sets. Not only do the sets link together to form vast underground networks, but they also have a teleological hunger for manifestation. Peirce seems to have a view of the unconscious and its associational structures that diverges significantly with that of psychoanalysis. For Freud, of course, unconscious material remains hidden until it can be compelled into view by indirect analytic means (which must overcome great resistances). Peirce's model is teleological in the sense that the skeletal-sets drive toward the light of awareness so that their structures can be known. This view is of a piece with Peirce's pragmaticism, which is optimistic concerning the ability of the sign-using self to penetrate into the depths of the world. By the same token, the self can bring its own vast unconscious fields of awareness into the transforming light of consciousness.

But we must remember that we are operating within a dialectical structure. The unconscious associational skeletal-sets must themselves experience the pressure of external reality. After all, contiguity and resemblance are principles operating on both sides of the subject/object split. Objects and events outside of the self (remembering that the spatial images of "inside" and "outside" are questionable in Peirce's anthropology) form into their own associational patterns and the self must honor these if it is to survive. "Experience may be defined as the sum of ideas which have been irresistibly borne in upon us, overwhelming all free-play of thought, by the tenor of our lives. The authority of experience consists in the fact that its power cannot be resisted; . . ." [CP 7.437]. Thus the conscious self (not consciousness per se, which is deconstructed by Peirce) is caught between its unconscious skeletal-sets and the forces coming to it from experience (as the domain of secondness). There is, of course, a strong convergence between our skeletal-sets and the external world ensuring a positive trajectory for the sign-using self.

In an untitled manuscript ca. 1900 Peirce describes his detailed experiments designed to show that the self can make very subtle discriminations in sensation. The experiments focused on color sensibility as measured by the human eye under highly controlled conditions. The subject sits in front of an enclosed box painted black into which a small shaft of light penetrates. Color samples are shown to the subject, who has to make a quick identification. Peirce carefully computed the rate of success and the subtlety of these discriminations. The result of many months of experimentation convinced Peirce that the self can learn to increase its ability to make certain sensations more vivid, and thereby to disclose their makeup more accurately. Interestingly, he made the abduction from these experimental results that the self is constituted with many non-discrete layers (although the better concept might be that of "dimensions"), each with its own intensity of sensation. This abduction enabled him to make further startling claims about the unconscious.

Since Peirce has already deconstructed consciousness and the individual ego, the self is left with its semiotic series (ideas of sensation, for example) that actually form the field previously known as consciousness. In several places, Peirce uses the analogy between consciousness and a lake:

> . . . that our whole past experience is continually in our consciousness, though most of it sunk to a great depth of dimness. I think of consciousness as a bottomless lake, whose waters seem transparent, yet into which we can clearly see but a little way. But in this water there are countless objects at different depths; and certain influences will give certain kinds of those objects an upward impulse which may be intense enough and continue long enough to bring them into the upper visible layer. After the impulse ceases they commence to sink downwards. [CP 7.547]

At the bottom of the lake (referred to elsewhere as a kind of "generic soul," cf. CP 7.592) can be found all of the previous experiences of the self, which, as we already saw, are gathered together into clusters (skeletal-sets). These clusters have their own magnetic power to bring new material into their orbit. Peirce's model here is very similar to that of Jung, who argued that the personal unconscious is constituted by what he called "feeling toned complexes," each of which has a strong image or feeling at its center. This core of the complex acts like Peirce's skeleton to bring new material into its integrity. The unconscious for both thinkers is very active and dynamic, constantly forming gestalts of great depth and power.

For Peirce, in keeping with his sense of teleology, the deeper layers of the lake/consciousness can be brought into the light of awareness, thereby regaining their lost intensity. There is a flow of energy moving in both directions within the self. As an image moves toward the surface, it gains in intensity and energy. As the same image moves back down into the unconscious, it loses intensity and energy. This process, insofar as it admits of purpose, is anti-conservative; that is, it allows for a genuine increase in energy and order (under the impress of self-control).

The image of the lake proves to be a rich one for Peirce. Ideas are likened to raindrops falling on the surface of the lake. As the drops sink below the surface they enter into the vast relational chains already found just beneath the surface. Associational and suggestive patterns exert their inertial pressure on new ideas, assuring that they will have a place to become efficacious in the general psychic economy. Energy is, of course, conserved, but there is also the possibility for an increase in the available energy for the self. Peirce moves quickly from his color-sensation experiments to the idea that the self traffics in intensities that can be enhanced through discipline and purpose.

Ideas form into unconscious complexes (to use Jung's language) and move up and down the lake of consciousness. It takes effort for the self to probe into the deeper structures of consciousness. Peirce shows the continuity between something as specific as color sensation and the deeper structures of awareness that connect us to the "generic soul." He sees two factors operating in psychic dynamics. The first is the "momentum" that moves an idea from a dim to a vivid state and back again. The second is a "buoyancy" that brings certain ideas to the surface:

> Still another factor seems to be a certain degree of buoyancy or association with whatever idea may be vivid, which belongs to those ideas that we call purposes, by virtue of which they are particularly apt to be brought up and held up near the surface by the inflowing percepts and thus to hold up any ideas with which they may be associated. The control which we exercise over our thoughts in reasoning consists in our purpose holding certain thoughts up where they may be scrutinized. The levels of easily controlled ideas are those that are so near the surface as to be strongly affected by present purposes. [CP 7.554]

The function of purpose is to bring ideas into the sphere of scrutiny and self-control where they may support positive habits and beliefs. Peirce does not use the psychoanalytic language of resistance and repression here (not simply because it was not available to him, but because of an aversion to its way of framing the problem), but the Humean language of vividness and dimness. While he is fully aware that feeling forms the background (as firstness) for awareness, he still sees ideas in terms of their quasi-visual or iconic aspect. The closer to the surface a given idea, the easier it is to bring it into the forms of control pertinent to pragmaticism.

There is a general psychic economy that is finite. Each layer of the self is finite in its capacities. The social self, the individual ego, and the realm of percepts and their perceptual judgments are all finite in different respects. Only the generic soul (or spiritual consciousness) is infinite (and known through the most basic vague background feeling).

The image of the lake is more faithful to the depth structures of the self than the image of our "glassy essence." A lake is constituted by numerous life forms with their own evolutionary laws and associational patterns. Peirce makes it clear that the self is the locus of nature's forms of semiosis, but this fact can be dealt with in a variety of ways. The image of the "glassy essence," while it allows for perspectival shifts (refraction properties), remains too passive. The image of the lake, on the other hand, evokes a sense of the true unconscious dynamics that continue to exert their pressure on all surface phenomena. Ideas (as tied to experience/secondness) come into the lake and enrich its contents. The raindrop is more dynamic than the ray of light in that it can enter into the psychic/chemical constitution of the self and become transformed by the encounter. More importantly, lakes can contain hidden associational chains that are self-moving to new structures. A glass or prism is not self-moving, but must serve the ambient light that enters into it.

Like Jung, Peirce hints that the depth structure of the self reaches right down into the mind of the creator. This possibility should not come as a surprise, given Peirce's emphasis on continuity and the ubiquity of mentality and semiosis in the universe. In a ca. 1893 manuscript entitled "Short Logic," he opens the door to the deepest structure of the sign-using self:

> Thus all knowledge comes to us by observation, part of it forced upon us from without from Nature's mind and part coming from the depths of that inward aspect of mind, which we egotistically call *ours*; though in truth it is we who float upon its surface and belong to it more than it belongs to us. Nor can we affirm that the inwardly seen mind is altogether independent of the outward mind which is its Creator. [CP 7.558]

There is a direct logical connection between the pragmatistic belief in critical common sense and the belief in a mind of nature that is itself rooted in the divine mind. The self has a kind of inner light of nature that brings it into harmony with the laws and habits of the evolutionary universe. This light is not an intuition but a general capacity to form truth-generating habits in the long run. We could almost say that the innate light of nature is a gift of the creator to the sign-using self so that it can explore the depths of its own and nature's mind. The critical common-sensist is also an explorer of the unfathomable depths of the personal and generic soul.

With this highly expansive and capacious conception of mind in its largest sense, it would seem to follow that the mind cannot be located in, or at least confined, to the human brain. This is precisely the implication that Peirce draws. In his 1902 manuscript, "Minute Logic," he explores a further set of issues in the field of psychology, renamed by him "psychognosy." Traditional psychology has privileged the concept of consciousness and has located this consciousness within the brain. Peirce firmly rejects the mind/brain identity thesis in favor of the view that the mind can be located in a variety of places. We recall his discussions about the importance of the tongue (which he brings up again in the current manuscript) as the locus of personality via its language. He also says, by way of amplification, that an author's mind may be more present in one of his or her books than in some alleged interior psychic realm.

Peirce distinguishes between the interior and exterior aspects of the self in an unusual way. The interior realm is the realm of feeling and he goes so far as to say that "What is meant by consciousness is really in itself nothing but feeling" [CP 7.364]. The exterior aspect of the self is the mind. Hence, as in his earlier essays (1868–1869), the true locus of our mental life is the external realm of signs and forms of signification. From this it follows that psychology (or psychognosy) does not study consciousness or self-consciousness but external mind. If consciousness is nothing but feeling, and feeling is in the domain of firstness and immediacy, it does not have enough 'content' to be a proper subject of study. Inquiry cannot take place without some secondness and reaction among elements. Feeling can be grasped and understood in its vague outline and presence, but it is not, per se, a subject of psychological study. Further, as noted earlier, Peirce has an intentional theory of feeling; namely, one that asserts that feelings are always about some object other than themselves. Hence to study feelings is to study objects.

When the mind turns to introspection it can only find its intentional products, never its actual operations. The mind in itself is extremely elusive. It is driven to create products that mark its complex trajectory through time. Consequently we must read backward from the mind's creations to its hidden operations. "As for the mind's watching its own operations, no such thing is possible. It is a pure delusion" [CP 7.376]. Any train of thought will be mappable, but the processes by which each aspect of the train was created will be beyond the ken of the introspective gaze. The entire weight of Peirce's psychological theory is on the side of objective intentional referents. These referents belong to the larger mind, which is not confined to the human brain. It is important to note that the spiritual consciousness *and* personal mind are both larger than the human brain that is alleged to house them.

Peirce remains suspicious of any concept of pure unmediated simplicity. Every aspect of the self involves mediation and inference. Even the so-called simple sensations are already highly complex: "The truth is that the phrase *simple sensation* is devoid of all meaning, unless by simple be meant important" [CP 7.376]. As we will remind ourselves shortly, the structure of perceptual judgment, as tied to the percept, is complex, inferential, and fallible. Hence we can find no absolute beginning point for sensation.

We have seen the link between critical common-sensism and a belief in the unconscious with its own internal laws and associations that serve to guide the sign-using self through time. Peirce augments this link by referring to the tensions between what he calls the "Instinctive Mind" and the "Rational Mind." The instinctive mind is much the more important of the two and functions to guide the self in its everyday decisions. He even goes so far as to see the rational mind as an immature version of the instinctive mind, especially because it is so prone to error and confusion. Peirce eulogizes the powers of the instinctive mind and the plastic quality of instincts. If the rational mind sinks into rigid and a priori forms of reasoning, the instinctive mind, with deep unconscious roots, remains supple and mobile as its various instincts and habits shape the self/world transaction. Psychology (psychognosy) privileges the rational mind and thus fails to illuminate the true phylogenetic structures that guide life. Peirce's privileging of the instinctive mind is of a piece with his affirmation of critical common-sensism and the innate but self-transforming skeletal-sets of the unconscious.

We will complete our analysis of Peirce's conception of the human process by briefly looking at his 1903 manuscript, "Telepathy." In this essay, Peirce does not say much about the phenomenon of telepathy per se, remaining skeptical of much of the literature and theorizing about the topic, but he does say some important things about the nature of perceptual judgment and its relation to the percept. This is done in the context of showing how perception remains a problematic guide for such sciences (or pseudosciences) as psychical research. In looking at percepts, perceptual judgments, and what Peirce calls the "percipuum" we come full circle and return to the issues that animated him in the 1860s.

At the beginning of this chapter we saw how Peirce linked perceptual judgments to inferences (as being the limiting case of abduction). At this point, we can add some crucial distinctions pertinent to epistemology, which in turn shed light on how the self comes to grasp essential features of the world. Peirce is especially clear here on the distinction between the percept and the perceptual judgment: "The perceptual judgment is all but in the same relation to knowledge and belief as is the percept. . . . If one *sees*, one cannot avoid the percept; and if one *looks*, one cannot avoid the perceptual judgment" [CP 7.627]. Seeing is forced and direct, while looking involves the shaping of a judgment about what is seen.

In terms of the three primal ontological categories, the precept is correlated to firstness and secondness. That is, the precept is a brute something that imposes itself on the subject. As such, the percept does not have any representative status. The percept is not about anything other than itself. In this special sense, the percept cannot be false, since to be false it would have to represent something in some respect. The perceptual judgment is correlated to thirdness precisely because it does represent something, namely the percept, in some fashion. Consequently, the perceptual judgment can be false, although these judgments are automatic, unconscious, and based on instinct. Peirce gives the example of his yellow chair with a green cushion. The yellowness of the chair is imposed on the mind (the firstness and secondness of the percept). The self has a little latitude in making the judgment "this is a yellow chair," although that too will be largely compulsive.

Peirce uses the term "percipuum" to denote the combined reality of the percept and the perceptual judgment. Since it is impossible to distinguish the percept from its perceptual judgment by an act of introspection, we are left with the fact that they come to us as a combined unit. By a process of analysis we can separate them in principle, but we must remember that we are actually dealing with the percipuum, rather than with either of its constituents.

When a perceptual judgment is imposed on a percept, the correlation is one of predication, not one involving a copy, icon, or a drawing. The relation between the perceptual judgment and its percept is a perceptual relation (an operation within perception). There is a crucial temporal dimension to the percept/perceptual judgment correlation: "In a perceptual judgment the mind professes to tell the mind's future self what the character of the present percept is. The percept, on the contrary, stands on its own legs and makes no professions of any kind" [CP 7.630]. Percepts are brought into the structure of time by their mediating judgments. Consequently, thirdness, as ingredient in all perceptual judgments, makes full temporality actual for the realm of percepts.

The epistemological implications are clear. The psychical researcher is probing into the nature of highly unusual percepts. Yet, if the investigator does not understand that the percipuum has two parts, only one of which is making anything like an affirmation, he or she fails to see that the judgment lying at heart of the percipuum may be false. Put differently, to fail to distinguish between the compelling percept (as partaking of firstness and secondness) and the less compelling perceptual judgment (as partaking of thirdness) is to give too much credence to the percipuum. For Peirce, while a percept cannot be false, a percipuum can be in error: "There is no percipuum so absolute as not to be subject to possible error" [CP 7.676].

Thus, for example, when the psychical researcher deals with such a phenomenon as telepathy, in which a thought moves from mind to mind without using any of the known physical senses for its encoding, transmission, and decoding, there is a fallible percipuum involved that can admit of alternative perceptual judgments. The percept is what it is regardless, but its perceptual judgment, as temporal and general, can be other than it is. It is, of course, especially difficult to break open a percipuum to see its two components, but it is enough to know that it has these two logically and categorically distinct dimensions. We can admit that there is a class of unusual and deeply intriguing phenomena to investigate, but we need not accept that their meaning is always given in an unambiguous or unmediated way.

There is something liberating in thinking in terms of a fallible percipuum, rather than in terms of some given sensum that comes to the self clean. The various phenomena available to the psychical researcher, such as clairvoyance, psychokinesis, precognition, and telepathy, all come to the self in the guise of a percipuum that blends givenness and interpretation in ways that can never be fully decoded. This insight gives a certain humility to the task of rendering the world of psychic phenomena intelligible. Abductions from an evocative percipuum must be made with great circumspection and care.

The picture of the self emerging from these many papers, letters, and manuscripts is a complex one. Peirce's philosophical anthropology covers a vast terrain and links his theory of the self to his logic and his theory of the community. We start on the most basic level of our sensations and find that we are in fact dealing with a percipuum, which is itself a complex blend of a given percept (firstness and secondness) and a perceptual judgment (thirdness). The perceptual judgment is rooted in the unconscious and has the status of an inference, but one in which the antecedent and the consequent both seem to be given directly. Hence, the perceptual judgment seems to be both in time and out of time. It is in time in the special sense that it represents the future dimension of the self, while it is out of time in the sense that it seems to be an immediate inference/predication that did not unfold through a temporal sequence. Be that as it may, the perceptual judgment is the more important element in the percipuum because it embodies thirdness and at least hints in the direction of abduction proper.

Moving on to consciousness itself, we see how Peirce deconstructs the Cartesian notion that the self is some kind of thinking substance, knowing itself through introspective acts. Consciousness so-called is actually a locus of internal feeling. The individual self correlated with consciousness is also deconstructed. Both consciousness and the finite ego are fictions and are to be replaced by intentional and external forms of semiosis. The self builds itself up through time and becomes the locus where the sign/object/interpretant triad unfolds most clearly. The present self refers to its past self (which obtains as an object) in a certain respect so that a future self (interpretant) can emerge to give identity to the self as a whole. The self is not a consciousness or self-consciousness (contra Hegel) but a sign series that continues to add more and more interpretants to its evolving contour. Self-knowledge is obtained by translating backward from external and public signs toward an elusive inner realm of feeling.

Consciousness and the personal ego, once removed, give way to a semiotic self that is fully communal. The social self is the true self insofar as it is the locus for those public signs and interpretants that operate to give the individual some sense of semiotic identity. The identity relation (at least in the realm of the human process) is a species of self-control. That is, the self becomes what it is through self-controlled semiotic acts that point toward an emancipatory future. The heart of self-control is hope, not a simple belief in the success of the infinite long run, but a radical hope that the self and its communities will be fully transformed in their depth structures.

The social self operates through contrast to mold and transform the individual self so that it can come into conformity with the larger semiotic orders. The social self does not function thorough some kind of bare conformity or consensus, a mistake made by neopragmatists, but by binding itself to the natural semiotic structures of the evolving universe, which moves via cosmic habits/thirds toward the full realization of concrete reasonableness and the *summum bonum*. The social self uses the method of science to overcome provincial distortions so that the plenitude of nature's semiotic structures can become known to each sign-using self. Outside of the community, the individual is as nothing and has neither self-control nor self-identity.

More basic than the social self is the spiritual consciousness or generic soul. For Peirce, this primal soul is given to awareness in a vague way. While we are embodied we tend to ignore this spiritual consciousness because of the sheer semiotic noise of the illusory private ego and the larger social self. Peirce uses the argument from continuity to show how we make the transition from life to death in an unbroken momentum that serves to illuminate the depth dimension of the self that is there all along. The spiritual consciousness is the background of all backgrounds, appearing to us as a kind of pure feeling (or primal firstness). Immortality is attained in the present and does not depend upon some kind of soul substance or substrate that can be isolated from the rest of the self. Our immortal self is fully continuous with our mortal self and partakes of the same ontological structures. Again, we see how Cartesianism is overcome with its insistence that the immortal soul must be ontologically distinctive from the mortal and embodied part of the human process.

The self is thus multidimensional, although it does not have an isolated or ultimate substrate. Consciousness gives way to external and public sign series that receive their validity and vector directionality from the social self. Yet underneath the social and individual aspects of the self is a vast unconscious that has personal and transpersonal elements. I have deliberately used the commensurate language of Jungian archetypal psychology because I am persuaded that Peirce moved toward an awareness of the collective unconscious. He certainly has structures parallel to Jung's feeling-toned complexes. We will look into the question of the archetypes in the final chapter. His image of the lake augments, and in many respects surpasses, his image of our glassy essence. The lake is constituted by personal and prepersonal elements, each of which is shaped by skeletal-sets that lie beneath the surface of the water. The laws of continuity and association, working through resemblance, contiguity, and contrast, guide the formation of the unconscious gestalts. By an effort of will and self-control, the individual can bring much of this underwater material to the surface of consciousness. When this is done, given ideas increase in vividness and energy, thus overcoming the principle of the conservation of energy if only for a brief time. External experiences (raindrops) replenish the lake and gives the self an unending supply of new signs and interpretants.

Self-control is central to the growth of the self and has an ethical and ontological dimension. Ontologically, self-control is what it is because of the depth structures of cosmic habit within the universe as a whole. Habits of cosmic scope emerge into full manifestation/thirdness because of the self-control of the universe. The human process derives its energies and vector directionalities from the universe. Ethically, self-control emerges in the context of the social self, which functions to reign in the imperial drives of the individual. Rejecting psychological and ethical egoism, Peirce insists that the individual prefers self-sacrifice to the quest for pleasure. Of course, the community must intervene to show the individual just what its needs truly are. But this process is a healing one in which the individual welcomes the larger community into its self-constitution. Without this ethical and social dimension of self-control, the individual would fail to satisfy its own cognitive and emotional needs.

In the end, the self must struggle to integrate its public semiotic structures with its vast unconscious sets and powers. Self-control links public space to the more elusive momentum of the unconscious so that a future-directed picture of wholeness can guide the self. Ironically, it seems as if the individual, who has no real consciousness or self-consciousness, is caught between two vast realities that are not compatible with its being. Yet, for Peirce, the structures of the community and of the unconscious are crucial for giving the self its ontological location within the world. Whether we are a glassy essence or a bottomless lake, we derive our scope and integrity from social, religious, and unconscious forces that eclipse us and reach down into the semiotic origins and goals of the universe. We are a small part of an infinite semiotic web that has neither beginning nor end, but which promises to bring completion to the individual and its chosen communities. The theonomous heart of the sign-using self brings us both subjective and objective immortality in our present existence. The mere loss of an individual ego thus seems a small thing in the face of the larger universe of signs.

Notes

1. In this regard, see the otherwise excellent works: *Charles Peirce's Empiricism*, by Justus Buchler (London: Kegan Paul, Trench, Trubner & Co. Ltd., 1939), reprinted in 1980 by Octagon Books, and *The Thought of C. S. Peirce*, by Thomas A. Goudge (Toronto: University of Toronto Press, 1950), reprinted by Dover Publications in 1969. Buchler, one of the outstanding systematic philosophers of the age, failed to recognize the centrality of Peirce's later philosophical theology for his overall perspective. Goudge, whose book remains one of the best on Peirce, divides Peirce into two halves; namely, the "naturalistic" and "transcendental" halves. I am persuaded that a different conception of naturalism (an ecstatic naturalism) animates Peirce's metaphysics and that his perspective is both deeply religious and consistent throughout. Unfortunately, most of the Peirce scholarship at midcentury expressed the philosophical prejudices of the time, i.e., a kind of cryptoposi-

tivism with its narrow views on nature and method. It is interesting to note that Buchler moved toward a much more encompassing perspective after his dissertation on Peirce and created one of the most important works in systematic thought since Whitehead's *Process and Reality*; namely, his *Metaphysics of Natural Complexes* of 1966, recently republished in an expanded edition, ed. by Wallace, Marsoobian, and Corrington (Albany: SUNY Press, 1990).

2. Vincent Colapietro, *Peirce's Approach to the Self: A Semiotic Perspective on Human Subjectivity* (Albany: SUNY Press, 1989), pp. 95–96.

Chapter Three

Firstness, Secondness, Thirdness: The Universe of Signs

The discipline of semiotics, the systematic study of those complexes known as signs, has had a long and rich history, stemming from its origins in ancient Greek thought, working its way through the medieval period, and culminating in the contemporary period. Two major contemporary traditions have been identified, although there are other, perhaps less prominent species, and they have evolved into fairly distinctive alternatives. Continental semiotics stems from the writings of the structuralist Ferdinand de Saussure, who privileges language and the allegedly arbitrary cultural codes within which signs function. The American tradition, on the other hand, derives its inspiration from Peirce's pragmaticistic semiotics with its emphasis on the deeper natural and evolutionary structures of signs. Structuralist and pragmaticistic semiotics move in different directions and have their own implications for the status of semiosis within the universe.

Peirce did not develop his semiotics in a vacuum, nor did he privilege human language as the paradigm for all other forms of sign activity. As we have seen, Peirce locates sign activity within the self and its communities, as these in turn are located within an evolving universe that is itself "perfused with signs." Peirce's position can thus be defined as a "pansemioticism" in which each order encountered is at least potentially or virtually semiotic.[1] Nature is a self-recording sign system that leaves traces of its semiotic evolution throughout its innumerable orders. Some commentators have missed the naturalistic foundations of Peirce's semiotics because of a contemporary bias toward human forms of signification (anthroposemiosis). By the same token, these commentators often mute or downplay the metaphysical categories that animate and shape Peirce's semiotic theory. In what follows, we will correlate Peirce's semiotics with his most basic metaphysical categories so that it becomes clear how Peirce wishes to measure anthroposemiosis by a far more general semiotic metaphysics that honors indigenous sign activity no matter where or how located.

Peirce's interest in metaphysical categories started early, largely through his encounter with Kant's *Critique of Pure Reason*, which struggled to establish the transcendental conditions for intelligibility. At the same time, Kant regrounded the traditional logical table of judgments so that he could lay the foundations for a different kind of ontology. Both Peirce and Kant put pressure on established metaphysical categories and procedures, yet both remain friendly to some kind of generic-level analysis of the basic structures of intelligibility. As noted previously, Peirce's rhetorical blasts against metaphysics refer more to his interlocutors, living and dead, than to the enterprise itself. To fail to understand Peirce as a metaphysician, first and last, is to fail to grasp the crucial support conditions for pragmaticism.

Put more precisely, Peirce shaped his semiotics at the same time that he was shaping his metaphysics. As he came to move semiotics more and more to the center of his vision, he refined and clarified his categorial structure so that it could illuminate the nature of sign activity. In our exposition we will exhibit the categorial structure first, with references to the semiotic. The second half of the chapter will then focus more specifically on the makeup of the sign and its various forms of relation to objects and other signs. We will conclude with an analysis of the naturalistic implications of his pansemioticism.

The Three Primal Categories

The most important early document for an understanding of Peirce's metaphysics and semiotics is his 1867 paper "On a New List of Categories," published the following year in the *Proceedings of the American Academy of Arts and Sciences*. In this brief and highly condensed essay, Peirce develops his own categorial structure and shows its implications for semiotic theory. He points in the direction of his more mature classification scheme of firstness, secondness, and thirdness, and lays the foundations for his basic semiotic triad of icon, index, and symbol (which refers to the three ways in which a sign can refer to its object). While Peirce came to prefer a different language for his basic categories, he is surprisingly consistent in his sense that the world ultimately devolves into three primal categories, no one of which can be further reduced to another. At the same time, he insists that sign function must take place according to the basic categories and that it cannot take place without reference to the sovereign ontological structures.

Peirce begins his analysis by making the Kantian claim that the function of categories is to reduce the manifold of sensations to some kind of unity. To validate a general category is to see if it is absolutely indispensable; that is, that it is impossible to reduce the manifold to unity without it. Once its necessity has been established, it can be correlated to the structures of the sign. In looking at the manifold of sensation, it soon becomes clear that there is a basic underlying something that obtains prior to any attempt at predication or qualification. This basic 'something' is referred to as "it." At the same time, the *it* can be defined as the "present in general"; namely, as the nonunified something that stands before us and claims our attention. "This *it* is thus neither predicated of a subject, nor in a subject, and accordingly is identical with the conception of substance" [W 2.49 & EP 1.2]. Since the *it* cannot be a predicate or a quality, it has no intrinsic features that make it distinctive. The *it* is substance in general, or pure "thatness" rather than whatness or quality. Consequently, anything we say about the *it* will involve a different order of reality and analysis. Once we leave the pure *it* we are in the realm of judgment. As we saw in the previous chapter, the realm of perceptual judgment is the realm of unconscious predication and thus has already leaped beyond the *it* to a higher level of designation. We get to the *it* by a process of prescinding in which we strip away all features and qualities of substance so that the *it* can emerge. Of course, we never live in the world of the *it* any more than we can encounter pure substance. The conception of the *it* involves a positing that infers that and what it is, although, strictly speaking, it has no "what."

The plot thickens when we go from substance/*it* to being. Like Kant, Peirce argues that being cannot be a predicate; that is, it cannot be a real quality of an object. Rather, it is a connective term linking some quality to substance. As such, being is somewhere between substance and its qualities and serves to link them together. In Peirce's example, to say that "the stove is black" is to say that the quality of blackness belongs to the stove (qua *it* or substance). The copula "is" merely brings a quality and a substance into conjunction. Being does not affect or alter the substance but it does open up a realm of indeterminate predication such that something can be affirmed of the *it*. In this sense, being is a powerful enabling condition for the determination of objects. Consequently, being's 'neutrality' is a complex one. It can facilitate predication, yet it avoids invading the substance that is predicated. Put in even simpler terms, being, as a concept, has no content, even though is makes it possible for content to find a 'home' in the *it*.

Both being and substance serve as the beginning and end points of reflection. By this is meant that they both hold and, in a different way, enable all qualities. They hold qualities by giving them a sphere of relevance. They enable categories by providing the momentum of predication. While being is not a predicate, it is the enabling ground for all predication. In this sense, being is a dynamic concept. As we move backward, as it were, from being to substance, we encounter quality. A quality emerges whenever the opening created by being gets filled in by specific content. As noted, being creates an opening by securing the possibility of predication. The actualization of this general possibility takes place through the category of quality (which is a general trait). It is important to note that the quality is not given immediately to perception and is not available to the self through an act of alleged introspection. Rather, the quality is itself the product of a hypothetical inference. Consequently, the blackness of the stove is brought into relevance to the *it* of the stove itself. When this takes place, we can link proper predicates with their underlying substance.

Refining his nascent categorial scheme still further, Peirce distinguishes between the concepts of "respect," "quality," and "ground." He correlates them as follows:

> Moreover, the conception of a pure abstraction is indispensable, because we cannot comprehend an agreement of two things, except as an agreement in some *respect*, and this respect is such a pure abstraction as blackness. Such a pure abstraction, reference to which constitutes a *quality* or general attribute, may be termed a *ground*. [W 2.52–53 & EP 1.4]

The quality of blackness is the respect in which the particular *it* belongs to a genus or class and can thus enter into structures of relation and comparison. This general respect or quality serves as a ground; that is, as an enabling and empowering condition for specificity. Peirce, as we will see, ties power to specificity insofar as there must be a movement toward actualization for a substance to become efficacious in the world. Even the most general categories are specific in some respect; that is, are respects or grounds that demarcate one thing from another. There is no real contradiction between the link of power and specificity, on the one hand, with the move toward generality on the other. Purely open or vague generality, the realm of the *it*, has less power than the qualified generality of true quality or whatness.

In addition to the ground/respect/quality triad is what Peirce calls the "correlate," which serves as a linking third term holding divergent predications together. The correlate emerges through the psychological laws of association, which are manifest in the concern with similarity and contrast. His example is that of the English noun "man" vis-à-vis the French equivalent "homme." Both terms refer to the same two-legged creature. Consequently, the correlate is the reference relation that brings the two terms of comparison into unity, i.e., it shows their similarity. Another of his examples puts this even more clearly. For every murderer there must be a murder victim. One cannot have one without the other. These two realities are correlated together through the mediating relation, the correlate. This unique relation links qualities together in specific ways. Yet the correlate does not link terms together through a new and higher term, something reserved for the interpretant.

To return to the stove example, blackness makes the stove what it is and serves as the ground and respect for its inner dynamism, both in terms of self-identity and in terms of its relational possibilities and actualities. These ontological relations carry with them their own semiotic relation. Peirce points toward his more mature semiotic theory when he enunciates the emergence of what he calls the "interpretant":

> By a further accumulation of instances, it would be found that every comparison requires, besides the related thing, the ground, and the correlate, also a *mediating representation which represents the relate to be a representation of the same correlate which this mediating representation itself represents.* Such a mediating representation may be termed an *interpretant,* because it fulfills the office of an interpreter, who says that a foreigner says the same thing which he himself says. [W 2.53–54 & EP 1.5]

This is a highly complex structure but we can open it up a little more clearly so that its inner dynamisms become clarified. We started with the substance or the *it* that obtains prior to predication or qualification. Qualities are brought into correlation with the substance through the copula "is" that is the enabling ground for predication. Yet all predication must be correlated to objects and other qualities; that is, must be brought into relationship with larger orders of relevance. The murder victim is correlated with the murderer and linked through a mediating or third structure. The intelligibility of this correlation is made public through the "interpretant" which is the mediating sign. Peirce here links the concept of "interpretant" to that of "interpreter" but he is clear in most contexts that they are to be separated. That is, the interpretant is the mediating sign that makes all categorial and semiotic linkages public (specifically, in the form of arguments). The interpreter is the person who takes over the interpretant and modifies it in such a way as to create yet new interpretants. As we will see, there is no end to the number of actual and possible interpretants (which, Peirce hints, may exist even where there are no interpreters—although this is a controversial point).

Peirce makes the correlation of his categories with number clear: "This passage from the many to the one is numerical" [W 2.55 & EP 1.6]. The sensuous manifold, in good Kantian fashion, is a many-fold chaos awaiting its unification. As we go 'up' the scale of categories we bring more and more unity into the manifold. Reading between the lines, we can point to the mature categorial scheme and show how Peirce adumbrates and foreshadows it here in this 1867 essay. The *it*, as substance, as the present in general, is without determinate shape and content. Consequently it is almost akin to the domain of pure possibility. Therefore it is roughly equivalent to the category of firstness. The correlate, on the other hand, works through similarity and contrast to bring two items into some kind of connection. Therefore it is roughly equivalent to the category of secondness. The interpretant is the mediating link holding representations together. Consequently it is less roughly equivalent to thirdness. The *it* is the ultimate preformal 'matter' that takes on predication and quality, via the enabling yet undetermined power of the copula. The correlate emerges to show identity or similarity, or in another order of relevance, a link between two items (e.g., the murderer and murdered). The interpretant mediates between the *it* and the correlate by sustaining the more general and intelligible aspects of quality.

Peirce elaborates on these distinctions and makes further refinements, but they are not directly pertinent to our delineation of the basic ontological categories. The exciting shift comes when he links his nascent metaphysics with his semiotics. His triadic distinction between icon, index, and symbol (as the three relations between signs and their objects) emerges into some clarity, even though he uses slightly different terms here:

1. Those whose relation to their objects is a mere community in some quality, and these representations may be termed *Likenesses*.
2. Those whose relation to their objects consists in a correspondence in fact, and these may be termed *Indices* or *Signs*.

3. Those the ground of whose relation to their objects is an imputed character, which are the same as *general signs*, and these may be termed *Symbols*. [W 2.56 & EP 1.7]

This paragraph lays out the basic terrain and Peirce never wavered from these insights. In the dimension of firstness, the sign refers to its object via likenesses. This relation is termed "iconic" in later writings. An icon shares some quality with its denoted object, although this likeness need not be a literal pictorial form. For example, a series of descriptions can be iconic insofar as they show the link between qualities common to the sign and its object. As we will see in more detail, the concept of "quality" functions in the dimensions of firstness *and* thirdness, but in different respects. The second relation is indexical and involves a causal connection between the sign and its object, what Peirce calls a "correspondence in fact." This is the domain of secondness and entails that two items are brought into correlation. This relation is natural in the sense that it occurs throughout nature and is not the result of a human stipulation. One of his oft-cited examples is that of the weather vane that is a sign in an indexical relation to the wind. Its direction is causally determined by a natural phenomenon that it, qua sign, faithfully measures and indicates. Another example would be a medical symptom, say a fever, that points indexically to an underlying causal agent.

On a much higher level of sophistication is the symbolic relation between a sign and its object. This involves intelligibility and thirdness. These signs are general in the sense that they point to more basic and recurrent features of the world. However, unlike the indexical relation, which is causal and natural, the symbolic relation is one involving an "imputed character"; that is, a character that comes from conscious human contrivance. A national flag, for example, is a symbol pointing to its object in an imputed or conventional way. Unless the perceiver understands the created correspondence between the particular flag and a given nation, its symbolic power is mute. Generality is, to some extent at least, rendered intelligible through human manipulative acts.

At the conclusion of "On a New List of Categories" Peirce adds yet another triadic distinction to the others. This refers to the inner logic of semiotic reference and exhibits the ways in which symbols move from the most basic forms of pointing toward a participation in larger argumentative structures:

. . . first, the direct reference of a symbol to its objects, or its denotation; second, the reference of the symbol to its ground, through its object, that is, its reference to the common characters of its objects, or its connotation; and third, its reference to its interpretants through its object, that is, its reference to all the synthetical propositions in which its objects in common are subject or predicate, and this I term the information it embodies. [W 2.59 & EP 1.10]

The symbol, as tied to the category of thirdness and intelligibility, refers directly to its object, which must itself be general in some respect to be 'worthy' of a symbol. Thus it denotes its object and renders it present to conscious sign-users. Yet this dimension passes over to that of connotation in which the symbol illuminates the basic qualities (characteristics) of its object. The scope of these qualities may increase as the symbol takes on richer shades of meaning. The full extent of these characteristics represents the connotative dimension of the symbolic relation. Finally, the symbol illuminates a field of interpretants that can link together into synthetical propositions. Peirce uses the Kantian term "synthetic" to underlie the fact that the string of interpretants emergent from the symbol actually adds new knowledge to the world. A merely analytic proposition would simply unfold the self-contained predicate of the subject. Interpretants are thus efficacious in enhancing the reach of genuine knowledge.

In the second half of this chapter we will see how the concept of "information" works semiotically. At this point it is important to remember that signs serve to open out the structures of nature and human culture for interpreters and that they are not purely arbitrary. Even symbols, with their imputed or conventional character, have some relation to extrahuman realities. Peirce remains a semiotic realist and naturalist in the sense that signs penetrate down into nature and function within prehuman orders. His objective idealism is, as noted, of a piece with his naturalism insofar as the world of nature is also, and more importantly, the realm of muted mentality.

To summarize what we have seen thus far, Peirce links the move from the many to the one with a basic triadic structure. The basic categories, whether called firstness, secondness, and thirdness, or the *it*, the correlate, and the interpretant, are irreducible to each other. By the same token, there is no room for a fourth category to somehow complete the list. Any attempt to show that there must be a fourth can be further analyzed into triadic structures that do the same ontological work. Signs also function triadically and mirror the three primal ontological categories. There are a number of triads pertinent to the life of signs and these will be unfolded in turn. As Peirce's thought matured, he applied his primal categories to more and more areas of nature, from the most basic protoplasm to the divine natures themselves. He never abandoned his triadic scheme and found no limitations to the instantiation of firstness, secondness, and thirdness.

Jumping ahead to ca. 1890, we can see how Peirce makes a number of bold and imaginative moves that push his three categories into all corners of the universe. One of the most evocative of all of his writings is his manuscript "A Guess at the Riddle," which is an outline for a proposed book of that title. In this essay Peirce links his ontological triad to psychology, cosmology, philosophical theology, neurology, and evolutionary theory.

Peirce begins the essay with a brief reflection on the status of number in the history of thought, noting that some thinkers have preferred to think in dyads, while others prefer to think in terms of fours or fives, etc. The important point for Peirce is that all numbers refer to nature and ". . . go down to the very essence of things" [CP 1.355 & EP 1.248]. We do not simply cast out a series of numbers and hope that they have some fit with the antecedent structures of the world. It follows, for Peirce at least, that his primal choice of the number three is manifest repeatedly in the orders of the world, and every area of inquiry will evoke triadic structures, no matter how thought proceeds. The number three is thus built into the basic woof and warp of nature.

The three categories can be articulated fairly clearly, although they will exhibit a blinding variety of forms within the organic and inorganic orders of nature:

> The first is that whose being is simply in itself, not referring to anything nor lying behind anything. The second is that which is what it is by force of something to which it is second. The third is that which is what it is owing to things between which it mediates and which it brings into relation to each other. [CP 1.356 & EP 1.248]

The category of firstness refers to a monadic reality that abides in itself and that prescinds from relations. Strictly speaking, we cannot even speak of self-identity in the realm of firstness (as the identity relation will be what Peirce calls a "degenerate" form of secondness). Secondness, by contrast refers to the force that demarcates one thing from another. We are already in a dyadic tension that is brute and immediate, and, at this stage, bereft of intelligibility. Thirdness, as a category, refers to the power of mediation that brings the earlier dyadic structure into a higher form of relationality, a relationality that is intelligible and that manifests lawlike regularity. Any given order of relevance will manifest all three categories, but may privilege one or two over the other(s). Peirce argues that we rarely find these categories manifest in a 'pure' fashion and that we must work toward them by a process of prescinding, which is a kind of ontological sub-traction process in which regnant features are intensified and lifted out of their ambiguous and embedded context.

Let us take a closer look at each of these three categories and their forms of instantiation in the realms of nature. The category of firstness is the hardest to describe, precisely because it occupies a domain that could be called preverbal. Every time we attempt to describe firstness, we stain its purity and make it other than it is. This puts the category of firstness in a peculiar position. Peirce argued that there can exist nothing that is not cognizable in some respect. Yet the category of firstness seems to be uncognizable and unavailable to the life of com-munication and public signs. How are we to resolve this seeming paradox in Peirce's categorial structure? His answer, at least, is that we can arrive at a sense of firstness thorough a process that moves backward from the more obvious and public features of secondness and thirdness toward their ultimate enabling condition. Here we see the lingering Kantianism even in the mature Peirce. For Kant, we can make deductions (akin to legal arguments) from the observed traits of experience to their necessary (a priori) transcendental grounds. There is a sense in which Peirce is reworking this strategy, a form of tran-scendental argument, in the context of ontology. Consequently, firstness will emerge as the necessary ground for any dyadic or triadic struc-tures of interaction and intelligibility.

With these methodological comments in mind, we can say a fair amount about what firstness is. Peirce lists a variety of predicates that qualify firstness, although, strictly speaking, firstness is prior to all predication. Among its attributes are: freshness, presentness, imme-diacy, newness, originality, spontaneity, freedom, having no unity, having no parts, feeling, and pure quality. Firstness cannot be thought or asserted and remains outside of the structures of induction, deduc-tion, and hypothesis (abduction). Firstness is thus: "What the world was to Adam on the day he opened his eyes to it, before he had drawn any distinctions, or had become conscious of his own existence, . . ." [CP 1.357 & EP 1.248].

Adam came upon a world that he had not made but that as yet had no name or shape. Religious myths of a primal garden or of a golden age are imaginative ways of pointing toward pure firstness. The flight from the garden is equivalent to the emergence of secondness, with all of its distresses. Hence, sin brings secondness into the world. It is important to note that Peirce's Adam does not even have self-con-sciousness at this stage. He is pure awareness, moving through the world without guile or any sense of its underlying structures and powers. It is almost as if Adam got back to the Kantian manifold of sensation and lived in a realm prior to the categories of the understanding (as forms of thirdness). Of course, all such dreaming innocence must give way before the powers of secondness.

The metaphysical aspects of firstness pertain to its modal properties, that is, its relation to the dialectic of possibility and necessity. For Peirce, firstness is not yet actual, not a center of necessary interaction:

> The first is full of life and variety. Yet that variety is only potential; it is not definitely there. Still, the notion of explaining the variety of the world, which was what they [the pre-Socratics] mainly wondered at, by non-variety was quite absurd. How is variety to come out of the womb of homogeneity; only by a principle of spontaneity, which is just that virtual variety that is the first. [CP 1.373 & EP 1.257]

Firstness is not yet "there," is not a sphere of actuality that can shape other orders. Yet it is the spawning ground of all of the world's orders and supports them. In this passage, Peirce argues that the pre-Socratic quest for a homogenous principle, e.g., water or fire, for explaining the later plurality of the world, is based on a misunderstanding of firstness. The ground of the world, pure firstness, is a heterogenous and self-othering momentum that spawns the things of nature but has no unity of its own. It is tempting to see firstness as a unified ground, or foundation of all foundations. However, Peirce clearly saw that it must be pure variety, pure possibility, and pure indeterminacy. Peirce denied that all manifest orders were strictly necessary, insisting that chance is a real power in the universe. On the deeper level of firstness, there are no necessary structures, only pure heterogenous momentum.

Secondness is much easier to describe since we are surrounded with concrete examples. The category of secondness refers to any interaction involving two elements. Among the attributes assigned to secondness, which can be predicated in a straightforward manner, are: compulsion, effect, effort, independence, result, negation, relation, and occurrence. Each of these predicates point toward a causal relation in which one object/event transforms another. While firstness has a certain "tender" quality, secondness is "hard" and "tangible." It involves a brute shock that makes its presence known. In fact, Peirce links the concept of secondness more directly to that of experience. The term "experience" has a variety of meanings. The pertinent meaning here is the colloquial one in which someone says, "She has a lot of experience with this issue." In this sense, "experience" refers to a depth of knowledge that can only come from numerous encounters. Secondness is akin to the concept of "experience" in this special sense. As experience is shaped and molded by the world, we are shaped by the innumerable forms of secondness that surround us. His image is that of a sailing vessel that sails out to sea with new sails, but that returns later with torn and weathered features. The new ragged edges come from secondness.

Firstness does not admit of levels or types. There is only firstness per se. Secondness, however, has a degenerate case in which the fullness of secondness is not yet manifest. The term "degenerate" is not meant to be used in a moral or ethical sense. It merely denotes an incomplete stage or manifestation of the primal category. The pure stage of secondness is that involving two distinct objects/events in direct interaction. The degenerate case, on the other hand, is a mere relation of reason, rather than of fact. For example, a resemblance between two items of the world, especially when these two items are not causally involved with each other, is a degenerate case of secondness. It is degenerate in that, while that *are* two terms/items of comparison, their relation is in the mind only (a relation of reason). A more interesting example is that of self-identity in which a thing is internally identical to itself. Strictly speaking, we do not have two actual items in relation/opposition, yet we do have a degenerate form of twoness. Genuine secondness thus involves real external relations of two events/objects. Degenerate secondness involves rational and internal relations, either between two nonconnected items or between an item and 'itself.'

Thirdness is the most complex of the three categories, not least because it has two degenerate cases. If firstness is the hardest to describe, and secondness is the most obvious on the immediate level of lived experience, thirdness is the most important for the life of the self and the evolving universe. Thirdness serves, among other things, to bring secondness and firstness together. The momentum of the three categories is hierarchical in that there is a nonreversible dependence relation as we move up the scale. Firstness is not dependent upon anything for its 'existence.' It merely obtains on its own. Secondness, on the other hand, could not be at all were it not for the firstness from which it emerges. By the same logic, thirdness could not be at all were it not for both firstness and secondness. While Peirce is antifoundational in his epistemology, he has a lingering form of foundationalism in his ontology. Firstness founds secondness and thirdness, while neither can found firstness. Secondness founds thirdness, while thirdness cannot found secondness. However, firstness is not more real than either secondness or thirdness. It is only more basic to the structure of the world.

Thirdness, then, emerges out of the realms of firstness and secondness. There is a sense in which thirdness is the teleological fulfillment of the other two ontological categories/structures. For Peirce, even with his modified developmental teleology, which insists that all goals are subject to the finite conditions of the world and are self-corrective, there is a deeper kind of primal purpose in the world governing the unfolding of secondness and thirdness out of the womb of firstness. That thirdness exists at all seems to be part of a larger cosmic plan. However, the particular thirds that are manifest in a given cosmic epoch may very well be freely chosen cosmic habits that do not represent a specific divine plan. As we will see in the next chapter, the concept of theodicy or of a providential plan becomes profoundly modified in Peirce's philosophical theology.

Thirdness is general and involves a quality that is distinctive and pertinent to specific orders. The universe is moving toward an increase in the scope and 'amount' of thirdness. This is manifest in the growth of cosmic habit and centers of concrete reasonableness. While Peirce distances himself from Hegel on many occasions (yet he doth "protest too much"), his category of thirdness has strong family resemblances to Hegel's concept of the "concrete universal." Both a given third and a concrete universal link together the dynamics and power of causal orders with the purposive momentum of the universe. Thirdness is the combination of habit and purpose. It gathers habits together into larger orders of relevance, while shaping these very habits by a purpose that remains partially open.

The basic triadic structure is not only a vertical hierarchy, but is deeply relational. As noted, Peirce argues that the triad cannot be reduced to a dyad or set of dyads. His prime example proving this claim is that of gift giving. The subject "A" gives a gift "B" to a subject "C." The relation of giving cannot be reduced to the two dyads of: A does B and C receives B. These two dyads would have no internal connection. The act of giving, as purposive, entails an internal relation between A and C. Consequently, the triad of A gives B to C is irreducible to any dyadic pairing. This formal relation mirrors the deeper ontological structures of the world. Any event, from a protoplasmic cell to the divine life, will function according to the primal triadic structures that are ubiquitous.

To bring this point home with even more force, Peirce cites an example that brought him to tears in his childhood. The story involves what could be called a degenerate form of thirdness, a mere comparison between two events that, while causally related, are not related through purpose (an essential ingredient of thirdness). The story also involves an A, B, C structure, which is why it is pertinent (cf. CP 1.366 & EP 1.254). A shopkeeper threw away a stone that inadvertently hit and killed the son of a local ruler. The shopkeeper is punished for a 'crime' that he did not commit. The shopkeeper (A) throws a stone (B) which in turn brings about the death of the son (C). Yet this relation is not a full triadic relation of thirdness insofar as it involves two disconnected dyads. The dyads (A-B and B-C) *are* connected through a causal relation, but they are not connected through purpose. Consequently, the relation of killing is far from being a genuine relation. To assign blame in this case is not only immoral, but it is illogical. Moral blame can only be assigned when there is a genuine triad involved, one involving purpose/thirdness. Thus the difference between "giving" something and inadvertently "causing" something is a fundamental ontological difference with direct moral and logical consequences. Thus all relations are either triadic or degenerately so, and hence not full relations.

On the level of a simple living cell, for example, the triad is manifest in the relations of: sensibility, motion, and growth. Insofar as a cell can be aware of its surroundings, i.e., can be irritated in some fashion, it involves firstness, the domain of possibility and feeling. Insofar as a cell will move from one spatial coordinate to another, it will exhibit secondness, the domain of interaction with an other. Finally, insofar as a cell will express growth, thereby taking on habit and reasonableness, it will embody thirdness. Peirce argues that the basic units of neurology function triadically and that some primitive form of purposive behavior can be seen in nascent mentality.

On the much more complex level of human consciousness, the basic triad is manifest both internally (to consciousness) and externally (in terms of the relations of subject and object):

> It seems, then, that the true categories of consciousness are: first, feeling, the consciousness which can be included with an instant of time, passive consciousness of quality, without recognition or analysis; second, consciousness of an interruption into the field of consciousness, sense of resistance, of an external fact, of another something; third, synthetic consciousness, binding time together, sense of learning, thought. [CP 1.377]

Human consciousness encounters both its own structures and the antecedent powers of the world. On the first level, it is a feeling, taking place in an instant. There is a sense in which firstness is not in time.

The pure feeling, which is passive and open to a sense of quality, does not occupy a stretch of time. Firstness is the generative source *of* time, rather than a product of time and its flow. Again, we are reminded of the Kantian elements in Peirce. Firstness is the condition for the possibility of time (ontologically, however, and not merely cognitively).

Moving past passive feelings of quality is the domain of "interruption." The dreaming field of firstness is interrupted by an external shock that breaks into the innocence of the primal layer of awareness. The self senses a resistance that must be overcome. Secondness negates firstness and forces it into a domain of energy and power. The Hegelian concept of "determinate negation" is pertinent here. Secondness is manifest in innumerable (determinate) seconds that shape awareness. Each second is a negation of the field of possibility and feeling. Yet it negates this primal field in a specific way. The self carves out its unique trajectory amid the exploding world of seconds.

Thirdness is the domain where the time process becomes fully manifest to the self. If firstness is a kind of nascent present of all presents, and secondness is a kind of rudimentary before and after, then thirdness is the domain of genuine tridimensional temporality. Past, present, and future arch out from the heart of the self and provide the 'space' within which internal dialogue can take place. By the same token, the self-world dialectic emerges into its own form through the time opened up by thirdness. The self is what it is because of the time granted by thirdness. Again, we are reminded of Kant. For Kant, of the two inner senses, that of space and that of time, the sense of time is the more basic in that it applies to both the outer and inner realms. Firstness makes time possible, while failing to actualize it. Secondness splits the realm of firstness into the rudimentary before and after. Thirdness, not tied to the Kantian transcendental unity of apperception, pushes time out into the self and its world.

Many commentators argue as if the three primal ontological categories are a classification device for making the world intelligible. The truth runs far deeper. For Peirce, firstness, secondness, and thirdness are enabling powers that spawn the world and its structures of interaction and intelligibility. In the next chapter we will examine the tensions within Peirce on the issue of the eternity of the three categories. The question will be: are the three categories preexistent and eternal, or are they products of an evolving universe? There are reasons for picking both alternatives, but a judicious transformation of the argument can provide a mediating third possibility.

As we have seen, the three categories apply to the structure of everything from the protoplasmic cell to the inner dynamics of the human process. How do they relate to cosmogenesis? At this point we can only hint at the full use of the categories, but a preliminary perusal is appropriate:

> Out of the womb of indeterminacy we must say that there would have come something, by the principle of Firstness, which we may call a flash. Then by the principle of habit there would have been a second flash. Though time would not yet have been, this second flash was in some sense after the first, because resulting from it. Then there would have come other successions ever more and more closely connected, the habits and the tendency to take them ever strengthening themselves, until the events would have been bound together into something like a continuous flow. We have no reason to think that even now time is quite perfectly continuous and uniform in its flow. [CP 1.412 & EP 1.278]

The "womb of indeterminacy," the self-othering realm of pure firstness, spawns the orders of the world. An initial flash (proto-second) is soon 'followed' by another. When two flashes emerge from the womb of nature, the domain of secondness begins to take shape and form. As the number of flashes (events) multiplies, there is a tendency for them to group together. Habit seems to be an intrinsic constraining force in the world, gathering up the foundlings that have emerged from the womb of firstness. When a "continuous flow" emerges from the flashes, thirdness has become manifest. Time, Peirce hints, is not an antecedent linear structure, but has a nonuniform flow. Each of the three categories instantiates time differently. Firstness is pretemporal, but generative of time. Secondness is temporal in a deficient and binary sense. Past and present obtain in the domain of secondness, but the future remains mute. The full power of the future only emerges with thirdness (as we saw when examining Peirce's pragmaticism). With the rise of thirdness, time becomes fully actualized.

Peirce continued to expand and enrich his concept of the three categories. In a ca. 1894 manuscript "The List of Categories: A Second Essay," he sharpens his analysis further and links the categories to some more traditional notions. We will take a brief look at this manuscript before moving on to his 1903 Harvard lectures on pragmatism (briefly touched upon in the first chapter). In this ca. 1894 manuscript, Peirce links firstness to the concept of being or "suchness" and perhaps unwittingly indicates just how radical this concept is:

> The pure idea of a *monad* is not that of an object. For an object is over against me. But it is much nearer an object than it is to a conception

of self, which is still more complex. There must be some determination, or suchness, otherwise we shall think nothing at all. But it must not be an abstract suchness, for that has reference to a special suchness. It must be a special suchness with some degree of determination, not, however, thought as more or less. There is to be no comparison. So that it is a suchness *sui generis*. [CP 1.303]

Firstness, the "monad," suchness per se, is ontologically distinct from either the object or nothingness. Peirce recognizes that firstness is unique (*sui generis*) and that there are no direct analogies linking it to the realm of determined objects. It is even further removed from the nature of the self (which has far too many delimited features). It would be tempting to simply equate firstness with nothingness, but Peirce was aware that firstness had to have some qualities so that it could be the object of some kind of thematic reflection.

Suchness is prior to "whatness" (essence) but remains relevant to the seconds that emerge in the world. Nothingness would have no relevance to anything other than itself. That is, it would merely negate anything that participates in being. Firstness, on the other hand, is 'responsible' for its offspring in the sense that it has an inner dynamism that ejects the seconds of the world. There is a strong neo-Platonic dimension in Peirce's account of firstness. It functions as a kind of primal ground that is stained when it enters into the transactions of the world.

Peirce explicitly links firstness to Kant's "manifold of sense," insofar as it manifests itself in ". . . unlimited and uncontrolled variety and multiplicity; . . ." [CP 1.302]. Here he moves away from neo-Platonism insofar as it insists that the primal reality, the One, is a unity beyond multiplicity. For Peirce, firstness is sheer heterogeneity and self-othering momentum. There is a deep irrationalism at the heart of Peirce's ontology that is often overlooked because of the more obvious and accessible domain of thirdness/rationality.

As noted, the concept of "quality" is pertinent to the domains of firstness and thirdness. The key difference is that on the level of firstness, quality is not yet conscious and obtains as a mere possibility. Put differently, the qualities of firstness are free-floating possibilities that do not have an internal purposive or intelligible structure. In the domain of thirdness, quality becomes conscious, purposive, and funded with intelligence. Peirce uses the term "quality" to cover both cases because it connotes something general and pervasive, making it akin to feeling.

Firstness is the domain of potentiality or possibility; consequently, it is not yet actual, does not have "existence." In most contexts, Peirce confines the term "existence" to the realm of secondness, the realm of dynamic impaction and actualization. The pure suchness of firstness does not yet exist. Something exists only when it is actualized from out of the ground of suchness. Existence entails, for the self at least, a sense of resistance and effort. There is no intelligibility on this level: "It is to be noted that existence is an affair of blind force" [CP 1.329]. The innumerable seconds that impinge on us are all part of the realm of blind force. We are grooved and shaped by this force, while exerting our own counterresistances whenever we are able.

The basic distinction between the ego and the nonego is made possible by the domain of secondness. Resistance and conflict separate the self from its world, and, in a different way, from its own inner structures. The ego not only sets itself up against the rest of the semiotic universe, it must feel the compulsive power of the orders within the world. "It [secondness] is the compulsion, the absolute constraint on us to think otherwise than we have been thinking that constitutes experience" [CP 1.336]. There is a quality of shock or surprise in secondness. Peirce cites the example of a loud train whistle breaking in on our consciousness. This creates a shock that splits consciousness into a before and an after. In some passages, Peirce almost equates secondness with the pain of experience. If firstness is, as noted, "tender," secondness fills us with numerous painful shocks and breaks that continue to punctuate the life of awareness.

Thirdness is a healing force for Peirce. The breaks created by secondness are stitched together by the mediating power of thirdness. The concept of continuity, discussed in the first chapter, is central to that of thirdness. A given third is a continuous quality that manifests law and habit. "Continuity represents Thirdness almost to perfection" [CP 1.337]. The realm of action (secondness) passes over to the higher realm of conduct (thirdness). Action is little more than a species of reaction, while conduct involves self-control and the growth of reasonableness. The core of conduct is the self-control that lifts the self beyond its provincial semiotic interests. Yet there is an even deeper layer found in thirdness than that of self-control. The real core of conduct is what Peirce calls "sympathy." The goal of the moral life is to increase the scope of sympathy in the world. Peirce has an almost literal sense of sympathy as a continuous force that serves to bind selves together. Feeling, found in the domain of firstness, becomes moral when it participates in the higher sympathy manifest in the domain of thirdness.

We have seen that thirdness makes the ethical realm possible. Firstness is beyond good and evil in the sense that it has no actualized moral qualities. Secondness is too brute to have any directionality that could be morally appraised. Only thirdness has a moral force. Peirce often argues as if the domain of thirdness is moral per se, not unlike the early Plato who eulogized the forms and equated the good with the generic. The move from mere behavior to self-controlled conduct is a move possible only because of the power of thirdness. The self actually participates in vast thirds that lend their reasonableness to the individual. Just as Peirce makes the strong link between continuity and thirdness, he makes the equally strong equation between self-control and thirdness. If thirdness entails continuity, which overcomes the breaks of secondness and evokes self-control, then it follows that thirdness must be put in the honorific category. Peirce did not always separate the descriptive from the evaluative elements in his metaphysics. In describing thirdness, he at the same time gives it a strong moral cast.

The connection between thirdness and meaning is equally clear. Meaning cannot obtain unless there is comparison and generality. What kind of meaning can be found in firstness? There is a sense in which firstness makes meaning possible (as it does with time), but it does not follow that it 'has' meaning. What kind of meaning can be found in secondness? Do two causal events, bereft of purpose, mean anything? Peirce denies that they do. Consequently, if meaning is to obtain at all, it must be in the domain of thirdness. Here Peirce links the concept of "thirdness" with his crucial concept of the "interpretant," which is the carrier of meaning, both for the human process and within the larger orders of nature. Interpretants form into series that have neither beginning nor end, and are thus infinite in scope and complexity. An interpretant carries forward some kind of idea. As a component of thirdness, the interpretant participates in the structures of continuity and points toward the future (in which a final interpretant would be manifest).

Before moving on to an analysis of Peirce's semiotic theory, we will return to his 1903 Lectures on Pragmatism. In the first chapter we discussed the seventh lecture, which dealt with abduction. We are now ready to take a brief look at the earlier lectures, especially where they contribute toward our understanding of the three primal categories. While these formulations are not as speculative or daring as those we examined from "A Guess at the Riddle," they do serve to give even more precision to our previous formulations.

Peirce discusses his own conception of "phenomenology" which he defines as the science of that which is common to ". . . whatever is *experienced* or might conceivably be experienced or become an ob-

ject of study in any way direct or indirect" [CP 5.37]. The three categories are the most basic elements to be found within experience (as
traits of what he calls the "phaneron"). Consequently, phenomenology works in consort with metaphysics to describe the manifestations
of firstness, secondness, and thirdness. Since the 'object' of phenomenology is nothing less than all of experience and its objects, it follows that it is more primary and foundational than the other more
delimited sciences. Peirce is explicit in his belief that he is giving a
pragmatic reconstruction of Hegel's phenomenology, which had as *its*
concern the description of the various shapes of self-consciousness as
they unfold within the science of the experience of consciousness. A
pragmatic phenomenology gives more weight to secondness and strives
to render the three categories intelligible: "The business of phenomenology is to draw up a catalogue of categories and prove its suffi-
ciency and freedom from redundancies, to make out the characteristics of each category, and to show the relations of each to the others"
[CP 5.43].

A phenomenological analysis of the three categories is not a normative evaluation. Peirce contrasts phenomenology with what he calls
the three normative sciences. On the 'top' is the science of logic (also
defined as general semiotics) that has as its concern the description
of forms of reasoning (deductive, inductive, and abductive). More basic
than logic is the normative science of ethics that tells us how we ought
to think. On the most basic level, hence at the 'bottom,' is the science of aesthetics, which tells us what the highest good is, and which
is thus the ultimate goal of both logic and ethics. The three normative
sciences are concerned with separating out right from wrong uses of
method, and with demarcating good and bad purposes and goals. Phenomenology, on the other hand, is nonnormative, and chooses to make
morally neutral descriptions of the various manifestations of the three
ontological categories. Of course, Peirce is rarely consistent in his
effort to separate normative from descriptive tasks. As noted, he in-
trudes honorific norms into his categories and thus gives a normative
edge to his phenomenology.

In the context of these Harvard lectures, Peirce is asking his interlocutors to engage along with him in a sustained phenomenological
description of the three categories. His strategy is to start with the
most simple and inescapable facts of immediate experience, and then
to move toward more complex and attenuated structures. He notes that
three skills are needed by the phenomenologist: the ability to look
directly at what stares us in the face, the power of resolute discrimi-
nation that separates off elements from each other, and the generaliz-

ing power of the mathematician. When these three skills are combined, it is possible to complete a phenomenological description that delivers the same results as an independent logical or metaphysical analysis of the categories.

As is often the case, he distances himself from Hegel's procedure, even though he moves along parallel tracks. Like Hegel, he starts with something akin to "immediate sense certainty" and shows how it underlies and empowers all subsequent forms of awareness. He asks the members of the audience to envision the simplest possible form of awareness:

> Imagine, if you please, a consciousness in which there is no comparison, no relation, no recognized multiplicity (since parts would be other than the whole), no change, no imagination of any modification of what is positively there, no reflexion—nothing but a simple positive character. Such a consciousness might be just an odour, say a smell of attar; or it might be one infinite dead ache; it might be the hearing of a piercing eternal whistle. In short, any simple and positive quality of feeling would be something which our description fits that it is such as it is quite regardless of anything else. [CP 5.44]

His examples are intriguing. Try to envision a pervasive smell that is not yet designated as a *particular* smell. For persons who live in a town with a paper mill, there is a strong smell that permeates the atmosphere. After a while, the residents of the town cease to smell that odor as a particular and nameable smell of such and such a type. Yet, should someone leave town and come back after a suitable absence, the smell could be recognized in a distinctive way, and be part of the realm of secondness or thirdness.[2] While we are bathed with the quality of firstness, we are only dimly aware of its presence. Phenomenological descriptions of firstness must live in the ambiguity of an awareness that is pervasive and given, yet which remains elusive precisely because of its immediacy.

If firstness is given over to the mind in its simple positive character, secondness comes to us through struggle. Peirce cites the example of direct muscular struggle in which we push against a partially open door. The resistance of the door, felt in the constriction of our muscles, compels us to acknowledge the power of the nonego. Put in simple terms, existence is what resists us. Firstness cannot resist us because it is a monadic background feeling that has no directionality or force. Secondness resists us in an obvious way. Another example of this is that of the strong arm of the sheriff upon one's shoulder. A mere court order is a bare possibility, a first. When this possibility is actualized by the sheriff, it becomes a brute second, and wrenches the self out of its complacency.[3]

Secondness comes to us in a series of surprises. It is as if the self is constantly overtaken by seconds that enter from the fringes of awareness to impose their vector directionalities on consciousness. Peirce's example in this context is that of a flash of lightning in total darkness. The surprise of the flash overtakes the self and opens up in a dramatic way the dyadic tension between the ego and nonego. Put in direct terms, the action of consciousness is "a series of surprises" [CP 5.51]. These surprises are preintelligible and call forth perceptual judgments to render them into some meaningful shape.

Peirce spends far more time on the concept of thirdness and locates his own conception against the background of the history of philosophy. He remains consistent in his rejection of nominalism, insisting that the evolutionary perspective rendered nominalism obsolete (although it also lacks any kind of logical status). The doctrine of essence returns in force, with the important modification that essences are in some sense in the future, even while manifest in the present.

While other philosophers have had conceptions that are analogous to the three categories, they rarely allow them to have any status in reality. Peirce makes a quick tour of the history of philosophy so that his audience is clear on how pragmaticism represents a distinct advance on the other alternatives. He lists seven systems of philosophy, each but his own representing a partial understanding of the three categories.

The simplest system is one that only privileges firstness. He refers to this system as a nihilistic one, or one that relies on mere qualities of feeling. It is nihilistic in that it has no conceptual elements whatsoever; that is, it is bereft of even the minimal degree of reason. The second system is one that privileges secondness. This is expressed in a kind of simplistic corpuscular or atomic metaphysics that sees only dyadic reaction. Moving 'up' the ladder we come to the third system that honors thirdness alone. Hegel is the chief exemplar of this third type of system. He has a place for firstness (immediate sense certainty or pure being) and secondness (via determinate negation), but these become *aufgehoben* (sublated) into thirdness. Thus thirdness alone is the really real. The fourth type of system privileges secondness and thirdness alone. This can be seen in the thought of Descartes, Spinoza, and Kant. Descartes, for example, expresses secondness in the irreducible tension between extended and nonextended substance. At the same time, he expresses thirdness in his geometric method that uses generic categories to frame a conception of the world.

Kant is a more complex case. The critical perspective leaves firstness behind, as a 'mere' chaotic manifold of sensation, so that the a priori structures of intelligibility (thirdness) can assume center stage. Secondness is manifest in the tension between the noumenal and phenomenal 'halves' of the self. The fifth type of system will privilege firstness and thirdness, and hence have no role for genuine dyadic reaction. Bishop Berkeley is the premier exemplar of this type of system. The supposed secondness of spatial relations is reduced to a form of intelligibility, itself tied to the immediate qualities of perception. The sixth system of philosophy will stress firstness and secondness, and have no sense of true universality. Peirce refers to this type as that of ordinary or moderate nominalism. Thirds are linguistic fictions and have no evolutionary or purposive force outside of the conventions of human language.

The seventh system gives equal status to all three categories. No category can be transformed into another and each remains fully intact, even in the realm of thirdness that seems to transcend firstness and secondness. Peirce refers to his own pragmaticism as a kind of Aristotelianism "of the scholastic wing, approaching Scotism" [CP 5.77n]. By which he means that the world is constituted by possibilities (firstness) that become actualized (secondness) and take on the features of true universality (thirdness). The Aristotelian dimension is the underlying naturalism that believes in real genera as belonging to a vast organic realm. The Scotistic dimension is the sense that universals are extralinguistic and belong to the orders of the world.

Peirce admits that his own perspective is close to that of Hegel, but faults Hegel for not honoring secondness, and for working out of an inferior logic. Hegel's case is especially instructive because he has a place for all three categories, but lets thirdness ride roughshod over the others. Of course, one can argue that this is not a fair reading of Hegel. The conflicts within the various shapes of self-consciousness do involve secondness in a very direct way. The obvious example is the famous master/slave dialectic from the *Phenomenology of Spirit* in which Hegel describes how the master shapes the nascent self-understanding of the slave, who in turn shapes the self-understanding of the master. One suspects that Peirce would call this correlation a form of thirdness (perhaps in a degenerate sense). Peirce's example of secondness is not that of the look or gaze of the other, but that of a sharp stick in the back. It is an open question whether or not Hegel has the same role for the shock of an irrational second.

To shed more light on the problem of degeneracy in thirdness, Peirce cites the example of self-consciousness. Whenever a self attempts to understand its inner being (a dubious concept for Peirce) it fails to have a true representation of itself. Put differently, so-called introspection does not use interpretants in the full sense. Peirce gives a striking illustration of his conception of this type of degenerate thirdness. Suppose we wish to draw a map of a country. That map must have a microcosmic analogue for all of the features of the country itself. There must be a point-to-point correspondence between the map and that to which it refers. However, the map is now a genuine part of the country and must thus be represented on the map. So the map will have an image of itself at the proper place. However, this new image is now also a part of the country and must be represented. This process generates an infinite regress, with no final map. What is the relation between any map in the series and the country itself? Is this relationship that of genuine thirdness? Peirce argues that it is not, for the simple reason that there is no intervening third (representation) linking the map to the country. The relation is more than a relation of secondness because it is not causal and it involves structures of intelligibility. Therefore the relation is a form of thirdness, but in a degenerate case. The relation of map to country is analogous to the relation between a self and itself. We remember that the identity relation in prehuman realities is a degenerate form of secondness. When we deal with human forms of awareness, which entail conscious mentality, we move to thirdness. Self-consciousness must thus be a degenerate form of thirdness rather than a degenerate form of secondness.

Before moving on to our analysis of Peirce's semiotics, we must say a few more words about the relation between thirdness and nature. For Peirce, "*Thirdness* is operative in Nature" [CP 5.93]. This is most clearly manifest in the force of natural law and our ability to make reliable predictions. I can drop a stone and know that it will fall because the law of gravity is a third that is operative within the innumerable orders of the universe. Peirce ties his own version of scholastic realism to his pragmaticism. That we have the power to make predictions is a consequence of natural universals. Peirce gives a succinct summary:

> Reality consists in regularity. Real regularity is the science of Reality. Real regularity is active law. Active law is efficient reasonableness, or in other words is truly reasonableness. Reasonable reasonableness is Thirdness as Thirdness. [CP 5.121]

The universe is evolving toward a state in which perfect reasonableness will be realized, although, strictly speaking, we must still say "would be" realized. We have noted that Peirce sees a correspondence between the structures of the human mind and the depth structures of the world. Evolution has compelled us to honor the seconds and thirds that surround us and that have their own forms of resistance. When we ride on the growing tide of thirdness, we come closer to finding our own destiny in the world. Everything that we do, fashion, or say derives its power and validity from the ubiquitous forces of thirdness, forces that are reasonable and deeply friendly to human need and aspiration.

The World of Signs / The World as Signs

We have seen that Peirce's perspective is semiotic through and through. From his early papers of 1868–1869 to his most mature reflections in his final years, he probed into the structure and dynamics of signification. He lavished unusual care on the internal and external nature of signs, developing triadic lists that have such complexity as to numb the imagination. At the same time, he examined the communicative and social aspects of sign activity so that the logic of sign linkage could be rendered intelligible. We have referred to Peirce's perspective as that of a "pansemioticism" in which, using his 1905 phrase, "the world is perfused with signs." Sign activity is tied to mentality and it follows that nature must be perfused with mentality. There is a direct correspondence between Peirce's pansemioticism and his panpsychism (the doctrine that matter is "effete mind"). Some scholars have been vexed by the panpsychist elements in Peirce, seeing them as a late aberration that shows a flaw either in his metaphysics or in his very thought processes. These views betray more about the lack of philosophical elasticity in Peirce's interlocutors than about Peirce's semiotic and metaphysical theories. As will emerge even more sharply in the next chapter, Peirce's commitment to panpsychism does not negate his naturalism, but gives it a different dimension of meaning. In the final chapter we will probe into some of the implications of the conjunction of panpsychism and naturalism. At this point it is pertinent to note that pragmaticist semiotic theory has the scope and power that it has because it is rooted in a vast conception of nature, a nature that, at the very least, is hospitable to the emergence of centers of mentality.

Certain elements of Peirce's semiotic theory have emerged in the context of our analyses of other categories. One of the difficulties facing any student of the semiotic elements in Peirce is that there is

nothing analogous to the classical series of papers previously examined. To find out what Peirce has to say about signs it is necessary to
pull together fragments from a variety of sources. However, once this
is done, it soon becomes clear that Peirce is strikingly consistent in
his basic categorial analyses.[4] While there is some evolution in his
views, he remains committed to the basic triadic scheme and to the
belief that the universe is best understood in semiotic terms. What
makes Peirce especially evocative is his detailed and future-directed
correlation of metaphysics and semiotics.

In looking at his 1868–1869 papers we saw that Peirce redefines
the self in semiotic terms. So-called 'inner life' is actually an
introjection of public and external signs. The self becomes the locus
of vast semiotic chains that intersect with it. Each of these chains has
its own inner dynamism and manifests continuity. There is no first
sign in the series, nor, barring an absolute negation, will there be a
last sign. The self carves out its own unique trajectory within the
semiotic options given over to it by an evolving universe.

One of the most basic semiotic triads has already been mentioned—
that pertaining to the relation between a sign and its object. These
relations are: iconic, indexical, and symbolic. We have also taken a
brief look at the triad of sign, object, and interpretant. This second
triad pertains to the ways in which signs become efficacious in the
world and form into vast semiotic series. The concept of the
"interpretant" has emerged as one of the most important concepts
within the recent history of the semiotic movement and will receive
more extended treatment in what follows. While this exposition cannot exhaust the complexity of Peirce's semiotic theory, and it is doubt-
ful that any exposition could, it will provide an initial orientation into
the basic structures of pragmaticist semiotics.

It must be remembered that the concept "sign" is exceedingly broad
in Peirce. Anything whatsoever can function as a sign. An object becomes a sign when it can point to something other than itself. As we
saw, the causal relation is itself semiotic in that it correlates one event
with another and lets the second event point indexically to its causal
antecedent. The fulfillment of a sign relation requires the emergence
of purpose, and hence thirdness, but the less complete or virtual stages
of semiosis can obtain in their own right. The distinction between a
sign and an object is a functional one. From one perspective, a sign
is an object, while from another, an object is a sign. The choice as to
terms is forced by the context. If the context is one that favors the
manifest structures of intelligibility and communication, then the term
"sign" is used. If the context is one that favors the hidden and dy-

namic aspects of the situation, then the term "object" is used. Objects are 'behind' signs, yet they also live 'in front' of them, goading them toward an increase in scope and meaning.

To clarify this we need to introduce an important distinction. Peirce was aware, in good Kantian fashion, that objects have both manifest and hidden components. For Kant, of course, this meant that any object actually has two incommensurate dimensions: the phenomenal appearance directly available to us in an intuition (*Anschauung*) and the unknown and unknowable depth dimension of the thing-in-itself. We can never get any closer to the thing-in-itself. It is forever beyond our reach (although God can have intuitions of the thing-in-itself). Peirce recasts Kant's distinction in pragmatic terms. The so-called depth dimension of the object is what he called the "dynamic object," while the present aspect is what he called the "immediate object." Peirce distances himself from Kant by insisting that inquiry can actually get us closer to the true dynamic object. There is thus a growing convergence between the immediate and dynamic objects. Science will (would) bring us closer to the pragmatic version of the thing-in-itself. If Kant leaves us with an absolute abyss, Peirce puts us on the road toward true convergence in the infinite long run.

The distinction between the immediate and dynamic objects (or immediate and dynamic aspects of *the* object) is an important entrance point to Peirce's semiotic theory. The dynamic object does not simply 'hang out' awaiting its eschatological appearance, but actually lives as a goad to sign activity, compelling it to honor the antecedent *and* emergent aspects of the object. The sign serves the object insofar as it lives to unveil the traits of the object itself. Signs are self-effacing in that they wish to provide a clearing within which objects can appear. If the sign remains too tied to the immediate object, it fails to reach deeper down into the objective structures and powers that animate the immediate dimension. Insofar as the sign feels the pressure of the dynamic aspect of the object, it reveals the telic and dynamic aspects of the real. Put in simpler terms, signs do not exist to draw attention to themselves alone, although they certainly do at least that, but to serve the objective powers of nature.

The implications of the immediate/dynamic distinction can only be seen as we unfold the details of Peirce's semiotic theory. Yet we can already see that a distinctive tone has been sounded. Sign activity is not confined to an internal realm of self-reference, but points outward into fields of relation that may be only virtually semiotic, yet relevant to semiosis nonetheless. If structuralist or poststructuralist semiotic theories remain solipsistic or confine themselves to human language, pragmaticist semiotics honors the objective relations of the world.[5] The dynamic object exerts a continual veto power over the signs that cluster around the immediate object.

There are thus several constraints built into the semiotic process. We have the constraint of method, flowering in abduction and interpretive musement. We have the constraint of self-control that guides the individual. We have the constraint of the community of inquiry that extends the reach and scope of the individual interpreter. And, finally, we have the constraint of the dynamic object that lives just 'underneath' the sign that wishes to point toward the depth dimension of its object. Together, these forces keep sign activity relevant to the world that spawns signs. The mystery of nature is that it is both a world of signs and the creative ground of sign activity. This mystery will be probed further in the last chapter.

As noted, the early papers pointed toward a convergence of the three categories and the various semiotic triads. Firstness is correlated with the iconic dimension of sign relation. Secondness is correlated with the indexical dimension of sign relation. And thirdness is correlated with the symbolic dimension of sign relation. The iconic relation is one that shares some feature or quality in common with the object. For example, a blueprint of a building is an iconic sign that shares, via a method of projection, spatial features with the object. A photograph, on the other hand, which seems to be iconic, is actually an indexical sign in that it is directly caused by the object. Of course, it has strong iconic features but its basic structure is indexical. Here is a perfect example of a sign that can function in two modes at the same time. For a Christian, for example, a cross functions symbolically to refer to the events of death and resurrection that point to the inner heart of the divine/human transaction. Yet the same cross can function iconically insofar as it is of the same general shape as the historical cross itself.

Consequently, the three categories become embodied and efficacious through signs. The correlation between semiosis and power is clear. There can be no effective power in the world unless there are media of embodiment and transmission. Put differently, the three primal categories are mute until and unless they are concresced into signs (remembering that the term "symbol" is a subset within the larger class of signs). Once a category is expressed through a sign it can find a sphere of operation. Peirce has an incarnational sense of the categories; that is, a sense that they fulfill themselves through their participation in the orders and events of the world. Categories are not free floating. It is almost as if each category hungers to find a home in the innumerable signs of nature, thereby clothing itself in the rich colors of meaning.

With these general comments in mind, let us look more closely at the textual material. In 1885 Peirce published "On the Algebra of Logic" in *The American Journal of Mathematics*, in which he adumbrates his theory of signs as an introduction to an elaborate analysis of mathematical notation. He refers the reader back to his 1867 discussion of the icon, index, and symbol, but adds important new material to his growing semiotic theory. In particular, he probes into the relation between semiosis and mentality. This 1885 essay is a transitional piece, moving past some of the 1867 formulations, but not yet to the point where the now-familiar language of the later reflections emerges.

Peirce starts with a description of the 'highest' dimension of the sign/object relation; namely, that of the symbol (termed in this paper a "token," a term that changes its meaning in later years). He ties the symbolic domain to that of habit and mental association:

> A sign is in a conjoint relation to the thing denoted and to the mind. If this triple relation is not of a degenerate species, the sign is related to its object only in consequence of a mental association, and depends upon a habit. Such signs are always abstract and general, because habits are general rules to which the organism has become subjected. They are, for the most part, conventional or arbitrary. They include all general words, the main body of speech, and any mode of conveying a judgment. For the sake of brevity I will call them *tokens*. [CP 3.360]

The sign, in this case the symbol ("token"), points to a thing and to a mind for whom the sign has meaning. The correlation of a sign and its object is through a habit. Habits are general modes of interaction that participate in thirdness. The sign is assigned to its object through an arbitrary and conventional act, an act that comes from antecedent habits of personal and social life. Peirce gives us concrete examples, in the form of class designations, of true signs/symbols. Any general term, e.g., a common noun, will be a symbol. There seems to be a tension in this passage between a realist (Scotistic) conception of thirdness and a merely conventionalist understanding of the sign/object relation. This tension remains unresolved in Peirce although I am increasingly persuaded that he was struggling toward a nonconventionalist understanding of how symbols function to unveil objective and generic features of nature.

The second sign relation, the indexical, is nonconventional and involves a 'real' relation with an object. If the symbol is linked to the object through a specific human act, the index is related to the object in a compulsive and quasinecessary manner:

> Supposing, then, the relation of the sign to its object does not lie in a mental association, there must be a direct dual relation of the sign to its object independent of the mind using the sign. In the second of the three cases just spoken of [i.e., the pairing of: sign/object, sign/mind, and object/mind], this dual relation is not degenerate, and the sign signifies its object solely by virtue of being really connected with it. Of this nature are all natural signs and physical symptoms. I call such a sign an *index*, a pointing finger being the type of this class. [CP 3.361]

The mind comes upon a relation already in place and merely registers what the indexical sign has to convey about its object. This relation is not a degenerate version of thirdness so much as straightforward causal relation that brings the object into a much tighter correlation with its unveiling sign. He cites as examples of an indexical sign/object relation demonstrative and relative pronouns insofar as they denote things without actually describing them. They function like the pointing finger to illuminate an objective structure or relation.

The third type of relation, the iconic, is bereft of the generic power of the symbol/object relation and lacks the brute causal force of the index/object correlation. Yet it has its own unique structure that actually makes the other more complex forms possible:

> The third case is where the dual relation between the sign and its object is degenerate and consists in a mere resemblance between them. I call a sign which stands for something merely because it resembles it, an *icon*. Icons are so completely substituted for their objects as hardly to be distinguished from them. Such are the diagrams of geometry. [CP 3.362]

The term "degenerate" is unfortunate here, but the upshot of the passage is clear. An iconic relation is one in which the sign, in its material aspect, shares a number of key regional features with its denoted object. There is a sense in which a very good icon can be so like its object that they become indistinguishable. The concept of "resemblance" should not be taken too literally, however. A musical score has no literal resemblance to the sounds coming from a group of musicians, as spatial and acoustical structures belong to different orders of relevance. Yet there is a direct translation mechanism by which the spatial becomes the auditory. The musical score and the music heard belong together in an iconic relation. The icon (musical score) may remain unactualized. The object (music as heard) need not be present for the sign relation to obtain. When the music is played the musical score can take on an indexical role in causing the sounds to occur, although it must be understood that this is an unusual use of the concept of causality. Here, however, the relation runs from sign to object rather than the other way, as would be appropriate in a true indexical relation.

Any given sign will privilege one of the three relational possibilities. Yet the others will be manifest in some degree. A phenomenological analysis of semiotic relations requires an intense focus on 'pure' cases so that the more common, and deeply ambiguous, cases can become clarified. Consider a complex sign such as a sunrise in a nature painting. Envision a sun emerging over a mountain. The rays of the sun pour over the mountain valley and cast both light and shadow. The sun is a complex sign. In its iconic dimension it presents immediate qualities that show its direct likeness to the sun as experienced. The color, texture and shape of the painted sun all point toward the stellar appearance. Does this same sun have an indexical quality? Here the plot thickens. There is no direct causal relation between the sun itself and the act of painting. However, there is an indirect causal relation in that the painter could not have derived his or her image from any other object of relevance. There is an indirect causal/indexical relation connecting the sun and the sun as painted. Here we see how thirdness emerges as more important than secondness. The sun is painted according to the aesthetic norms of the reigning genre and cultural era. These norms are somewhat arbitrary and involve the imposition of thirdness onto the material of aesthetic contrivance. On a deeper level, the painted sun could connote or denote some spiritual quality, such as the awakening from a dogmatic sleep. In this context, the rays of the sun could refer to the power of the spirit to quicken and transform nature. These symbolic elements may or may not be intended by the artist, yet they can augment the qualitative and semicausal aspects of the sign/object relation. Consequently, the sun in the painting functions on all three levels to illuminate its object. Our attempts to interpret the painting add new interpretants to the web of signs already available.

In a ca. 1896 manuscript "The Logic of Mathematics; An Attempt to Develop My Categories from Within," Peirce sheds further light on the internal relations among the sign, its object, and its interpretant. We took a brief look at this triad in the first half of this chapter, in the context of a discussion of his 1867 paper "On A New List of Categories." Peirce does not change his position in the twenty-nine years separating these two essays, yet he continues to find more and more applications for his basic semiotic categories. The true semiotic triad is as follows:

> But a *thoroughly* genuine triad is separated entirely from those worlds [of the first two categories] and exists in the universe of *representations*. Indeed, representation necessarily involves a genuine triad. For it involves a sign, or representamen, of some kind, outward or inward, mediating between an object and an interpreting thought. [CP 1.480]

Peirce's desire to separate the semiotic structure from the other categories should not mislead. He is not saying that signs are disembodied or that they shun the categories of firstness and secondness, but that they can be delineated and described in relative independence. He wants to say that in some basic sense signs are not matters of fact or matters of law, but that they belong to the living domain of thought. There are times when it is a mistake to take Peirce too literally. His deeper intent in making a distinction is often fairly clear and his analyses can be rescued from some of his unfortunate formulations.

Be that as it may, the sign takes on a mediating role. The concept of "mediation" is absolutely central to Peirce. The sign is itself a third insofar as it brings the realms of the object and mind together in a meaningful way. The sign opens up the object so that it (the object) can spawn a thought. The thought can itself mediate between the sign and the object by creating yet another sign (the interpretant) that augments and, hopefully, deepens the original sign (the representamen). The term "representamen" often stands duty for the term "sign" yet there is a sense in which the representamen is the sign in its original position; that is, prior to its evolution into the realm of the interpretant. This sounds more complex than it actually is. Both the terms "representamen" and "interpretant" refer to stages within semiosis. Yet both stages can be characterized as stages of the sign. The representamen is a sign in its original or nascent state while an interpretant is a sign in its more 'mature' and developed state. There are good tactical reasons for having three terms here. If the term "sign" alone were used there would be confusion about the current status or role of the sign within the mediating structures of meaning.

It is also important that we avoid a linear or spatial reading of the sign/object/interpretant triad. It is not as if we have a simple forward progression *from* the sign *to* the object, and thence *to* the interpretant (interpreting thought). The relation is far more dialectical. In one movement of the dialectic the object can come first, and hence spawn the sign and, through a different movement, the interpretant. In another movement of the dialectic the interpretant can come first and shape the contour of the representamen and the object. In yet another movement of the dialectic, the sign (representamen) can shape the immediate object and its interpretant(s). There is a sense in which the sign/object/interpretant triad is a functional one, although this point can be overstated.

There is a certain hunger lying at the heart of semiosis. Signs are rarely 'satisfied' with their current configuration. Objects are self-moving in their dynamic dimension and carry new signs and interpretants in their wake. Interpretants are the most fecund of all in that they link up with other interpretants in a bewildering variety of ways. Peirce was fully committed to the principle of plenitude; namely, the notion that the universe is continually 'filling up' its cracks with more and more semiotic material. We have noted the restlessness in each of the three categories. This carries over into the behavior of signs.

Moving now to later manuscripts, Peirce unfolds the utter complexity of semiotic structures and enriches his ontology so that the three categories become even more relevant to the life of signs. In one of his most succinct statements, from a manuscript ca. 1897, Peirce lays out his distinctions yet again, but with an important refinement:

> A sign, or *representamen*, is something which stands to somebody for something in some respect or capacity. It addresses somebody, that is, creates in the mind of that person an equivalent sign, or perhaps a more developed sign. That sign which it creates I call the *interpretant* of the first sign. The sign stands for something, its *object*. It stands for that object, not in all respects, but in reference to a sort of idea, which I have sometimes called the *ground* of the representamen. [CP 2.228]

The original sign, the representamen, unveils some particular feature of its object. Peirce is very clear that signs are not self-referential. They point to something other than themselves. And they point in specific ways so that an idea (meant by Peirce in a Platonic sense) enters into a mind. The idea, the respect in which a sign refers to its object, is the ground of the sign (qua representamen). The concept of "ground" is a very rich one in Peirce. Umberto Eco uses the Wittgensteinian concept of a "universe of discourse" to denote the ground relation of the sign. By this he means that the ground is a framework within which specific discourses (sign relations) can occur. The ground takes on a mediating role in that it lets the object transform itself into a general quasi-Platonic idea that can locate itself within the mind of an interpreter (remembering that Peirce usually distinguishes between the interpretant and the interpreter).

Each moment within the triad, as supported by the ground (as a kind of 'fourth') can mediate for the others. The ground mediates by bringing the object and a mind together via an idea. The representamen mediates by holding an object and an interpretant together. The object mediates by keeping open lines of objective relevance that hold signs and subsequent interpretants together in the same semiotic series. Is the ground semiotic in its nature or does it point to a presemiotic realm? This is a difficult question to answer. There are senses in which the ground is semiotic insofar as it provides particular ideas (respects or capacities) to the sign/object/interpretant triad. Yet there is a more elusive sense in which the ground is a kind of mysterious enabling condition that empowers semiosis without itself being caught up in it in a public and embodied way. Some might find this way of describing the ground to be too mystical, yet it must be admitted that the ground relation is different in *kind* from the other semiotic relations. I am persuaded that the ground is both semiotic and presemiotic but in different respects.

We are ready to move on to some more complex triads. The triad of sign/object/interpretant is a kind of ontological triad telling us what there is in the world. The triad of icon, index, and symbol is a relational triad, telling us how signs refer to their objects. But this is only the beginning of the story. In a ca. 1903 manuscript "Nomenclature and Divisions of Triadic Relations, as Far as They are Determined," Peirce unfolds other structures:

> Signs are divisible by three trichotomies; first, according as the sign in itself is a mere quality, is an actual existent, or is a general law; secondly, according as the relation of the sign to its object consists in the sign's having some character in itself, or in some existential relation to that object, or in its relation to an interpretant; thirdly, according as its Interpretant represents it as a sign of possibility or as a sign of fact or a sign of reason. [CP 2.243]

The second triad is that of icon, index, and symbol. The first triad is a new one. Peirce distinguished between the "Qualisign," the "Sinsign," and the "Legisign." This triad refers to the nature of the sign in itself, prior to any relational possibilities and actualities.

The Qualisign is the sign qua quality; that is, as a pure quality that is not yet embodied. The Sinsign is an actually existing thing or event (occurring only once) that is now embodied. The Sinsign must 'contain' several Qualisigns so that it has some specific content. The Legisign is a "law that is a Sign" and is established in its content by human stipulative acts. The Legisign, unlike the Sinsign, is a general type rather than a singular instance. The Legisign can only be at all if it 'contains' Qualisigns (qualities) and Sinsigns (embodied particulars). Legisigns do not signify their laws or generals through a kind of vague reference, but must work through the intermediary of a "Replica." The Replica is a particular, and hence a Sinsign, but a special type of Sinsign, i.e., one that has a general content in addition to its particularity.

The first triad in the passage quoted above is thus a prerelational triad that exhibits the features of the sign in itself. The Qualisign is the most elusive of the three, precisely insofar as it partakes of firstness, which is itself elusive. The Sinsign is the material, particular, and pregeneral sign; the here-and-now sign that 'contains' specific qualities. The Legisign is the general sign (thirdness) that, ironically, remains mute until it becomes embodied in Sinsigns. All universals derive their power from their 'willingness' to become particular. Should a Legisign remain outside of the 'taint' of the here and now, it would have no efficacy within the world of signs. Any given sign will manifest the three dimensions of Qualisign (quality), Sinsign (particularity), and Legisign (law), but, as to be expected, with varying degrees of force.

The third triad described, that dealing with the interpretant, consists of the "Rheme," "Dicisign" (or Dicent Sign), and "Argument." These three dimensions refer to the relation between a sign and its interpretant (remembering that the second triad of icon, index, and symbol describes the relation between the sign and its object). Thus we see three basic structures: sign in itself, sign to object, and sign to interpretant. The third triad breaks down as follows. The Rheme is a sign of qualitative possibility. That is, it represents a possible object for its interpretant. Like the Qualisign, the Rheme is prerelational, or, in this context, preinformational. It does not carry forward a body of information that we can somehow circumscribe and point to. Yet it has the potential for information. The Dicent Sign is a sign of actual existence. Like the Sinsign, which also denotes actual existence for the sign in itself, the Dicent Sign must 'contain' features of its antecedent member of its triad, in this case, the Rheme. A Dicent Sign (sign/interpretant correlation) as referent to an actual existent (particular) will manifest the possible qualities, now actualized, of the Rheme. An Argument will be a sign of law, and will by definition embody the qualities of the Rheme relation and the particularity of the Dicent Sign relation.

It is a little misleading to use the term "sign" in each of these cases. In the triad of Qualisign, Sinsign, and Legisign, the term "sign" is more appropriate in that it denotes the features of the sign in itself. Yet in the triad of Rheme, Dicent Sign, and Argument, we are dealing with the sign/interpretant *relation* rather than with the features of the sign in itself. This applies equally to the second triad, that of icon, index, and symbol. The reader must work especially hard to keep all of these distinctions in mind. Peirce's texts are not always helpful in showing the different configurations of the various triads. The following passage does, however, illuminate the key features of the third triad:

> An *Argument* is a Sign which, for its Interpretant, is a Sign of law. Or we may say that a Rheme is a sign which is understood to represent its object in its characters merely; that a Dicisign is a sign which is understood to represent its object in respect to actual existence; and that an Argument is a Sign which is understood to represent its Object in its character as Sign. [CP 2.250]

It is important to note that Peirce develops his semiotics in the context of his general logic, which has as its concern the structure of arguments. Peirce had a great confidence in the power of an argument, when well crafted, to move the mind toward a valid comprehension of the basic features of the world. In placing the concept of "argument" at the culmination of his third triad (that of sign to interpretant) Peirce is indicating that the entire point behind general semiotics is the creation of grounded and powerful arguments that can sustain a generic portrayal of the world.

Let us look at the above passage in more detail. The Argument is a sign pointing toward its interpretant in such a way as to exhibit the presence of law. A law is a general, manifesting self-control and intelligibility. The Argument gathers up the possible qualities in the Rheme, combines them with the particularities of the Dicent Sign, and comes to a conclusion as to the true essence of the sign and its interpretant. Signs are linked together through a number of means. They can be linked through simple contiguity, or through the resemblance of qualities. They can be linked through a series of causal connections that may lack purpose and intelligibility, but that have their own inner dynamisms nonetheless. And they may be linked through the power of arguments that connect full-blooded signs to a vast rational network of intelligibility.

The centrality of the argumentative structure, which is future directed, comes out sharply in the inner momentum of the third triad. If the first triad (sign/object/interpretant) can be called the "ontological triad," and the second triad (icon/index/symbol) can be called the "unveiling triad," then the third triad could be called the "argumentative triad." While Peirce does not use these terms, I think that they are as reasonable as any others for denoting how the three triads differ. The logic of the argumentative triad points toward a growth in reasonableness:

> The Interpretant of the Argument represents it as an instance of a general class of Arguments, which class on the whole will always tend to the truth. It is this law, in some shape, which the argument urges; and this "urging" is the mode of representation proper to Arguments. The Argument must, therefore, be a Symbol, or Sign whose Object is a General Law or Type. [CP 2.253]

The unveiling triad does not present an argument; rather, it makes it possible for features to emerge into the light of awareness. The ontological triad shows us what the world is 'up to' and how it functions. The argumentative triad has a different role to play. Its concern is with generating and sustaining a conceptual framework in which truth emerges in the form of specific arguments. The argument "urges" us toward law and truth. Arguments are purposive and deeply embedded in the semiotic structures of the world. The argument emerges in the nexus connecting the sign to its interpretant. The role of the interpretant is to enhance the original sign and to give it greater scope and efficacy.

As is to be expected, what we have called the "ontological triad" (sign/object/interpretant), the "unveiling triad" (icon/index/symbol), and the "argumentative triad" (rheme/dicisign/argument) can be combined together to form yet more complex triads. Thus, for example, you can have a rhematic iconic qualisign; namely, a sign that would combine the firstness of the rheme (the sign itself) with the firstness of the sign/object relation (icon) with the firstness of the sign/interpretant relation (qualisign). The example here would be the possibility of a feeling of red. At the other extreme would be an argument symbolic legisign; namely, a sign that would combine the thirdness of an argument with the thirdness of the symbol (the sign/object relation) with the thirdness of the legisign (sign/interpretant relation). The example here would be a general law and its commensurate general object. There are ten such combinations (of the components of the three triads). We will not explore these various possibilities. They are fairly clear cut and can be examined in CP 2.264 where Peirce has a diagram depicting each of the ten triads.

By way of recovering some earlier ground, and by way of opening up some further distinctions, we will spend some time looking at Peirce's letters to his English admirer and interlocutor, Lady Victoria Welby. While Peirce and Lady Welby never met, they engaged in a lively correspondence from 1903–1911. The letters reveal many facets of Peirce's personality and give an indication of the stresses under which he lived in his relative confinement in Milford, Pennsylvania. At the same time these letters provided Peirce with an important forum for his mature ideas on semiotics. His style is far less involuted than in his manuscripts, and he lays out the basics in a way that helps us separate out the wheat from the chaff.

Peirce asks the important question: what, exactly, are signs for? That is, what role do signs play in evolution and in giving meaning and stability to the self? His answer is, as one would expect, a combination of pragmatic criteria with evolutionary theory:

> It appears to me that the essential function of a sign is to render inefficient relations efficient,—not to set them into action, but to establish a habit or general rule whereby they will act on occasion. . . . Knowledge in some way renders them efficient; and the sign is something by knowing which we know something more. [SS 31–32]

The sign not only represents a place where the three categories (read here as ontological powers) can appear, but it also serves to make all transactions, whether causal or purposive, more efficient. The ultimate goal of sign activity is to increase the number of positive and general habits in the world. Peirce does not directly link signs to action here, but makes it clear that a general rule (habit) will generate the right kind of actions.

The referential structure of the sign is crucial. Signs have their own material properties, but their deeper momentum is to help us "know something more." Signs are to some degree mental and bring knowledge into the various meaning horizons of the self. This new knowledge is not only pertinent to the life of signs, but points to the structures of the world and its innumerable objects. Signs are about other signs but they are also about independent realities.

Peirce plunges into his triads and makes some of our above discussed connections a bit more concrete. Interestingly, he relates the icon/index/symbol (unveiling) triad to the sign/dynamic object correlation. We will quote the relevant passages at some length because they tie together several features that often remain perplexing:

> I define an Icon as a sign which is determined by its dynamic object by virtue of its own internal nature. Such is any qualisign, like a vi-

sion,—or the sentiment excited by a piece of music considered as representing what the composer intended. Such may be a sinsign, like an individual diagram; say a curve of the distribution of errors. I define an Index as a sign determined by its dynamic object by virtue of being in a real relation to it. Such is a Proper Name (a legisign); such is the occurrence of a symptom of a disease (the symptom itself is a legisign, a general type of a definite character. The occurrence in a particular case is a sinsign). I define a Symbol as a sign which is determined by its dynamic object only in the sense that it will be so interpreted. It thus depends either upon a convention, a habit, or a natural disposition of its interpretant, or of the field of its interpretant (that of which the interpretant is a determination). Every symbol is necessarily a legisign; for it is inaccurate to call a replica of a legisign a symbol. [SS 33]

The icon (iconic relation of sign to dynamic object) is a sign that has an internal nature linking it to its object. Any qualisign (the sign itself 'prior' to its relational actualities) will also be like its object. Peirce uses the terms "vision" and "sentiment" to denote the iconic relation (and its product). A vision is a kind of undifferentiated feeling that corresponds to a parallel dynamic object. A sentiment is an internal qualitative configuration, certainly linked to feeling, that is evoked by the icon. If I hear a Mahler symphony, for example, its iconic dimensions will evoke a sentiment in me that may correspond to the mind of the composer when the work was written (and/or performed). The music as heard can function as a qualisign insofar as it is a sphere of possible feeling-qualities ready to become relevant to a dynamic object.

The indexical relation is a "real" relation in the sense that it is inescapable (necessary) and does not involve human contrivance or subjective variation. A medical symptom is a perfect example of an indexical sign. The symptom (say a ringlike rash) is the product of a dynamic object (say Lyme disease). The rash is a direct product of the underlying disease itself. It does not emerge to satisfy some purpose, but to manifest an antecedent reality. At the same time, the symptom is a legisign in that it points to a particular class of illness that can be decoded by the physician. The rash is an indexical legisign because it is caused by the dynamic object (Lyme disease) and refers to a general law. Yet the particular rash here and now is also a sinsign. Consequently, the rash is an indexical sinsign legisign. It manifests secondness and thirdness. Yet the rash is, qua rash, not yet a symbol because it does not involve human convention.

The symbolic relation, on the other hand, involves habit and the will to interpret. Any symbol will be conventional in the sense that human communities determine its meaning at a given time. The rash *could* function as a symbol if we willed to interpret it as a sign of human vulnerability to disease and decay. This would add another dimension to the indexical structure. The symbol is also a legisign in that it points toward a general law. The symbolic relation stresses the generic features of the dynamic object and points to the future.

As an example, consider the sun in the painting discussed earlier. The sun rises over the mountain and conquers the darkness. The sun could thus be a symbol of the emergence of a new spiritual consciousness that would transfigure human nature. Is the sun in the painting a legisign. Of course, in that it is depicting a general law about how we correlate consciousness with light. Is the sun also a qualisign? Yes, in the sense that it is a field of possible qualities that can emerge in specific ways. The sun is a muted index in the sense that it could spawn further aesthetic elaborations in other painters. The symbolic and iconic dimensions are the more important. The indexical is the least important. Consequently, the sun is less likely to emphasize the relation of the sinsign or the dicisign.

With Peirce, it never hurts to repeat ourselves on occasion so that the full richness of his categories becomes even further clarified. Peirce asks Lady Welby to think on the biblical phrase "Cain killed Abel," which involves the basic A/B/C triad we discussed above. Cain (A) is in relation B (murderer) to Abel (C). This relation cannot be reduced to that of two externally connected dyads. Cain had a purpose in killing Abel and thus manifested thirdness. Peirce takes the A/B/C triad and works it through the icon/index/symbol (unveiling) triad:

> Of course, an Icon would be necessary to explain what was the relation of Cain to Abel, in so far as this relation was *imaginable* or imageable. To give the necessary acquaintance with any single thing an Index would be required. To convey the idea of causing death in general, according to the operation of a general law, a general sign would be requisite; that is a *Symbol*. For symbols are founded either upon habits, which are, of course general, or upon conventions or agreements, which are equally general. [SS 70]

We cannot actually see Cain or Abel, as they are fictitious beings, but we can form images of them that bring them out of the realm of possibility to the realm of imagined actuality (which is not a contradiction of terms because imagined beings can be quite efficacious). The proposition "Cain killed Abel" can be broken down into parts. The two subject terms (Cain and Abel) are icons that can become indexes insofar as we encounter the particular dimension of each imagined person (a Sinsign). The relation of killing follows a general law and enters into the realm of the symbol. The plot thickens when it is recognized that the proposition "Cain killed Abel" can also function as a general cultural symbol of treachery and the violation of family norms and values. Fratricide is one of the most serious of all crimes and is subject to strong social taboos.

In the same letter, Peirce makes it clear why the icon/index/symbol triad may be best termed the "unveiling triad." He links each of the three possibilities (of the sign/object relation) to stages in appearance:

> Thus the Icon represents the sort of thing that may appear and sometimes does appear; the Index points to the very thing or event that is met with,—and I mean by an *Occurence* such a single thing or state of things; and finally, the Symbol represents that which may be observed under certain general conditions and is essentially general. [SS 71]

It is interesting to observe that the iconic relation still partakes of possibility. The thing may or may not appear. The logical point is that the icon provides the conditions for the possibility of appearance. As we have noted several times, Peirce transforms Kant's transcendental framework into a pragmaticist ontology in which the transcendental conditions for the possibility of experience become grounded in the ontological conditions for the real. Thus the icon makes genuine ontological manifestation possible.

The index points directly to something that, by definition, *is* manifest. The thing becomes available to the sign-using organism through the power of the indexical relation that provides a 'place' for the object to appear. The appearance of the object is not, however, a mere ephemeral manifestation. With the emergence of the index, the object becomes empowered to enter into further causal relations and structures. The index participates in secondness, the category of existence, and thus the index not only unveils the object as a here and now existent, but lets its own inner powers become efficacious. If the icon makes appearance *possible*, the index takes a genuine appearance and bestows power on it (although it actually does so by letting the object's 'internal' power come out).

The symbol, as general, provides for the most generic conditions within which further appearances can occur. The symbol thus unveils the object in its full relational and internal actualities. The unique power of the symbolic relation (between sign and object) is that it participates in the concrete reasonableness of thirdness and thus links the object to the more powerful orders of relevance that permeate the universe. As Peirce says elsewhere, "Symbols grow" [CP 2.302]. They grow along with the evolving universe and the underlying dynamic objects that empower them. There is thus a dialectic (or economy) of power in the unveiling triad. Icons, indexes, and symbols are enhanced in *their* power by the dynamic objects that they serve. Yet, in a different way, the underlying dynamic objects are enhanced in *their* power by the signs that bring them more and more into concrete orders of relevance.

If we wish to use spatial imagery, signs seem to occupy a specific, if shifting, territory. They have a 'place' within nature and this place can be measured. There is a sense in which sign systems compete for limited semiotic space and must make their claims within a general evolutionary environment that may or may not be congenial to their particular powers. Peirce uses an interesting equation to denote how a sign functions to convey information. He links the concept of information to that of space. A given sign (or sign system) will occupy an area. In this area it will have its own quanta of information that can be roughly measured. He introduces this concept in the context of a discussion of his existential graphs, which are simple circular and oval-form drawings (much like complex Venn diagrams) that replicate logical/semiotic functions.

The diagrams denote the "information" that is contained in a given semiotic case. Peirce has a straightforward equation: "breadth × depth = area" [SS 99]. "Area" here means "information." The total information conveyed by a sign is a product of its breadth (i.e., its extension or denotation) and its depth (i.e., its comprehension, signification, or connotation). A sign will have a shifting extension in terms of its referential or denotative power. By the same token, it will have a shifting richness in its connotative power. Both dimensions are necessary and both work together to increase the area/information of the sign. For example, take a sign such as poem. The poem itself may, qua sign, denote particular orders of relevance. The poem thus has a breadth insofar as it refers to or invokes certain events or objects in the extratextual world. At the same time, the poem will have its depth dimension insofar as it clothes those objects or events in rich connotations that enhance the depth of the poem. The full "area" of the poem cannot be fathomed until its denotative and connotative powers are probed by the reader/interpreter.

The concept of semiotic area is a valuable one. It points to the fact that each and every sign carves out a domain and carries that domain with it throughout its various transmutations. Whether we are speaking of a representamen or an interpretant, the same equation (breadth × depth = area) applies. The area of a sign is constituted by innumerable subaltern orders of meaning, attained or possible. Today we are inclined to see information in terms of binary bits of data, whose true information power is measured in terms of the surprise value of a given bit or stream of bits. Peirce's spatial model is richer in that it allows for an intimate correlation of connotation and ambiguity that cannot be confined to binary structures. The depth of a sign is not something that can be readily circumscribed. In other contexts Peirce talks about the necessity of vagueness in our concepts and perceptions. In the context of his semiotic theory, this vagueness is manifest in the elusive richness of the connotative dimension of signs.

In terms of the dynamics of signification, the concept of the "interpretant" remains uppermost. The interpretant is the resultant sign that emerges from the functional dialectic of the sign and its object. The interpretant moves outward into the world (with breadth and depth) and gives the original sign its objective immortality. Yet the concept of the "interpretant" has its own triadic structure which must be delineated. The interpretant, as a public and mobile sign, has three dimensions or modes of operation. In his letters to Lady Welby he uses the terms "Dynamical," "Final," and "Immediate." In other places he uses a parallel, if slightly different, triad of terms: "energetic," "logical," and "emotional." We will look at both formulations and see that they are for the most part equivalent.

We must remember that the interpretant is the mature sign that has already been augmented (and hence has greater semiotic density than the representamen). The interpretant is always underway toward further interpretants and seems to 'hunger' to link up with larger and larger units of meaning. The interpretant exists within the mind of an interpreter. This 'mind' need not be human. Peirce allows that prehuman forms may function as interpreters in some minimal respects. Yet the mind of the interpreter is merely the 'place' where interpretants reside. We have noted that Peirce usually distinguishes between the interpretant and the interpreter. The interpretant has a life of its own and can be analyzed on its own terms. In the ontological triad of sign/object/interpretant, the final actuality is the one that is most pertinent to the life of communication and the growth of concrete meanings within the various time processes of nature. If the sign/representamen is the originating source of meaning, then the interpretant is the consummated phase of meaning, yet a phase that is always open to further augmentations in scope and depth of semiotic value.

Let us look at how he frames the interpretant triad in his letters to Lady Welby. In a letter dated March 14, 1909, Peirce is especially lucid in his formulations and indicates how the interpretant can obtain in three distinct modalities:

My Dynamical Interpretant consists in direct effect actually produced
by a Sign upon an Interpreter of it. . . . My Final Interpretant is, I
believe, exactly the same as your Significance; namely, the effect the
Sign *would* produce upon any mind upon which circumstances should
per-mit it to work out its full effect. My Immediate Interpretant is, I
think, very nearly, if not quite, the same as your "Sense"; for I understand the former to be the total unanalyzed effect that the Sign is
calculated to produce, or naturally might be expected to produce; and
I have been accustomed to identify this with the effect the sign first
produces or may produce upon a mind, without any reflection upon it.
[SS 110]

The immediate interpretant, as the most basic level, and hence tied
to firstness, is actually "an abstraction, consisting in a Possibility"
[SS 111]. That is, the immediate interpretant is a potential interpretant
that brings a sphere of possible meanings to an interpretive situation.
The dynamical interpretant, on the other hand, as akin to the category
of secondness, is the actual impact of meaning in each given case.
The dynamic interpretant may vary from interpreter to interpreter. It
is a direct and given effect that, qua secondness, impinges on the
interpretive process. The final interpretant, as a manifestation of
thirdness, is the last interpretant that inquiry would come upon at the
end of its labors. Yet it is important that the concept of "final" not
mislead. As Ransdell argues, the final interpretant is not simply the
last one in an infinite series, but it also, in good Hegelian fashion,
'contains' all of the earlier members of its series and gathers them
together under one penumbra of meaning. Thus the final interpretant
is the series and its consummation, all prevailing at the same 'time.'[6]
Returning to our example of the nature painting with the sun rising
over the crest of a mountain, we see how all three modes of the
interpretant operate. The painting is what it is and not something else.
This simple observation is refined when this identity is understood in
terms of the immediate interpretant. The painting, qua immediate
interpretant(s), is a field of possible interpretants awaiting actualization by interpreters and further interpretants. The immediate interpretant maintains some possibilities and denies other. When the painting is actually viewed by an interpreter it gives birth to dynamic
interpretants. Each interpreter may encounter a different dynamic
interpretant. One may see a highly stylized pastoral painting while
another may see a deeply religious work that opens up the depth dimension of a self-transcending nature. The 'sum' of all dynamic
interpretants point toward the final interpretant that gathers up all other
interpretants and gives them a final and fulfilled meaning. The community of inquiry, given the 'time' of the infinite long run would find

the final interpretant of the painting, remembering that the final interpretant does not forget from whence it came. Put in colloquial terms, the final interpretant is generous to its forebears and gives each of them a place in the fulfilled kingdom of meaning.

There is a sense in which the final interpretant is "destined to come" [SS 111] from out of the future. In our discussion of abduction we stressed the eschatological elements in Peirce; namely, the religious sense that truth, meaning, and value come to the self from out of a pregnant future that promises to redeem the present and past. The same religious sensibility animates Peirce's semiotics. The final interpretant is promised for each and every object in the world. Whenever a sign, qua representamen, points toward an object (either iconically, indexically, or symbolically) it also points toward the final interpretant that would come to bring the object into its final transparency. The object becomes what it is when the dynamic and immediate dimensions are wedded together. The final interpretant performs the sacrament of marriage by providing the bond that frees the dynamic object from closure. When the final interpretant emerges, all facets of the object enter into the light of public semiosis and the object is known by the community as it is known by God.

In a manuscript ca. 1903 Peirce uses the different terms mentioned above for his description of the interpretant triad. For the term "immediate" he uses the term "emotional." For the term "dynamic" he uses the term "energetic." And for the term "final" he uses the term "logical." The insights are the same in either case:

> The first proper significate effect of a sign is a feeling produced by it. . . . This "emotional interpretant," as I call it, may amount to much more than that feeling of recognition; and in some cases, it is the only proper significate effect that the sign produces. . . . If the sign produces any further proper significate effect, it will do so through the mediation of the emotional interpretant, and such further effect will always involve an effort. I call it the energetic interpretant. The effort may be a muscular one, as it is in the case of the command to ground arms; but it is much more usually an exertion upon the Inner World, a mental effort. It can never be the meaning of an intellectual concept, since it is a single act, [while] such a concept is of a general nature. But what further kind of effect can there be? In advance of ascertaining the nature of this effect, it will be convenient to adopt a designation for it, and I will call it the *logical interpretant*. . . . [CP 5.475–476]

This redefinition of the terms of the interpretant triad sheds light on the human responses to interpretants. In the case of the emotional interpretant, there is a bare feeling of recognition that has a limited significative effect on the self. His example is that of listening to a piece of music, which is manifest to the interpreter as a series of feelings. Yet this soon gives way to more lasting and compelling effects, thus giving birth to the energetic interpretant. Here we go beyond the passive state of entertaining feelings into one involving actual muscular effort. The command "ground arms" functions as an energetic interpretant in that it compels the soldier to move his or her rifle from the shoulder position to one parallel with the vertical body. As a command, this energetic interpretant is a particular case, not yet an intellectual concept. It is when we move to the logical interpretant that we go beyond muscular effort to a general idea.

Peirce does distinguish between the logical interpretant and the *ultimate* logical interpretant of the concept, thus pointing to his 1909 formulation to Lady Welby. Be that as it may, the logical interpretant participates in thirdness and points toward transformed habits for the self. In either classification (dynamic, final, immediate, or energetic, logical, emotional) the interpretant has a kind of autonomy and power that must be acknowledged by the interpreter. It is helpful to see each interpretant as a sphere of power and meaning in its own right. The interpreter is shaped and molded by the 'sum' of interpretants that enter into its trajectory. While the self is more than the 'sum' of its interpretants, it can never escape from their influence. Like Royce, Peirce places a great deal of emphasis on the will, yet he often prefers to see the self in more passive terms; namely, as a product of vast interpretant series that reach down into the heart of nature.

Peirce does not confine the sign or the interpretant to language. His naturalism, of the panpsychist variety, insists that signs are in and of a self-transforming nature. Since so much of recent semiotic theory has been confined to human languages, a position referred to as "glottocentrism" by Thomas Sebeok, it is crucial that Peirce's extralinguistic sense of semiosis be brought to center stage. Later in the same 1909 letter Peirce affirms his more generic stance:

> I think, dear Lady Welby, that perhaps you are in danger of falling into some error in consequence of limiting your studies so much to Language and among languages to *one* very peculiar language, as all Aryan Languages are; and within that language so much to *words*. [SS 118]

It is clear that icons and indexes can exist in the prelinguistic orders. The interesting question is: can a symbol exist outside of human language and convention? The 'obvious' answer is that symbols must be products of human contrivance. But this may turn out to be a less than obvious conclusion. We recall from the previous chapter that Peirce believed in a vast unconscious dimension of the self that could be called a kind of "collective unconscious." This depth dimension (more akin to a bottomless lake than a glassy essence) could very well be the ultimate seed bed for all truly general symbols. In this sense, the symbol would have a point of origin that is prelinguistic, even if it will manifest itself in linguistic terms, or be convertible to such terms.

There is some evidence that Peirce allowed for prelinguistic and prehuman forms of semiosis that manifested all of the basic features of signification. This is supported by his implied theory of the unconscious, both in the self and, so I would argue, in nature. In a manuscript from around 1907 Peirce applies the semiotic model to the prehuman:

> The action of a sign generally takes place between two parties, the *utterer* and the *interpreter*. They need not be persons; for a chamelion [sic] and many kinds of insects and even plants make their livings by uttering signs, and lying signs, at that. . . . However, every sign certainly conveys something of the general nature of thought, if not from a mind, yet from some repository of ideas, or significant forms, and if not to a person, yet to something capable of some how "catching on" . . . that is [,] of receiving not merely a physical, nor even merely a psychical dose of energy, but a significant meaning. [MS 318, pp. 00205–00206]

Insects and chameleons are utterers and interpreters of signs that have an immediate evolutionary value. When a chameleon changes its skin color to blend into an immediate object, it utters a new sign that can become an interpretant in the life of a possible predator. The skin is itself the object, the color is both object and sign. The color as interpreted, albeit unconsciously, is an interpretant. If this process, giving birth to the ontological triad, can apply to primitive insect or animal forms, why can't it apply to plants as well? And, we can infer, if it applies to plants, why can't we speak of a kind of virtual semiosis in the inorganic order?[7]

Metaphysically, this view harks back to the medieval sense that the world of nature contains traces of the divine, traces which can be seen in the most ordinary events. Peirce does not have a one-to-one sense of the correlation between nature and the divine, but does point to a dimension of ultimate meaning in which symbols become permeable to something that vastly eclipses the human process. Once we reject glottocentrism we are in a position to see each and every event of nature as potentially symbolic.

We have covered a lot of terrain in our discussion of Peirce's semiotic theory. The ontological triad of sign/object/interpretant tells us what there is in the world. There is a sense in which this triad denotes a functional distinction in that any one term in the triad can stand duty for (become) any other term. But this can be pushed too far. Objects are ontologically distinct from signs, and both of them are in turn distinct from interpretants. The functional analysis can go fairly far down the road, but then the inner nature of each of the three constituents will assert itself and make further translation impossible. The object itself has both a dynamic core and immediate facets that are available to the interpreter.

The unveiling triad, perhaps the most famous in Peirce, shows how signs can make objects manifest. Icons share features with their referents. Indexes are caused by single objects and do not share common iconic features with their referents (unless they also 'contain' iconic relations). Symbols refer to generals rather than particulars, and have a conventional or arbitrary relation to their referents. Any given sign will manifest all three layers, in either pure or degenerate forms. We abstract out (prescind) certain features for examination and often overstate their importance in a given case.

The interpretant triad, which has the two formulations of dynamic/final/immediate and energetic/logical/emotional, shows us how the interpretant becomes relevant to the growth of meaning. The second formulation refers more to the psychological aspects of the recognition of interpretants, while the first formulation (that presented to Lady Welby) refers more to the interpretant 'in itself.' It must be stressed that interpretants, no matter what their mode of operation, link together into vast networks that have neither beginning nor end. Nature is rendered intelligible through interpretants whose powers shape the self and its communities.

The argumentative triad of rheme/dicisign/argument points to the relation between a sign and its interpretant. The sign can present qualitative possibility (rheme), an actual existent (dicisign), or a law (argument). The upshot of this triad is that it moves semiosis into the sphere of argument so that a complex semiotic case can be made. The link between an interpretant and its sign is not a random one, but one that has very clear claims to make about the constitution of the total semiotic structure.

The triad of qualisign/sinsign/legisign points to the quality of the sign in itself; that is, outside of its possible or actual reference to either an object or an interpretant. As such, this triad could be called the "intrinsic triad" insofar as it refers to what a sign is or can be in its prerelational modes. It is intrinsic to a sign that it can represent the possibilities of quality, the particularity of a here-and-now correlation, or the power of general law. Insofar as the general law becomes efficacious it will find a place of operation through the sinsign.

All four triads, the ontological, unveiling, argumentative, and intrinsic, can be looked at functionally and ontologically. Clearly, the ontological triad is the most 'solid' in ontological terms in that it denotes the antecedent structures and powers of the world. Yet the three other triads also point to 'what is' in ways that cannot be converted into purely or reductively functional terms. Yet, at the same time, a functional analysis can be liberating insofar as it shows the innumerable permutations pertinent to the life of signs. Any given sign may have a very complex life history in which it moves from one status to another. A simple rhematic iconic sinsign could, in principle, become a rhematic symbolic legisign whenever it took on more generic powers of meaning. It would thereby increase its "area" (breadth × depth) and add its own sphere of meanings to the world as a whole. Signs are protean and open to novel augmentations of meaning.

What, then, is the upshot of Peirce's semiotic theory? It is clear that his semiotic structures are what they are because they participate in the three primal categories of firstness, secondness, and thirdness. Consequently, semiotics cannot be divorced from metaphysics. Animating both his semiotics and his metaphysics is a strong sense of the ubiquity of a self-transforming nature that lives as the 'sum' of all signs *and* as the ever-creative source for all semiotic possibilities and actualities. Nature spawns more semiotic orders than it can support. Some of these orders are condemned to be consumed by others, while some are destined to exert great power within their pertinent orders of relevance. Within these semiotic orders are those that can be termed "religious." Peirce was intrigued by religious questions all of his life. In his mature reflections he finds the language, largely derived from his metaphysical semiotics, to express his religious insights. In his analyses of the divine, and its relation to the self and its methods of semiosis, Peirce weaves together the seemingly disconnected threads of his perspective so that the highest orders of power and meaning can become relevant to the self. In the end, the ultimate goal of all of Peirce's elaborate reflections is to find the *summum bonum* that can promise a transfigured life.

Notes

1. For an evocative and profound treatment of the nature of "virtual" signs and their relation to general semiotics (which remains in dialogue with Peirce), see *Basics of Semiotics,* John Deely (Bloomington: Indiana University Press, 1990).

2. I owe this example to my former colleague Carl Hausman, who used it in our jointly taught graduate seminar in American philosophy.

3. For a correlation of this example with an event in Peirce's life, see "Charles Sanders Peirce and Arisbe" by William Pencak, in *Semiotics 1985,* ed. John Deely (Lanham, Md.: University Press of America, 1986), pp. 487–505.

4. The serious student of Peirce's semiotics must read at least the following works: "Charles Sanders Peirce" by Joseph Ransdell in *Encyclopedic Dictionary of Semiotics,* ed. Thomas A. Sebeok (Berlin: Mouton de Gruyter, 1986), pp. 673–695, and *An Introduction to C. S. Peirce's Full System of Semeiotic* (Toronto: Toronto Semiotic Circle, 1987), by David Savan.

5. For an excellent critique of structuralism from a Peircean perspective see John K. Sheriff's *The Fate of Meaning: Charles Peirce, Structuralism, and Literature* (Princeton: Princeton University Press, 1989).

6. Ransdell, "Charles Sanders Peirce," p. 682.

7. Cf. Deely, *Basics of Semiotics.*

Chapter Four

The Evolving God and the Heart of Nature

As his thought matured, Peirce became more and more concerned with the larger metaphysical framework that animated his perspective. His phenomenological analysis of firstness, secondness, and thirdness pointed toward an evolutionary cosmology in which the three categories worked to bring the universe toward an ideal convergence in which the highest good would become manifest. His highly detailed semiotic triads, and their seemingly endless permutations, unveiled traits of a cosmos that was semiotic through and through. Yet it was not until some of his more detailed reflections were completed that Peirce was in a position to probe into the fundamental principles of his cosmology. In transforming evolutionary theory to serve his own philosophical interests, Peirce was also compelled to rethink the nature of God in line with his unique form of objective idealism. His conception of God is incomplete, and has been the subject of intense scrutiny. There is some disagreement as to the upshot of his philosophical theology; some scholars insist that his views, though cast in his own unique language, remain fairly traditional, while other scholars see more radical things afoot in his attempts to correlate an evolving God with an equally dynamic universe.[1] In what follows, these tensions will become clarified and the radical nature of Peirce's philosophical theology should manifest itself.

The focus of this chapter, which will examine the most generic and sweeping of Peirce's metaphysical categories, will be on his reworking of evolution, the critique of necessitarianism, the redefinition of the human process, and the nature of divine growth. Animating these discussions will be a concern with the depth dimensions of nature and their pertinence to the human process and its communities. Peirce's evolutionism is not a simple extension of Darwin, nor is it just a reactionary move toward Lamarckianism, but represents a third option that attempts to honor what is viable in the earlier views.

We are fortunate in having a specific series of published papers as our focus. In the years from 1891 to 1893, Peirce published five articles in *The Monist*. In these essays he locates his own mature metaphysics against current or past alternative perspectives and defends his views against potential criticisms. The five papers are "The Architecture of Theories," "The Doctrine of Necessity Examined," "The Law of Mind," "Man's Glassy Essence," and "Evolutionary Love." These papers were written for a more general audience and contain some of the most exciting and evocative of Peirce's reflections on basic questions. At the same time, they serve to gather together many of the threads of his other reflections, particularly those that we examined in the context of his anthropology and phenomenology.

The Transformation of Darwin: Evolutionary Habits

The first article in *The Monist* series, "The Architecture of Theories" (1891), sets out the basic issues that are to be elaborated in the subsequent essays. In it Peirce probes into the status of natural laws and correlates them to his own conception of evolution. He examines the nature of space and sheds further light on his three primal ontological categories. The underlying commitment is to the view that philosophical theories are analogous to architectural principles and that thought cannot advance unless it takes the form of a vast interlocking conceptual structure similar to that of a well-constructed house.

Commentators have noted that Peirce was continually engaged in making additions to his house in Milford, Pennsylvania, during the time that he wrote these essays. He made many of the architectural drawings himself and devised the various building plans for these additions.[2] Consequently, it should come as no surprise that he saw a direct link between his efforts at home improvement and his struggles with the metaphysical structures of intelligibility. Less charitable scholars have been inclined to see both enterprises as ill-advised efforts ending in failure. For some, the late metaphysical essays give evidence to a marked decline in Peirce's categorial power, showing that he fell prey to a kind of romantic longing for a type of wholeness that continued to elude him in his personal and professional life.

A more sensitive and informed assessment will, I think, show that Peirce's power not only remain undiminished, but that he actually advanced his own problematic in these later essays and showed how pragmatism can gain greater strength and resourcefulness when it develops a grounding metaphysics. The categories of "synechism," "tychism," and "agapism," to name no others, serve to provide a kind of sweep and prospect for pragmaticism that lifts it out of the domain of mere methodologism. Even though most would be reticent to adopt or embrace Peirce's specific metaphysical commitments, many would honor their pertinence to his overall enterprise and admire the conceptual boldness with which he advanced on some of the most recalcitrant issues in philosophy.

Assuming, then, that at least the philosophical house building issued in a viable structure, we can examine how Peirce went beyond Darwinian principles and transformed evolutionary theory. As noted, Peirce links the framing of general theories to the activity of creating a solid and safe home. While the house uses material properties for its support, the philosophical architectonic, following Kant, uses generic categories to support its structure. Among these general categories, that of law assumes a special priority.

Peirce asks the intriguing question: why does the universe have laws in the first place? Can we simply take them for granted, or is there a sense in which their very existence is an issue? Peirce answers these questions by linking law with evolution:

> Now the only possible way of accounting for the laws of nature and for uniformity in general is to suppose them results of evolution. This supposes them not to be absolute, not to be obeyed precisely. It makes an element of indeterminacy, spontaneity, or absolute chance in nature. [CP 6.13 & EP 1.288]

A given law is what it is because it has emerged through time. It is crucial to note that the law is not absolute; that is, that it does not cover each and every case under its jurisdiction, but that there can be cases of variation that fall outside of the sweep of the law. The universe exhibits absolute chance. This chance is not in the mind of the beholder (as it would be for Kant), but is an objective feature of the universe. Laws are general habits, rather than absolute monarchs that do not tolerate deviation.

The universe thus moves from a heterogenous state of pure indeterminacy toward a state in which law becomes more and more the norm. Yet even in the growth of law, some element of chance will always remain. At the ideal 'end' of evolution, novel variations will still exist, showing that laws are generalized habits rather than eternal principles of inclusion. Any given law, not to mention the 'sum' of *all* laws, will be the product of organic and inorganic forms of evolution. Growth is an irreducible part of the universe and is manifest throughout evolutionary orders. Mere mechanical principles, which rely exclusively on efficient cause, cannot explain the presence of growth or novelty in nature. Consequently, a nonmechanical conception of evolution must be evolved that will find a proper place for centers of growth. Peirce is quite critical of Herbert Spencer (1820–1903), the British evolutionary theorist, for attempting to ground evolution on mechanical principles, thus utterly failing to explain the most obvious product of evolution, centers of growth in time.

Charles Darwin, on the other hand, advances the problematic insofar as he understands the means by and through which organisms come into the world and either flourish or perish. Peirce's succinct summary of Darwin's views shows that he had a good grasp of what was central to current biological theory:

> The theory of Darwin was that evolution had been brought about by the action of two factors: first, heredity, as a principle making offspring nearly resemble their parents, while yet giving room for "sporting" or accidental variations—for very slight variations often, for wider ones rarely; and, second, the destruction of breeds or races that are unable to keep the birth rate up to the death rate. [CP 6.15 & EP 1.289]

Random variation in the genetic material works against natural selection in the immediate environment of the organism. Evolutionary success is measured in terms of reproductive potency so that the death rate is lower than the birth rate. Peirce notes that variations are often slight (e.g., the change in the beak size or shape in a bird), and that the "room" for variations may not be very large in a given generation. Yet there are variations none the less and this opens up the possibility than new habits may emerge for the organic group. Darwin is superior to Spencer in that he admits a principle of chance (tychism) into the heart of his conception of evolution. Yet the Darwinian perspective lacks a deeper sense of purpose that could show us the inner dynamism of growth. To get a sense of purpose we must turn to Lamarck, even though we need not adopt his perspective wholesale.

Jean-Baptiste Lamarck (1744–1829), the French evolutionary theorist and friend of Rousseau, developed one of the first comprehensive theories of organic growth. He believed that nature contained a kind of perfecting power that guided evolution from the lower to the higher stages, culminating in the human process. The patterns of evolution exhibit some sense of purpose and have their remote origins in a divine author. Peirce concentrated on the less dramatic issue of where given characteristics in an organism come from. For Lamarck, a given individual can actually learn to add a new feature to its contour and then pass this acquired characteristic on to its offspring. Again, Peirce's summary is succinct and to the point:

> The Lamarckian theory also supposes that the development of species has taken place by a long series of insensible changes, but it supposes that those changes have taken place during the lives of the individuals, in consequence of effort and exercise, and that reproduction plays no part in the process except in preserving these modifications. [CP 6.16 & EP 1.289]

Here we see the emphasis on something like will or the use of effort to transform a situation from one that is unfavorable to one that is favorable. The organism can modify its behavior and add new habits to its repertoire. These new habits can enter into the inheritance patterns of the species by a process that remains mysterious. The dimension that appealed to Peirce is that of purpose and its role in shaping individual, and later, collective habits.

Peirce briefly discusses another theory of evolution that would now be called a "cataclysmic" theory; namely, one that emphasizes rapid and dramatic changes in the environment. Peirce has some sympathy for this concept, especially as applied to institutional change, but remains skeptical about its validity as a truly general theory. The Darwinian theory stresses the "haphazard" nature of evolutionary change, while the Lamarckian theory stresses the "inward striving" of organisms as a mechanism for change. The truth lies in some kind of synthesis (third) among the three alternatives of random variation, inward striving, and external cataclysm. Peirce's unique solution will be examined a little later.

After giving a brief synopsis of his three categories, Peirce takes the dramatic step of introducing his cosmological speculations. In looking at firstness, secondness, and thirdness, it is possible to avoid cosmology, as these three categories can be probed either logically or phenomenologically. Yet the categories also have profound implications for our understanding of the whence and whither of the universe as a whole, and Peirce did not shy away from making some striking claims. It should be noted that Peirce's metaphysical theories do not compete with contemporary astrophysical theories, such as that of the "Big Bang," but represent a different order of analysis and discourse.

In a sense, his cosmology is meant to provide a conceptual clearing *within* which his philosophical theology can unfold. I am not saying that Peirce thought of this correlation in these terms, but that the inner momentum of his system moves in this direction. His conception of God is so difficult to grasp precisely because it is located within and against a highly complex cosmology that contains process and nonprocess elements.

Peirce states his cosmogonic principles at the end of "The Architecture of Theories" and uses an image that has caused some trouble for his commentators:

> It [cosmogonic philosophy] would suppose that in the beginning—infinitely remote—there was a chaos of unpersonalized feeling, which being without connection or regularity would properly be without existence. This feeling, sporting here and there in pure arbitrariness, would have started the germ of a generalizing tendency. Its other sportings would be evanescent, but this would have a growing virtue. Thus, the tendency to habit would be started; and from this, with the other principles of evolution, all the regularities of the universe would be evolved. At any time, however, an element of pure chance survives and will remain until the world becomes an absolutely perfect, rational, and symmetrical system, in which mind is at last crystallized in the infinitely distant future. [CP 6.33 & EP 1.297]

The concept of a "crystallized" mind at the end of evolution tends to connote a rather static and ahistorical conception of the highest good. One reading of this passage has been that secondness, variation, and chance get squeezed out of the world as evolution marches toward its fulfillment. Hence the image of the perfect crystal seems to mock the pragmaticist commitment to growth and novelty. Once again we are confronted with a passage that can and should be read in a less literal way. We do not need to deconstruct the passage or look for some kind of elusive subtext so much as locate it within the larger contour of Peirce's cosmology.

The picture that emerges is a fairly clear one. The universe began as a kind of soup of pure possibility and indeterminacy. Yet this domain of possibility and potency is hardly passive. Built into the heart of nature is a kind of cosmic restlessness that insists on moving from bare possibility into the domains of existence (secondness). The "chaos of unpersonalized feeling" gives way to habits. It is interesting to note that the domain of cosmic firstness is that of unpersonalized feeling. For Peirce, like Whitehead and Hartshorne later, feeling is a form of relation in which one relata participates in another. Yet this chaos of primal feeling (relation prior to any existing relata) is unpersonalized. This is an intriguing prospect. Insofar as God will be somehow emergent from nature, God must come from a prepersonal ground. That is, the personal and anthropomorphic God that Peirce believes in must have an origin in the prepersonal. As we will see, this tension between prepersonal cosmic firstness and a personal God links Peirce's philosophical theology to certain mystical traditions that distinguish between the Godhead (*die Gottheit*) and God (*der Gott*). The Godhead is the God beyond the God of theism and is thus prepersonal, while God, in more traditional terms, remains personal.[3]

Be that as it may, the realm of pure arbitrariness gives birth to a generalizing tendency in which existents emerge and enter into relational groupings. These groupings in turn generate habits that introduce thirdness into the world. Yet pure chance remains in the world as a goad to evolution. The state of the perfect crystal would not tolerate chaos or novelty. Consequently there must be a way of combining the concepts of chance and pure totalization or perfection. The simplest answer to this dilemma is to remember that Peirce always talks of the "would be"; that is, of the state that the universe would attain given the infinite long run. Since the would be is not an actual envisioned state of affairs, there is no contradiction between the belief in chance and the hope of crystallized perfection. Elsewhere, Peirce questions the equation of perfection with a static quasi-geometric eternity (cf. CP 7.380) and insists that evolution and perfection are incompatible.

On a deeper level, the tension can be resolved by recognizing that the crystallized state of pure mind represents a rational system that combines concrete reasonableness with growth. As we have seen, there can be no growth in a mechanical universe. Nor can there be evolutionary development without some form of chaos (which need not be cataclysmic). Consequently it follows that while the crystal simile is inadequate, the underlying conceptual portrayal allows for novelty even within an imagined 'completed' universe (in the would be). We can also add that crystals are hardly as static as they appear to uncritical common sense.

To alter the imagery slightly, we can say that the crystal is a domain of thirdness that still admits growth and change. We must remember that thirdness is itself a 'restless' category and can only obtain if there is room for growth. As we will see shortly, mentality exists in the universe at large and any order funded with mentality will admit growth and change. Thus we can say that Peirce's crystal will certainly have an archetypal structure and core, but will also admit new traits and establish new lines of relevance as its own internal material changes. If we can stretch common sense even further, we can speak of a growing and self-aware crystal that feels the impaction of the extracrystalline orders.

The purpose of "The Architecture of Theories" is thus to open up the possibility that natural law is a product of evolution and that all orders of thirdness admit some growth and change. Peirce signals the reader that his own conception of evolution, to emerge more clearly later in the series of papers, will depart from both Lamarck and Darwin, while yet preserving what is viable in each. At the same time, Peirce opens up the door to the profoundly difficult questions of cosmogenesis, and, by implication, the ultimate goal of the universe.

In the second essay in *The Monist* series, "The Doctrine of Necessity Examined" (1892), Peirce attacks the then current and popular belief that all events in the universe can be fully explained without reference to any conception of chance or purpose. The necessitarian position seemed to many to be a direct extrapolation from the advance of science and its ability to render more and more of the world intelligible through causal principles of explanation. Peirce thus sees himself as a defender of chance *and* a defender of scientific method. He can defend both positions because he has a different conception of science than many of his contemporaries, a conception that he holds to be superior to the accepted one because it understands the new logic of probability and thus in turn understands the limits to exact description.

This essay drew some fire from other thinkers precisely because Peirce hit upon the most vulnerable spot of then contemporary scientism. His bold affirmations of the principles of growth, spontaneity, and chance challenged the prejudices of his era. What makes his case so convincing, however, is his use of arguments that come from the very sciences used to defend the necessitarian position. In effect, he turns science against scientism (the ideology of the mechanists and necessitarians).

Peirce takes a brief look at the history of philosophy and notes that the early Greek atomists (e.g., Democritus) believed that the world was constituted by discrete atoms (the smallest impenetrable units of reality), and that these atoms interact according to strict mechanical and efficient causal principles. Epicurus later added the famous (or infamous) "swerve" to Greek atomism that insisted that atoms are somehow moved from their courses by a kind of mysterious cosmic spontaneity. Peirce sees this later transformation of atomism as a move in the right direction. Unfortunately, nineteenth-century scientists and mechanistic philosophers ignored the Epicurean modification and moved back to the simpler metaphysics of the earlier tradition.

As always, Peirce is very careful to define the position he is attacking. We have noted in previous chapters his attention to the exact meaning of technical terms, not to mention his proclivity to invent new terms with what might seem like a careless abandon. He defined the concept of "necessity" in 1889 in Baldwin's *Dictionary of Philosophy and Psychology* and thus had already worked through the envisioned possibilities. His 1892 definition of necessitarianism is as follows:

> The proposition in question is that the state of things existing at any time, together with certain immutable laws, completely determine the state of things at every other time (for a limitation to *future* time is indefensible). Thus, given the state of the universe in the original nebula, and given the laws of mechanics, a sufficiently powerful mind could deduce from these data the precise form of every curlicue of every letter I am now writing. [CP 6.37 & EP 1.299]

The first thing to note is that the necessitarian believes in "immutable laws," a view attacked by Peirce in the previous article where he argues that laws are mutable; that is, they change along with the growth of the universe. The second thing to note is that the necessitarian believes that there is such a thing as "the state of the universe," as if the 'sum' of all states could be somehow pictured at once (thus denying real change or flux). The third thing to note is that the necessitarian believes in the "laws of mechanics," as if these were somehow a priori principles that do not admit of change or variation.

The necessitarian position is thus a very strong one in the sense that it makes rather grand claims about knowledge and its ability to probe into the heart of nature and its laws. Since it is such an extreme position, although it does not appear to be so to its followers, it is fairly easy to find means of criticizing it. Peirce attacks it in two general ways: first in its form as a postulate used to explain the order of the world, and second, from a scientific or observational perspective. He argues that the doctrine of necessity cannot be a universal postulate and that it is a fiction used to convey the sense that there is far more uniformity in the world than there actually is. The second move is the more interesting one because in it Peirce can use the tools of science against the scientistic ideology.

He insists that we do not observe necessity in nature, even though regularity is certainly a commonly observed feature of the world. All regularity is partial; it can never be exact or universal. In fact, the mathematics of probability, used so successfully in chemical theories, was developed precisely because there are deviations from law in given cases. In any large class of phenomena, such as molecules in a container, we must fall back on a probabilistic analysis and give up on the dream of finding the true "state of things" of the phenomenon itself. And this is not because we have failed to be precise enough, but because the world does not function through necessitarian or mechanistic principles.

In examining any law of nature we must see if it can be applied in an exact and universal manner. "Try to verify any law of nature, and you will find that the more precise your observations, the more certain they will be to show irregular departures from the law" [CP 6.46 & EP 1.304–305]. In fact, the more closely we look at a law, and its application to a genus or class of phenomena, the more likely we are to find these departures. The quest for exactitude will produce inexactitude. This conclusion has now become commonplace (as expressed in the Heisenberg "uncertainty principle"), but Peirce was clearer than most of his generation that science must honor the vague and indeterminate.

Looking more closely at specific sciences, rather than just at mathematical methods within science, Peirce observes that what he calls the sciences of "time" deal with objects and events that cannot be exhaustively explained in necessitarian terms:

> Question any science which deals with the course of time. Consider the life of an individual animal or plant, or of a mind. Glance at the history of states, of institutions, of language, of ideas. Examine the successions of forms shown by paleontology, the history of the globe as set forth in geology, of what the astronomer is able to make out concerning changes of stellar systems. Everywhere the main fact is growth and increasing complexity. [CP 6.58 & EP 1.307–308]

The universe manifests growth and complexity at every turn. To ignore these facts is to reduce science to some kind of ahistorical classificatory scheme, hardly a pragmatic conception of the scientific enterprise. Neither growth nor increasing complexity can be explained by necessitarian principles. A phenomenon grows through the power of spontaneity, which provides "room" for creative variation. If there is no chance there is no growth. By the same argument, the transition from a less complex to a more complex state can only occur because new options are provided for the phenomenon under question. These options are products of chance.

Thus, mathematics and observation both show that the necessitarian position is a false one. Not only does it fail to explain the actual facts, but it does not use proper scientific methods to probe into its subject matter. The universe contains pockets of novelty that break the hegemony of efficient cause. The belief in necessity is often found alongside of a belief in the self-sufficiency of materialism. The universe is explained along the lines of a vast material mechanism that follows strict causal laws. Evolution, where dealt with at all, is treated as yet one more manifestation of mechanical principles, from which it follows that nothing truly new or novel can emerge and that all subsequent states are prefigured in their antecedents. Peirce finds this view to be deadening both to science as an enterprise and to our sense of the role of mind in the world.

We have pointed to Peirce's panpsychism, the doctrine that mind is a more basic feature of the world than matter, and shown its relevance to his semiotic theory. In the context of his critique of necessitarianism he shows how a restriction on causal theory can open the door to mind:

> On the other hand, by supposing the rigid exactitude of causation to yield, I care not how little—be it but by a strictly infinitesimal amount—we gain room to insert mind into our scheme, and to put it into the place where it is needed, into the position which, as the sole self-intelligible thing, it is entitled to occupy, that of the fountain of existence; and in so doing we resolve the problem of the connection of soul and body. [CP 6.61 & EP 1.309]

Mind works through final cause and puts pressure on the various forms of efficient cause in the universe. Does Peirce go so far as to make final cause more basic than efficient cause? The answer seems to be that he finds a place for both and that neither assumes an absolute priority (unlike later process thinkers who make final cause the genus of which efficient cause is a mere species). The interesting claim here is that mind is the "fountain of existence." Mind lies underneath matter as its animating principle. Consequently, mind empowers all existents and links them together (through feeling) so that the relations between and among the objects of the world can be seen in terms of the power of mind to overcome distance and alienation. The link between the soul and the body is a paradigmatic expression of the link between any two items in the world. The soul serves as the animating principle of the body (à la Aristotle) rather than as a separate principle or special substance. Peirce's anti-Cartesianism comes to the fore in his panpsychism. He moves toward a monism in which mind seems to swallow up matter as one of its manifestations.

Peirce's position was attacked by the German philosopher Dr. Carus (in an article entitled "Dr. Charles S. Peirce's Onslaught on the Doctrine of Necessity," in *The Monist*, Vol. 2) who defended necessitarianism against the view that the universe contains genuine novelty and chance. Peirce was given an opportunity to reply to his critic in the pages of *The Monist*. We will take a brief look at how he augments his views to give them even greater argumentative power. Peirce gives a clear summary of the arguments that he advanced in his essay:

1. The general prevalence of growth, which seems to be opposed to the conservation of energy.

2. The variety of the universe, which is chance, and is manifestly inexplicable.

3. Law, which requires to be explained, and like everything which is to be explained must be explained by something else, that is, by non-law or real chance.

4. Feeling, for which room cannot be found if the conservation of energy is maintained. [CP 6.613]

We have looked at his understanding of growth and variety as irreducible facts that cannot be translated into necessitarian terms. The third and fourth arguments have a special force and scope that requires further comment. Peirce reverses the usual correlation that would start with an acceptance of the presence of law, and then moves toward an explanation of chance. He starts instead with the presence of real chance and moves backward toward the existence of law. Unlike most of his contemporaries, Peirce did not take law for granted, but wanted to understand just how it came into being. Chance has a certain metaphysical and cosmological priority over law. Put simply, chance was here first and is also more pervasive than often recognized.

The fourth argument is unusual in that it correlates feeling and energy. The concept of "feeling" is an especially general one. All relations are forms of feeling (not, except in unusual cases, human emotions). Feelings have a tendency to spread and grow. Consequently, they seem to violate the principle of the conservation of energy, which insists that energy can be neither created nor destroyed. Feelings can be created and can add their power to the world. Peirce envisions creation as a continual process rather than as a once-and-for-all happening. Each moment adds new created reality to the evolving world. The necessitarian position, insofar as it speculates about cosmogenesis,

sees the act of creation in purely antecedent terms, something perhaps 'done' by a divine being at the beginning of time.

Peirce sheds further light on this first state of affairs, this first
"germinal state of being" that antedates all existence, yet which still
obtains in the present as a power for diversification. He talks of a
kind of primal nothingness prior to the world of seconds and thirds.
Yet even this is not primal enough:

> Even this nothingness, though it antecedes the infinitely distant abso-
> lute beginning of time, is traced back to a nothingness more rudimentary
> still, in which there is no variety, but only an indefinite specificability,
> which is nothing but a tendency to the diversification of the nothing,
> while leaving it as nothing as it was before. [CP 6.612]

The true originative power of the universe is a deep nothingness
that is more of a tendency than an actual pool of diversified possibilities. We could call this the domain of nature's potencies (to use a
term from Schelling, who is referred to with approval in this essay).
The potencies of nothingness are ontologically prior to the possibilities that obtain in what we could call the "lesser" nothingness. Lesser
nothingness is the domain of nothingness of cosmic possibility and
variety. This is a kind of storehouse of possible objects and events.
Prior to the storehouse is the deeper tendency *toward* diversification
that has no internal variety, but which will make variety possible.

These speculations might strike one as being without any genuine
relevance for Peirce's pragmaticist program. Yet, in a curious way,
they are highly relevant for his conception of science and the growth
of meaning within community. In distinguishing between two types of
nothingness, the "lesser" and the "greater" (terms not used by Peirce
here), he shows how the necessitarian clings to an incomplete understanding of the creative powers of the world, and thus fails to grasp
the true locus of chance. Lesser nothingness is the cosmic soup of
possibilities that can become actualized whenever emergents take on
habits. Deeper down is the greater nothingness that provides the metaphysical goad for cosmogenesis. That is, the deeper domain of the
potencies of nature provides the true restlessness that compels the
universe into existence. The locus of chance is thus to be found in the
greater nothingness that is continually spawning possibilities, and
through the 'agency' of lesser nothingness, actualities (seconds). Peirce
wants the necessitarian to go to the heart of nature, rather than cling
to its surface phenomena.

The depth dimension of the world is a state of "intensest feeling"
in which there is neither memory nor habit, but which has the internal

tendency to wed feeling to feeling. The order of the world can come from absolute chance, through the process in which bare tendencies become transformed into actual possibilities, which in turn become actualities, which in turn take on habits. Law comes from absolute chance (which lives in the greater nothingness). Science lives in the domain of attained law. Yet the heart of science must become open to the heart of nature and come to see that chance exists not only in the interstices between and among events, but in the continually active forces of cosmogenesis. The creative powers of greater and lesser nothingness continue to be operative throughout the universe and work to overturn the principle of the conservation of energy.

Peirce concludes his reply to Dr. Carus by reiterating his own commitment to the priority of the tendency toward diversity that is even more basic than chaos: "To explain diversity is to go behind the chaos, to the original undiversified nothing. Diversificacity was the first germ" [CP 6.613]. Thus the greater nothingness makes the chaos of the lesser nothingness possible. Greater nothingness is self-othering in the special sense that it pushes into chaos so that the realm of potency can birth the realm of possibility. Underlying both greater and lesser nothingness is the domain of feeling. The doctrine of "tychism" (from the Greek word for chance) pertains to the chaos of the lesser nothingness. Once this doctrine has been articulated, a second comes to the fore, that of "synechism," which deals with the tendency of feeling toward connectedness and relation.

The third article in *The Monist* series, "The Law of Mind" (1892), examines the role of feeling in defining mind. This is undergirded by an analysis of synechism as a basic feature of the universe, with a special clarity of manifestation in the domains of mind. This essay is especially rich in its metaphysical analyses of the logic and psychology of feeling and the concomitant doctrine of synechism. Peirce begins his examination by moving past tychism toward his unique form of idealism:

> I have begun by showing that *tychism* must give birth to an evolution-ary cosmology, in which all the regularities of nature and of mind are regarded as products of growth, and to a Schelling-fashioned idealism which holds matter to be mere specialized and partially deadened mind. [CP 6.102 & EP 1.312]

Evolution would not be at all were it not for absolute and relative forms of chance, which provide the space within which novel variations can occur. Law is itself a product of habit and thus would not be possible without the basic reality of chance from whence habits come.

The "Schelling-fashioned idealism" of these essays is a panpsychism and an identity philosophy. Matter is "partially deadened mind" rather than an autonomous or even grounding principle in its own right. The move toward identity can be seen in his anti-Cartesian rejection of mind/body dualism *and* in his sense that nature is characterized by the law of continuity. This is not to say that nature is one totalized order, or continuum of all continua, but that the world is constituted by innumerable forms of continuity that appear whenever feeling and mentality appear. In certain passages, Peirce seems to equate feeling with mind, as if the primary law of mind is to obtain as a spreading realm of feelings.

The doctrine of synechism thus refers to the tendency to see continuity within and among the orders of the world. Peirce was long fascinated with the nature of continua in mathematics and logic, and his application of the concept of synechism to the law of mind is in keeping with his other commitments. There is a sense in which Peirce takes the associational principles from British empirical psychology and supports them via the logic of continuity. Hume's principles of resemblance and contiguity receive a new depth and power of meaning when translated into the terms of the logic of continuity. Where Hume leaves us with a cluster of inner states, Peirce moves us toward a sense of the role of mind in the universe at large, in which most forms of resemblance and contiguity are mind-independent (that is, independent of the *human* mind) and belong to the structures of the evolving cosmos.

The law of mind, as a special application of the law of continuity, points to the tendency of ideas to spread and form connective bridges. Like signs, which have a hunger to participate in more than one sign series, feelings are restless and move outward into larger and larger orders of relevance:

> Logical analysis applied to mental phenomena shows that there is but one law of mind, namely, that ideas tend to spread continuously and to affect certain others which stand to them in a peculiar relation of affectibility. In this spreading they lose intensity, and especially the power of affecting others, but gain generality and become welded with other ideas. [CP 6.104 & EP 1.313]

We have noted in previous chapters that Peirce links the nature of feeling to ethics. The foundation of ethics is twofold. On one side, it is the self-control that brings the individual will into harmony with the needs of the interpretive community. On the other, and deeper, side, it is the feeling of sympathy that bridges the gap between selves.

Peirce believes that feeling is not only the mechanism of relation, but that it is profoundly revelatory of the life of other minds. Since feeling and mentality are almost commensurate terms, it follows that the mind operates through sympathy rather than analogy to gain access to other centers of awareness. This emphasis on feeling and sympathy brings Peirce's implied ethics close to that of Schopenhauer for whom only *mitleid* (sympathy) could ground ethics. The difference between them is that for Peirce, feeling is rational, as is the world at large. For Schopenhauer the world, in its depth dimension of will, is deeply irrational and fully indifferent to human need. Peirce's evocative sense of what we have called the "greater nothingness" points in the direction of Schopenhauer's irrationalism even though the two part company when it comes to their assessment of the status and scope of reason in the world as a whole.

Peirce considers time to be part of a continuum. He does not spatialize time (as did the Aristotelian tradition), but understands it as an infinite series in which each member blends into its antecedent and consequent. "We are thus brought to the conclusion that the present is connected with the past by a series of real infinitesimal steps" [CP 6.109 & EP 1.314]. These steps are "real" because the structures of time are not generated by (or confined to) the human mind. In spite of his many Kantian elements, Peirce rejected Kant's view that time is a product of the synthesizing powers of the transcendental imagination. Peirce has a much broader conception of mind and a much broader conception of those realities that exist outside of human structures of mentality. The law of mind (synechism) reveals that the life of time is that of a continuum in which each moment participates in those that surround it. The image of time is more like that of a moving tide of feelings than like a series of discrete and atomic moments.

Consciousness is thus constituted by an infinite series of feelings that have an internal tendency to spread out. The concept of a "private feeling" is almost a contradiction in terms. Feelings, as the relational structures of the world, are social right from the start. Yet these feelings are not oblivious to their own tendencies; that is, they have some kind of mentality that lets them know that and what they are. "In fact, this infinitesimally spread-out consciousness is a direct feeling of its contents as spread out" [CP 6.111 & EP 1.315]. Feelings are self-aware and seem to desire further scope for their relational networks. We noted in the second chapter that Peirce believes in something like Jung's "collective unconscious," which for Peirce would be an infinite network of associational possibilities and directed feelings. There is a sense in which feelings are purposive and thus manifest a tendency toward some kind of goal. Hume's associational descriptions (of resemblance and contiguity) manifest no purpose and do not point to the infinity of the life of feeling and time.

Ideas, feeling, and consciousness, not to mention the unconscious (both personal and collective), all participate in the law of mind. The law of mind, as a manifestation of the general principle of synechism, insists that no item within the mind obtains in isolation from other items. It is not always clear whether Peirce believes in a doctrine of strict internal relations—namely, that any given feeling is connected to all other feelings in the universe—but it is clear that he was consistent in rejecting any form of atomism that broke down the world into disconnected particulars. The world not only manifests real generality, but it shows how these generalities themselves hunger for an enhanced scope.

Peirce thus develops a theory of continuity that moves beyond those views that see the infinitesimal in terms of the mere continuing divisibility of a line (a mere metric conception). Kant, according to Peirce, makes the mistake of confounding this infinite divisibility with continuity (cf. CP 6.120 & EP 1.320). The real issue is not that of divisibility, or of finding a third between any two points on a line, but that of showing connection between antecedent, present, and consequent states. The doctrine of synechism is not a doctrine of divisibility but a doctrine of how moments (not instances) blend together through infinitesimal steps. The two prime examples of the operation of synechism/continuity are time and feeling.

Peirce asks the intriguing question: how is past time still present and not somehow locked up tightly in an unavailable past? His answer is that the past is still present in some respects, precisely because the law of continuity shows how each moment is linked to (blended with) each other. The present is especially rich in this sense because it is ". . . half past and half to come" [CP 6.126 & EP 1.322]. We noted in a previous chapter that Peirce's view of time combines the concepts of continuity and asymmetry. Time is a continuum in which the present is the 'place' for the continuing relevance of the past and the goads of the future. At the same time, the three modes of time are modally distinct and have different ontological features. The future is richer than the present in the special sense that it is more open to possibility. Yet the past is richer than the future in the special sense that it is the domain of attained feelings. As an element or event from the past becomes more remote from the present, its efficacy does fade (Peirce gives the example of his memory of the color red in a Cardinal's robe that fades with each passing year).

The past is thus efficacious in the present and is not really past, if by "past" is meant without any operation on the present or the future. The advantage of the principle of continuity is that it keeps the past fully alive in the present and denies that there are any absolute breaks in time's flow. Peirce makes it clear that spatial conceptions of time can cloud the issue and make it look as if time is composed of discrete instances. The connection between time and feeling is evocative in this context. Both realities illuminate the functioning of continuity. Yet feeling is even more basic than time. The reason for this is clear. Feeling has both a temporal and spatial dimension. More important, feeling is the most basic underlying structure of relation in the universe. Given Peirce's panpsychism it follows that something mental must be the locus of all forms of relation. Of all things mental, feeling is that which is most likely to spread and to form into webs of connection. Even in his early papers, Peirce refused to confine thought to finite human minds. It should certainly come as no surprise that he gave feeling the same sort of metaphysical privilege.

Feeling is thus spatial, temporal, and relational. It is the ultimate manifestation of the principle or law of continuity. The Cartesian tradition denied the correlation of feeling with space, preferring instead to bifurcate the world into nonextended versus extended substance. Nonextended substance, of which feeling would be an instance, could have no spatial predicates of any kind. For a Cartesian it makes no sense to find the spatial parameters for a thought or a feeling. Peirce's semiotic theory had already made it clear that all thought is in signs and that all signs are embodied in some sense. Hence it follows that all thought is embodied and in some sense spatial. The logic follows for feeling:

> Whatever there is in the whole phenomenon [an excitation in a "gob of protoplasm"] to make us think there is feeling in such a mass of protoplasm—*feeling*, but plainly no *personality*—goes logically to show that feeling has a subjective, or substantial, spatial extension, as the excited state has. This is, no doubt, a difficult idea to seize, for the reason that it is a subjective, not an objective extension. It is not that we have a feeling of bigness; though Professor James, perhaps rightly, teaches that we have. It is that the feeling, as the subject of inhesion, is big. [CP 6.133 & EP 1.324]

Even the simple protoplasm, as we saw in "A Guess at the Riddle," can be the locus of spatially extended feeling. Feeling prevails whenever there is any relation between one protomind (that is, prehuman mind) and another. Peirce never took seriously the Cartesian concern over the existence of other minds. Minds are already connected through feeling and there is no need for any 'explanation' of how one mind gets to know another (or know that the other mind exists). When any mind, no matter how primitive, has a feeling, that feeling will be as 'big' as its intended object. This anti-Cartesian conception of the size of feelings is of a piece with the concept that each feeling is connected with earlier and later ones through infinitesimal steps. These steps are not exclusively spatial, but they often have spatial manifestations, especially in the domain of feeling.

The 'content' of mind is ideas. Of course, ideas are no longer seen to be discrete sense data or atomic units of sensation. If perceptual judgments are inferences involving unconscious acts of predication, it should be clear that ideas are always and already general. This generality links the concept of idea to that of feeling:

> Three elements go to make up an idea. The first is its intrinsic quality as a feeling. The second is the energy with which it affects other ideas, an energy which is infinite in the here-and-nowness of immediate sensation, finite and relative in the recency of the past. The third element is the tendency of an idea to bring along other ideas with it. [CP 6.135 & EP 1.325]

The three categories are also present here. The quality of feeling in the idea is a preconceptual general possibility for the idea (firstness). The energy of the idea is its secondness, its here-and-nowness that makes it finite and relative to a specific past continuum. Finally, there is the larger generalizing tendency of the idea to form into series (semiotic series in the human order and virtually semiotic series in the prehuman orders). Ideas can be seen as concresced moments within the life of feeling. They have a dynamism and a relational power that make them agents for evolutionary growth and transformation. Hume failed to move past a passive and hopelessly anthropocentric conception of ideas, thus confining them to a fragmented personal 'identity.' Peirce dynamized the empiricist conception and located it within a much richer metaphysics.

The law of mind being laid out, it is necessary to make some observations concerning the status of personality in the world. The deepest and most primitive layers of feeling are prepersonal. Only in beings capable of self-consciousness and self-control is it possible to speak of personality as a distinct reality in its own right. How does Peirce move from ideas and feeling, undergirded by the principle of synechism, to the nature of personality? This transition is one of the most important in Peirce and harks back to our analysis of the self in chapter 2. What exactly is personality? Is it some special new fact that is added to the universe or is it a rearrangement of previous facts? Peirce opts for the latter view. He argues that ". . . personality is some kind of coördination or connection of ideas" [CP 6.155 & EP 1.331]. That is, a personality comes into being when mental ideas take on a special type of configuration.

This configuration is made possible by self-control and takes place across time. There is no such thing as a nontemporal personality. As fully temporal, the human personality is an emergent and fragile configuration that must be nurtured against the forces of decay and inertia. Peirce makes it clear that the existence of personality is made possible by special types of coordination and teleology:

> But the word coördination implies somewhat more than this; it implies a teleological harmony in ideas, and in the case of personality this teleology is more than a mere purposive pursuit of a predeterminate end; it is a developmental teleology. This is personal character. A general idea, living and conscious now, it is already determinative of acts in the future to an extent to which it is not now conscious. [CP 6.156 & EP 1.331]

We have noted previously Peirce's reconstruction of the concept of teleology. By rejecting the static Greek concept of an inborn and unchanging entelechy, Peirce was able to correlate purpose more intimately with an open future. He notes that the concept of personality requires that of an open future and this future can only remain open if teleological structures are amenable to self-control and self-development. A mind becomes a personality when it gains the power to reshape its own goals through self-control and a self-image that points toward the future. These developmental teleological structures are concresced in unconscious general ideas that will become manifest in consciousness at the appropriate time. Peirce's concept of "developmental teleology" represents a singular advance upon previous conceptions and put him in a position to redefine the self and to provide a conception of evolution that avoided the either/or of Lamarck versus Darwin. This is not to say that his third option, which reintroduces a modified conception of purpose, will satisfy contemporary neo-Darwinists, but that it is a novel and intriguing possibility that requires further exploration by the philosophical community.

Peirce brings "The Law of Mind" to a conclusion by throwing out even more general hints about the status of personality in the universe. His basic conception is that personality emerges developmentally from prepersonal feelings. When the ideas of mind become coordinated into a special self-aware integrity, personality emerges as a new quality in the world. But it is important to note that this new quality is not totally new insofar as it is prefigured in all of its antecedent feelings and ideas. It is really more of a transfiguration of the prepersonal. The same logic seems to apply to God. As we noted earlier, Peirce consciously adopted an anthropomorphic conception of the universe. If the universe is not exactly a person, it is at least a place in which the main features of personality are manifest, with particular intensity as we move from the less to the more complex evolutionary orders. God is in some sense at the 'top' of these orders and is thus the paradigmatic expression of personality. As we will see toward the end of this chapter, the plot is much thicker and Peirce hints about a prepersonal and irrational ground underneath God.

Until that possibility becomes clearer, we can confine ourselves to the more traditional aspect of Peirce's philosophical theology. In this essay he still wants to see God as the JudeoChristian creator of the world who is itself a full personality:

> . . . a genuine evolutionary philosophy, that is, one that makes the principle of growth a primordial element of the universe, is so far from being antagonistic to the idea of a personal creator that it is really inseparable from that idea; while a necessitarian religion is in an altogether false position and is destined to become disintegrated. But a pseudo-evolutionism which enthrones mechanical law above the principle of growth is at once scientifically unsatisfactory, as giving no possible hint of how the universe has come about, and hostile to all hopes of personal relations to God. [CP 6.157 & EP 1.331]

There is thus a correlation between the belief in a personal creator and the denial of necessitarianism. A personal creator can only prevail in a universe that manifests developmental teleology. This follows from the fact that personality and an open future can only obtain together. The intriguing question remains: does God, as the ultimate personality, manifest developmental teleological structures, and thus an open future? Put differently: is God's future as open, as undetermined, as ours? If so, what is God's future open to? Is there something 'greater' than God that provides God with possibilities or even potencies of transformation? My sense is that Peirce had the courage to open this door onto the prepersonal ground and abyss of God, but that his categories did not have the flexibility needed to open out this reality in its inner being.

Peirce asks a final question that was very much on the mind of his generation. Does telepathy exist? If so, what is it and how does it work? It should be remembered that both William James and Josiah Royce were deeply fascinated with this issue and spent some energy seeking an answer. Peirce remains somewhat skeptical about telepathy per se, but opens the door to ". . . other modes of continuous connection between minds other than those of time and space" [CP 6.159 & EP 1.332]. Remember that feeling is more basic than time and may even be more basic than space, even though it is manifest in spatial terms. Could the ground of feeling be prespatial? Is there a dimension of the unconscious, for example, that reaches down into a prespatial continuum? Peirce struggled to free the concept of continuity from its almost inevitable spatial connotations. Is there a unique kind of continuity in what we have called the "greater nothingness" or must continuity be manifest in 'solid' connections?

Taking a brief sidetrack for a moment, we can briefly explore how Peirce's concept of the infinitesimal might bear fruit in a way that many have not suspected, and thus show us how the prespatial can be operative. We have noted that Peirce rejects earlier conceptions of the infinitesimal that would see it as some kind of quantitative unit. Carl Hausman suggests a deeper possibility that casts light on just how radical Peirce's redefinition of continuity is:

> Both continuity and spontaneity are constitutive of the universe through the function of infinitesimals. These are the infinitieth possibilities that leave uniformities open to branching and the universe open to new laws. . . . Applied to pragmaticism, the synechistic conception of infinitesimals as potentialities for new continua (new laws) underlies the way spontaneity shows itself in the abductive or hypothetical innovations possible in inquiry, whereas the synechistic conception of continuity, as uniformity that contains infinitesimals, shows itself in the laws that hypotheses lead inquirers to discover and construct.[4]

Infinitesimals are not so much discrete units as they are potencies that compel continua into being, while, ironically, opening out forms of novelty and chance. The ontological status of the infinitesimal is unique. It is neither an order within the world nor is it pure nothingness. I suggest that the infinitesimal is a kind of ontological link between the depth dimension of nature (the greater nothingness) and the manifest world of phenomena. Hausman has probed into the true depth logic of the infinitesimal and shown how it is related to concrete forms of inquiry. The pragmaticist must have some goad outside of method to keep the world open. Pragmaticism is the method of methods that understands how infinitesimals, as potencies, give birth to both law and chance. The infinitesimal is thus on the cusp between pure diversification and general law. It is the ultimate ontological bridge between nothingness and thirdness. We cannot find an infinitesimal, if by "find" is meant that we isolate it as an object of inquiry. However, we can feel the pulsations of infinitesimals whenever we see continua grow and, at the same time, allow for diversity.

Infinitesimals are not specific determinations but ". . . the conditions for determinations," and yet also ". . . the locus of tychistic possibility—of the spark of evolutionary development."[5] Yet these conditions are not transcendental in Kant's sense, but fully constitutive of nature and its orders. A given infinitesimal, then, is a condition or a potency that makes determination possible. But all growth must also come from the infinitesimals that allow for, even compel, creative breaks within continua. A given continuum is thus a product of ontologically 'deeper' infinitesimals that condition what is to emerge into the world of interaction.

We can conclude from this that infinitesimals are in some sense prespatial and thus the true ground for the creation of spatial structures. In the case of time, for example, Peirce argues that it is a continuum that can only be broken into instances by an act of prescinding, an act that essentially distorts the true nature of time. Time in its essence is not a function of space. To spatialize time is to veil the prespatial infinitesimals from which time comes. Feeling, as the most basic manifestation of continuity in the world, is spatial in its expression, but like time, comes from the prespatial conditions for determination; namely, the infinitesimals.

The ontology of infinitesimals is parallel to the ontology of atoms. In the fourth paper in *The Monist* series, "Man's Glassy Essence" (1892), Peirce reworks molecular theory so that he can find a new correlation between the domains of the psychical and the physical. His redefinition of the atom enables him to break free from physical or material images and to show how molecular interaction is actually funded with mentality. This is not to say that an atom is an infinitesimal, but only that it has a similar role to play in the creation and maintenance of the world of manifest phenomena. Like the infinitesimal, the atom is not so much a spatial mass as it is a sphere of energy or power awaiting its full relational presence amid other atoms. The infinitesimal is, of course, preatomic in the sense that it is not an actual sphere of efficacy.

Peirce's anti-Cartesianism is not confined to his criticisms of modernist epistemology, but flowers even more dramatically in his panpsychism. Knowing full well that it is one thing to merely wish to overcome the split between extended and nonextended substance, and another to show how the world actually obtains as a continuum that cannot be so divided, Peirce plunges into molecular physics so that he can generate a coherent theory of molecular interaction on panpsychist grounds. In particular, he takes the case of protoplasm as his paradigmatic expression of a substance that seems to stand right in the heart of the old organic/inorganic divide. He finds far more going on in the world of protoplasm than others have seen and uses these insights and claims to advance further theories about the human process.

Before redefining protoplasm, he reshapes atomic theory to better correspond to his own metaphysical commitments. An atom is not some kind of impenetrable mass-point, any more than it is a hard surface with a specific spatial configuration: ". . . we have no logical right to suppose that absolute impenetrability, or the exclusive occupancy of space, belongs to molecules or atoms" [CP 6.242 & EP 1.335–336]. Spatial images are inappropriate on the deepest levels of analysis, whether we are dealing with infinitesimals or with atoms and their corresponding molecular structures. Harking back to the Jesuit natural philosopher Boscovich (1711–1787), whose novel atomic theories represent an alternative to the spatial view, Peirce insists that atoms are centers of energy: "In short, we are logically bound to adopt the Boscovichian idea that an atom is simply a distribution of component potential energy throughout space (this distribution being absolutely rigid) combined with inertia" [CP 6.242 & EP 1.336]. The energy of the atom, while having spatial parameters, is not confined to any given configuration. We can conclude that for Peirce an atom is a permeable center of energy that has deep relational connections with surrounding atoms. Put differently, an atom is a locus for intersecting energies.

Once we have transformed atomic theory we can move on to larger molecular units. Peirce retained a fascination for simple protoplasmic forms and their living features. The protoplasm exhibits all of the features essential to the panpsychist conception of the world. In particular, the protoplasm can grow, reproduce, take on habits, and, most strikingly, feel:

> It is that the protoplasm feels. We have no direct evidence that this is true of protoplasm universally, and certainly some kinds feel far more than others. But there is a fair analogical inference that all protoplasm feels. It not only feels but exercises all of the functions of mind. [CP 6.255 & EP 1.343]

The functions of mind referred to here seem to be those pertaining to the growth of feeling and the coordination of habits into new and more complex integrities. The protoplasm interacts with its surroundings and lets its outer world become part of its inner world of feeling. There are no absolute boundaries in any molecular structure, especially one that shows growth and habit. The seemingly simple protoplasm is a highly complex sphere of mental interaction that lets its environment become part of its internal development.

Habits are never exact but must adapt to complex and changing circumstances. The domain of habits lies between the two extremes of the "chance-medley of chaos" and "the cosmos of order and law" [CP 6.262 & EP 1.347]. The world attains the order that it has through general habits. Yet there is an interesting link between habit and feeling. Insofar as a given habit remains undisturbed there is less feeling. Yet when a habit is broken up by chance or novelty, that increased chaos brings about an intensification in feeling. It follows that more complex organisms have more complex habits, and in turn, risk more irruptions. Consequently, there is an increase in the amount or intensity of feeling as we ascend the organic ladder of being. The human process is the most feeling intensive in the known universe (with the exception of God) and the most vulnerable to a transformation of habit. However, there is a continuum linking the feelings and habits of the protoplasm with the feelings and habits of the human self.

Another way to rethink the so-called subject/object divide is through a perspectival shift between inner and outer. Peirce's redefinition of molecular and atomic theory represents one strategy used to efface the difference between subjective and objective orders. The second move, perhaps best called a hermeneutic inversion, shows how we can think differently depending upon whether we take an external or an internal view of a given phenomenon:

> Viewing a thing from the outside, considering its relations of action and reaction with other things, it appears as matter. Viewing it from the inside, looking at its immediate character as feeling, it appears as consciousness. These two views are combined when we remember that mechanical laws are nothing but acquired habits, like all the regularities of mind, including the tendency to take habits, itself; and that this action of habit is nothing but generalization, and generalization is nothing but the spreading of feelings. [CP 6.268 & EP 1.349]

The external view focuses on how a thing finds itself in causal interaction with other realities. It acts on other things and in turn reacts to their action. Yet an internal gaze (insofar as we can concretize such a prospect) shows that the thing is a domain of generalized and generalizing feelings. Both views are valid, but each alone gives only one half of the story.

The conjunction of external action/reaction and internal feeling reaches its culmination in the human process. The metaphor of our "glassy essence" was discussed in chapter 2. There we noted that it contrasts with Peirce's image of the bottomless lake in which the self contains an unconscious depth that cannot be fathomed. The social aspect of our glassy essence comes to the fore at the conclusion of this 1892 essay. The individual self is a confluence of ideas and feelings, galvanized by self-consciousness, and unified in a general idea. A person is ". . . only a particular kind of general idea" [CP 6.270 & EP 1.350]. But this general idea has a center that is manifest in self-control and the "unified living feeling" [CP 6.270 & EP 1.350] that makes the person unique. Where does the social dimension come in?

We are always and already fully social and our various forms of interaction are supported by a depth structure of sympathetic feeling. Peirce cites the example of a recent gathering of thirty thousand young members of the society for Christian Endeavor who met in New York City. Their gathering manifested a "mysterious diffusion of sweetness and light" [CP 6.271 & EP 1.350] that could only be explained on panpsychist grounds. The social unit of this particular group could not be a mere aggregate but must actually be a kind of social organism in which each member communicates with each other through an immediate bond of feeling. Peirce chides psychical researchers for looking for telepathy when they should be examining the "corporate personality" that is manifest in all significant social gatherings.

It is significant that Peirce brings this fourth essay in *The Monist* series to a conclusion with a strong affirmation of the centrality of sympathy and the group mind. One of the implications of his reworking of the concepts of the infinitesimal and the atom is that the doctrine of synechism has the subtlety to cross over the divide between fact and value. The facts of time and feeling are direct evidence of continuity. Yet it also follows that the values of ethics (both self-control and the aesthetic core of ethics manifest in the *summum bonum*) manifest a continuum between and among selves. Sympathy is not so much a chosen mental stance as it is an ontological structure. The self is what it is because of its permeability to other selves. This ontological core of value shows us that the universe is essentially friendly to the human process and that the true essence of reality is evolutionary love.

Divine Love and Divine Growth

In the fifth and final essay of *The Monist* series, "Evolutionary Love" (1893), Peirce links his theory of sympathy to his own reconstructed theory of evolution. The essay is unusual in that it gives some indication of Peirce's social philosophy and ties his theory of human forms of community to evolution. It represents a curious blend of moral outrage and conceptual boldness. In particular, Peirce takes the entire nineteenth century to task for its obsession with economic theory and with what he calls the "gospel of greed." His own revisionist theory of evolution is meant to provide an alternative to the greed philosophy that will, at the same time, show the convergence of science and theology around the issue of the purpose of evolution.

Peirce defines his own position in terms of the Gospel of John in the Christian New Testament. He argues that the essence of the world must be divine love and that this love is manifest throughout the orders of creation. The English language is somewhat impoverished compared to the Greek because it has only one word for something that has several manifestations. The Greek term *eros* is not appropriate because it connotes the love of the lower for what is higher. Peirce does not deal with the Greek concept of *philia* which deals with what could be called love of neighbor (although he certainly talks about this *type* of love). The only term that makes sense in his cosmology is *agape*, which tends to connote the love of God for what is inferior and, by definition, unworthy of love. The universe manifests *agape* throughout the evolutionary orders. The self comes into its own when it responds to the presence of this divine love.

Peirce's cosmology is dynamic and the operation of love in the world manifests this inner and outer dynamism: "The movement of love is circular, at one and the same impulse projecting creations into independency and drawing them into harmony" [CP 6.288 & EP 1.353]. This language of projection and return points to neo-Platonism, in which all of the created world is an emanation from the One that manifests itself not through a specific creative act but through a sheer overflow into the 'stained' world of space and time. Peirce never really decided between an orthodox Christian sense of *creatio ex nihilo* and a neo-Platonic sense of the emanation of the world from its hidden ground. His indecision betrays something more fundamental lying unsaid at the heart of his vision. The relation between the world and God is not resolved in Peirce's mature cosmology, but this failure actually holds open the door to a radical conception of God that is only now beginning to assume some clarity. We will postpone comment on this issue until the next chapter.

The universe manifests growth and this growth is only possible because of the presence of the dialectic of chance and law. Underlying this dialectic is cosmic love, which nurtures all growth in the world.

The universe is the 'place' where love works out its inner dynamism. We fail to see this love because we are trapped in the greed philosophy that sees all interaction in terms of self-love and the struggle for survival. Peirce ties Darwin to the general prejudice of the age and insists that *The Origin of Species* (1859) is but one more manifestation of the gospel of greed. He makes the rather strange claim that the obsession with philosophies of greed and cruelty comes from the fact that the age lives under the influence of anesthetic, both in the literal medical sense, and in the more general cultural sense. Because pain has been greatly reduced, there is a kind of perverse longing for a philosophy that shows the intrinsic painfulness of the world. The Darwinian theory of evolution plays into the hands of the reigning prejudice and its underlying longing.

Some of Peirce's formulations are unfortunate. His admiration for Darwin in other contexts gives way to a kind of superficial contrast that clouds his appreciation for what Darwin had accomplished. The contrast is that between the gospel of greed and the gospel of love:

> The *Origin of Species* of Darwin merely extends politico-economical views of progress to the entire realm of animal and vegetable life. . . . As Darwin puts it in his title-page, it is the struggle for existence; and he should have added for his motto: Every individual for himself, and the Devil take the hindmost! Jesus, in his sermon on the Mount, expressed a different opinion. [CP 6.293 & EP 1.357]

Needless to say, the biblical picture of Jesus is far more complex than Peirce indicates, not to mention the fact that the Darwinian perspective is not a simplistic defense of a kind of radical individualism and greed philosophy. By now, the differences between Darwin himself and the later social Darwinists has become clear to the average student of evolutionary theory. Put in its best light, what Peirce finds missing in the Darwinian/chance view of evolution is a kind of moral sympathy linking one organism with another. The Darwinian view lacks the social impulse that alone can quicken and reinforce the agapastic powers of the world.

We have noted in other contexts Peirce's strong commitment to critical common-sensism. This natural epistemological ballast stabilizes our knowledge transactions and keeps habits from sinking into endless self-doubt and reflexivity. The moral corollary to critical common sense is what Peirce here calls the "sensible heart." This sensible heart has a kind of moral insight into the social structure of the world. The agapastic theory of evolution is the only one that speaks directly to the sensible heart. The agapastic theory is anti-Darwinian in the sense that it stresses cooperation and love over natural selection and reproductive success.

As in his earlier essay in this series, "The Architecture of Theories," he contrasts three theories of evolution. The Darwinian stresses chance (random variation in the genetic material). Contrasted to this is a necessitarian position that stresses law and mechanical unfolding. The third view is his own agapastic conception that transforms aspects of Lamarck; in particular, the emphasis on the transmission of acquired characteristics. He gives a precise summary of the three views:

> Three modes of evolution have thus been brought before us; evolution by fortuitous variation, evolution by mechanical necessity, and evolution by creative love. We may term them *tychastic* evolution, or *tychasm*, *anancastic* evolution, or *anancasm*, and *agapastic* evolution, or *agapasm*. The doctrines which represent these as severally of principle importance we may term *tychasticism*, *anancasticism*, and *agapasticism*. [CP 6.302 & EP 1.362]

The first form of evolution, the Darwinian, fails to manifest purpose but does allow for chance variations in the transmission of characteristics from parent to offspring. The second form of evolution, the necessitarian, moves forward without the same use of variation and, as in the first form, fails to manifest purpose. The cataclysmic theory, touched on earlier, turns out to be a type of anancasticism in that it works through an external necessity to transform evolutionary structures. The third form of evolution actually includes elements of the first two but adds the key elements of purpose and sympathy (giving birth to the group mind).

Hegel is cited as the premier exemplar of anancasticism in that his philosophy shows a kind of necessitarian dialectic moving from one stage to the next without any true developmental teleology. Yet, Peirce's continual ambivalence about Hegel surfaces again when he indicates that Hegel brought philosophy to the threshold of the agapastic view. The agapastic conception of evolution shows how all dialectics evidence purpose while admitting chance. The Darwinian and necessitarian views are degenerate cases of agapasm. They point in the direction of evolutionary love but go only so far toward synechism and a sense of the continuity of feeling.

The term "advance" is crucial here. The two nonagapastic views of evolution fail to show that there is any real advance in evolution. For the Darwinian, whatever obtains in the present is simply whatever survived. It does not represent an advance or the triumph of purpose.

For the necessitarian, the current biological configurations are simply the result of mechanistic forces that unfolded according to the laws of efficient cause. To the agapist, however, there is genuine advance in all forms of evolution, whether organic or inorganic. This advance is a result of sympathy:

> In genuine agapasm, on the other hand, advance takes place by virtue of a positive sympathy among the created springing from continuity of mind. This is the idea which tychasticism knows not how to manage. [CP 6.304 & EP 1.362]

Here we see how Peirce's underlying panpsychism supports his critique of the tychastic or Darwinian view. If the universe is little more than dead matter, then it would follow that evolution cannot be a function of mind or sympathy and that the principle of synechism is a false one. The ontological commitment to the ubiquity of mind supports the various forms of continuity manifest in the world. Evolutionary love is a dramatic expression of synechism in that it is the true goad to organic growth. Evolution is quickened when one mind can communicate with another, not through sign series alone, but through a direct sympathy that enhances the scope and depth of the group mind. As the group mind grows in power, the individual members can acquire more traits that can be passed on to new members of the community.

Of course, the difficulty remains that of all neo-Lamarckian frameworks; namely, how to explain the mechanism by which new traits are actually passed on to offspring. Peirce does not inform us about this mechanism, preferring instead to speak of sympathy or the "immediate attraction for the idea itself" [CP 6.307 & EP 1.364]. It is as if ideas function to advance evolution by presenting alternative habits or generals that attract by their own internal appeal. Yet Peirce seems to confuse the structures of evolution per se with the processes of human thought. That is, human thought can proceed along the lines of random variation, necessity, or agapastic growth. A tychastic form of thinking takes place whenever the mind is invaded with sudden alien thoughts that represent new trajectories for thinking. The anancastic form of thinking takes place whenever the mind follows the principles of deductive or inductive logic. The agapastic form of thinking takes place whenever the mind is attracted to a larger, more encompassing idea that also manifests purpose.

This triadic view of thinking seems appropriate enough in its own terms. But it is unclear how it can be read back into the evolutionary process. Peirce seems to be moving from methodology, or an analysis of mind, toward the structures of evolution. Of course, he can do so because of his panpsychism. Nature is itself a mental process, at least via analogy, and manifests its own versions of tycastic, anancastic, and agapastic forms of thinking. Were Peirce to drop his panpsychism, his neo-Lamarckian view of evolution would have no legs to stand on.

Looking specifically at his views on thought, we can see how the agapastic form certainly enhances mental life by bringing about a unification of the mind under the guiding thread of purpose. If the mind only functioned by chance or by necessity, it would not be able to survive in a world that has a deeper directionality. Love is the true goad for mental growth:

> The agapastic development of thought should, if it exists, be distinguished by its purposive character, this purpose being the development of an idea. We should have a direct agapic or sympathetic comprehension and recognition of it by virtue of the continuity of thought. [CP 6.315 & EP 1.369]

Since the universe manifests a developmental teleology, it follows that the human mind, as the most centered sign system in the known universe, should also work according to the growth of sympathetic purposes. Will evolution be quickened in a dramatic way because of the entrance of human minds on the cosmic scene? Peirce does not make the same bold claims in this direction as the twentieth-century evolutionary thinker Teilhard de Chardin (for whom evolution is now moving past the biological sphere into the realm of attained mind—the "noosphere"), but he does at least hint that evolution is manifesting more and more instances of concrete purpose with each stage of its advance. Needless to say, the concept of "advance" is controversial enough in its own right, without bringing in the daring claim that the human process is moving evolution into a final transfiguration.

Be that as it may, evolutionary love is more basic than brute causality in guiding evolution toward some kind of convergence in the infinite long run (the "would be"). At the conclusion of this series of papers in *The Monist*, Peirce leaves us with a vast cosmology that tells us about the whence and whither of the universe as a whole, and informs us about our own role within it as moral beings dedicated to the spread of sympathy and positive communal feeling. He has attacked necessitarianism, defined the group mind, secured a place for real chance, opened the door to a radical new conception of God, shown the ubiquity of continuity, and replaced the Darwinian view of evolution with an astonishing view of evolutionary love. These various views are all consistent with each other and point to the richness of Peirce's late cosmology. While his reconstruction of evolutionary theory will fail to convince most people, his conception of continuity and its correlation to the "gospel of love" may find a place in metaphysical analyses of nature. In particular, his ambivalence about the nature of God and the God/world transaction stretches philosophical theology beyond its current limits. We will conclude our exposition of Peirce with some more observations about what he *did* manage to say about God.

The five papers just discussed mention God more or less indirectly in the context of other discussions. Yet Peirce did put down his more systematic reflections in other places. In the first chapter we examined his 1908 essay "A Neglected Argument for the Reality of God," which was more concerned with method than with an analysis of the divine natures.[6] He has much more to say about God per se in a ca. 1906 manuscript entitled "Answers to Questions Concerning My Belief in God," in which he works through some of the traditional conceptions of God in order to compare and contrast them with his own views. He poses a number of questions to himself that he then proceeds to answer. We must weave a larger fabric out of these fragments, but we can gain access to the emergent conception of the divine that was part of Peirce's larger cosmological speculations.

As is often the case, Peirce begins his reflections with considerations of methodology and language. He notes that the word "God" belongs to the vernacular and, like all such words, is somewhat vague. More precise terms, like "Supreme Being," which seem to advance our understanding, merely show the conceptual poverty of certain technical terms when they attempt to replace the richness and proper vagueness of the vernacular. Consequently, the term "God" is quite appropriate, precisely because it leaves room for creative elaboration and genuine ambiguity. It must be remembered that the concept of vagueness is in the honorific category for Peirce. The philosophical theologian must honor the term that has for centuries guided critical common sense.

The vague belief in God is fairly universal. Those who claim to doubt the reality of God are actually talking about a more abstract and less vague concept—a concept that may be ripe for critique because of its artificial precision. Peirce makes it clear that he is not talking of the "existence" of God, but of God's reality. The category of existence is confined to what reacts in the world (secondness), while the category of reality is correlated to the generals that are manifestations of reason. The ability of science to make valid predictions of the future provides evidence that we do have some insight into the reasonableness of the universe, and, by implication, the reasonable mind of God. For Peirce, we can catch a "fragment" of God's thoughts whenever we make valid predictions.

Hence the belief in the reality of God is an instinctual belief: "All the instinctive beliefs, I notice, are vague" [CP 6.499]. This vague instinctive belief needs to be refined on its own terms so that we can say something meaningful about the divine life and its patterns of growth. Peirce reminds us that God is not only real, but partakes of generality. The real is "that which holds its characters" [CP 6.495] across time and place. However, these real and general characters evolve from a less to a more determinate state so that they can be likened to evolutionary Platonic forms.

Peirce's developmental Platonism can be seen most clearly when he struggles to redefine the traditional concept of *creatio ex nihilo*, which affirms that God, as the highest being, created the world out of pure nothingness by a free act of will. The creation came into being at a specific time (although, as Augustine argued, time itself sprang into being with the creation of the universe), and the current configuration of things bears the marks of the original creation. Peirce's daring reconstruction challenges the concept of original creation and edges toward the neo-Platonic sense of emanation:

> "Do you believe this Supreme Being to have been the creator of the universe?" Not so much *to have been* as to be now creating the universe, . . . I am inclined to think (though I admit that there is no necessity of taking that view) that the process of creation has been going on for an infinite time in the past, and further, during *all* past time, and further, that past time had no definite beginning, yet came about by a process which in a generalized sense, of which we cannot *easily* get much idea, was a development. . . . I think that we must regard Creative Activity as an inseparable attribute of God. [CP 6.505 and 6.506]

God continues to create anew with each passing moment. There is a sense in which Peirce's concept of continuity affects his understanding of creation. The traditional view stresses a radical break between the 'period' prior to the primal act of creation and the created world in time (which is itself marked by a Fall from perfection). The Peircean view seems to be that there is a direct and unbroken continuum linking God's continual creative activity with the evolving orders of the world. Put in different terms, God continues to act within and between the orders of the world to insure that creative advance takes place in evolution. The pragmaticist must reject the doctrine of *creatio ex nihilo* because it makes it impossible to understand the continuing presence of evolutionary love. More importantly, it is a violation of the principle of synechism.

The world of creation manifests Platonic forms. These forms emerge from less determinate antecedent conditions. If, following Augustine, Peirce wishes to locate these forms in the mind of God, it follows that the mind of God must evolve along with the forms that are housed in that mind. In an 1898 manuscript, "The Logic of Continuity," Peirce sheds further light on the ontology underlying his developmental teleology:

> The evolutionary process is, therefore, not a mere evolution of the *existing universe*, but rather a process by which the very Platonic forms themselves have become or are becoming developed. . . .The evolution of forms begins or, at any rate, has for an early stage of it, a vague potentiality; and that either is or is followed by a continuum of forms having a multitude of dimensions too great for the individual dimensions to be distinct. It must be by a contraction of the vagueness of that potentiality of everything in general, but of nothing in particular, that the world of forms comes about. [CP 6.194 and 6.196]

It follows that God cannot have a preestablished world of Platonic forms in mind that can be used as archetypes in creating the general structures of the world. The mind of God, insofar as it is filled with attained forms, is as much a product of evolution as anything else. I am not persuaded that Peirce grasped the full radicality of his protoprocess view, but he certainly laid the foundation for a radical critique of orthodox philosophical theology.

The forms, then, emerge from the potentialities (potencies) of the universe and gain their distinctness when the primal vagueness of nothingness (what we have called the greater nothingness) contracts into something more and more particular. Each form is a particularization of the nothingness, yet, of course, attains the form of generality. Developmental Platonism puts the fulfillment of forms in the would be. Consequently, God must belong to the power of the would be and manifest a restlessness that can only come from the sense of incompletion.

Returning to "Answers to Questions Concerning My Belief in God," we see Peirce working through some of the other more traditional problems associated with philosophical theology. We have seen that his God, however vague, is, at least in the more precise mode of the Supreme Being, a coevolving creative power that must wait for the

Platonic forms to evolve on their own right. Does this mean that God is also partially shaped by the evolving universe? What inner logic determines the movement from greater nothingness (the potencies) to lesser nothingness (the possibilities) to the nascent world of generals (the forms)? Is God the agency within or behind this process, or is God too a product of this process? It is difficult to answer these inter-related questions because Peirce does not sense their urgency and thus fails to probe into some of the implications of his perspective. However, the general drift of his categorial scheme is toward a recognition of God's finite, fragmented, and evolving quality. It is as if God will only fully appear, both to us and in itself, at the end of history (cf. CP 1.362 & EP 1.251). Until that time, God remains underway toward its full plenitude in which the Platonic forms will become complete.

What is God's purpose for the universe? Peirce downplays the concept of divine majesty, which would entail that the purpose of the world and its creatures is to worship its creator. Instead, he makes a case for human autonomy, arguing that God is concerned with establishing independent creatures who do not seek to become part of an all-absorbing divine presence:

> In general, God is perpetually creating us, that is developing our real manhood, our spiritual reality. Like a good teacher, He is engaged in detaching us from a False dependency upon Him. [CP 6.507]

Using the language of emanation, we see that God continues to be the originating ground of our individual and collective existence, but that we are also being urged into an autonomous position in which we no longer need this direct connection with the divine energy. Is secondness part of God's pedagogy? How are we removed from the womb of firstness if not through the shocks of secondness and the lure of thirdness? Peirce hints that he has found a solution to the problem of evil in this notion that we are compelled into autonomy, thus taking on responsibility for the world's evils. Yet, on a deeper level, the evils associated with secondness are themselves part of a larger divine plan that would have us encounter evil precisely so that we can become free from a false identity with God.

Peirce continues his reflection by posing the traditional questions about divine omniscience, omnipotence, infallibility, etc. His overall conclusion is that our knowledge of God is so vague that it is impossible to gain full clarity on these issues. In each case we can answer the question: yes, in a sense. But the move toward clarification of this "yes" is fraught with difficulty. The same holds for the doctrine of miracles. We have no a priori reason for rejecting the possibility, but we do not have strong evidence either. In the end, we can say very little about God other than to make some attempts to link God to the general facts of cosmology.

Michael Raposa argues that Peirce locates belief in God in the unconscious and, in a refinement, in our instinctive beliefs. Such unconscious and/or instinctive beliefs are not always amenable to precise analysis. Philosophical architectonic must remain incomplete when it turns its energies to the most basic and primal realities. Of course, vagueness has a certain positive value for Peirce in that it can facilitate action in the world precisely because it does not give too narrow or 'clear' a portrayal of its object(s). For Raposa, we can clearly reject the notion that Peirce is a pantheist (i.e., someone who simply equates God with the world, such that there is no dimension of God left unentangled with the world that could transcend nature). At the other extreme, Peirce is clearly not a straight theist (i.e., someone who would so emphasize divine transcendence as to render the God/world transaction unintelligible). Peirce's position is thus a form of panentheism, which asserts that God is fully in relation to the world, but still transcends it in some basic respects. Raposa links Peirce's reconstruction of the theory of continuity with his implied panentheism:

> Nonetheless, God's relationship to individuals in the world might be roughly compared to that existing between a continuum and its topical singularities; these singularities may themselves constitute continua while still being determinate with respect to a given dimension of the embracing whole. Without wishing to belabor the mathematical underpinnings of Peirce's thought, such considerations really do illuminate his religious metaphysics. They suggest that Peirce, while definitely not a pantheist, might be properly labeled a *panentheist*, that is, one who views the world as being included in but not exhaustive of the divine reality. Such a view neither undermines the doctrine of creation nor collapses the distinction between God and the universe.[7]

Raposa is clearly correct when he sees an intimate connection between Peirce's theory of continuity and the various continua (topical singularities) that enter into the world and the inner life of God. My own reading of Peirce moves in a slightly different direction concerning the issue of creation. The greater nothingness is in some fundamental respect ontologically prior to God. There is a leap, not a smooth deductive transition, from the potencies of greater nothingness to the emergent and mobile possibilities of lesser nothingness to the continua manifest in and as the world of creation. God is as much a product of this series of leaps as is its world. I would characterize Peirce's position as that of a radicalized panentheism; specifically, what I will call an "ordinal monotheism" in which God is as much an emergent from nothingness as any other reality that partakes of secondness and thirdness. Yet there is a mysterious sense in which God is also a creative ground of the world. However, this primal creativity is most manifest in evolutionary love, rather than in some pretemporal once-and-for-all creative act.

Of course, one has to be especially careful in moving too quickly toward an 'understanding' of Peirce's doctrine of God. It is clear that he shied away from what could be called "dogmatics." His primary concern seems to be to find a tentative place for God within his cosmology. In probing into the whence and whither of the universe, Peirce was compelled to locate an evolving God within the tensions of the hidden whence and the triumphalist longings of the whither. He leaves us partially in the dark about the whence, but makes some clear affirmations about the whither. We will conclude with his thoughts about the ultimate goal of all life.

As we have seen, Peirce grounded ethics in aesthetics. If ethics tells us how we ought to think and act, thus providing a grounding norm for logic, aesthetics points to the highest good in which we are to find the true measure of our life. It remains a vexing question as to whether or not the *summum bonum* is itself an evolutionary growth or product. If it is, it is not ultimate in all respects. If the highest good is eternal and preexistent, then its ultimacy is clear. Put in another way: is God itself underway toward the *summum bonum* or can God be equated with it? My own sense is that God is an evolutionary emergent who is struggling toward a full realization of the highest good that somehow transcends it. This is of a piece with what I have called Peirce's implied developmental Platonism, which insists that all generals are evolving from an indeterminate to a more determinate state. God, as a locus of generals (in the guise of concrete reasonableness), is moving toward more and more determinateness. Yet God cannot go faster than the universe. That is, the universe of firsts, seconds, and thirds is God's body and God cannot outstrip its body. There is a sense in which the world represents a kind of ballast, keeping the divine from detaching itself from the real. God is thus embedded in nature and yet moving toward a highest good that is somehow just beyond its reach.

This conclusion might seem farfetched to those accustomed to see

Peirce in either traditional or process terms. The traditional view would simply absorb the *summum bonum* into God as one of God's attributes. The process view would be very friendly to this stress on value in the universe but would locate all value in the primordial mind of God. The alternative that I am presenting, that of an ordinal monotheism, would see God as the locus of all conditional and evolving values, but would insist that there are ultimate values that obtain in an order just beyond the divine plenitude. Peirce leaves us with enough ambiguities to open the door to this possibility. His late reflections on cosmology and evolutionary love point toward a transfigured theology in which the divine lives fully within the apagastic momentums of evolution, while still pointing toward a dimension of the world that lies on the other side of all creative advance. The whither of the world is not only locked in the mystery of the would be, but veiled from the view of the God who stands in the cleft between the ultimate nothingness and the final consummation of cosmic history. Peirce points us toward this cleft, but leaves us to contemplate this profound possibility alone.

Notes

1. Serious students of Peirce's philosophical theology must read the following two books: *Peirce's Conception of God: A Developmental Study*, by Donna M. Orange (Lubbock, TX: Institute for Studies in Pragmaticism, 1984), and *Peirce's Philosophy of Religion*, by Michael L. Raposa (Bloomington: Indiana University Press, 1989). Orange's book tilts more toward the process reading, while Raposa's tilts more toward a nonprocess account.

2. For an exhaustive study of the Peirce house ("Arisbe"), complete with photographs and architectural drawings see *Historical Structural Report: Architectural Data Section Charles S. Peirce House*, Pennsylvania, prepared by Penelope Hartshorne Batcheler (Denver, Colo.: National Park Service, 1983).

3. Michael Raposa makes a distinction between the "Absolute Mind" and "God," and sees Peirce as working through the conceptions of each in different ways. See his *Peirce's Philosophy of Religion*, pp. 35–62.

4. Carl R. Hausman, *Charles S. Peirce's Evolutionary Philosophy* (Cambridge: Cambridge University Press, 1993), pp. 190, 192.

5. Ibid., p. 188.

6. Raposa argues that Peirce rejected the argument from design, taking his cues from Hume, and that his use of the "Neglected Argument" in his 1908 essay is actually a form of the ontological argument. Orange takes the opposite position; namely, that interpretive musement points toward a modified argument from design.

7. Raposa, *Peirce's Philosophy of Religion*, p. 51.

Conclusion

Peircean Prospects

In our exposition of the philosophy of Peirce, several themes have assumed prominence. His detailed and insightful phenomenological descriptions of the categories paved the way for his mature reflections on cosmology and the divine natures. His earlier reflections on method, culminating in his portrayal of abduction and interpretive musement, moved him past the scientisms that marred the nineteenth century. The transition from pragmatism, which appeared to Peirce to be too nominalistic and dyadic, to pragmaticism, which emphasized synechism and triadic structures of knowledge, brought Peirce into the vicinity of a renewed conception of the extrahuman orders and their intrinsic semiotic properties. His profound semiotic theory, built on a vast architectonic of innumerable triads, opened the path to the prelinguistic and extracultural orders of sign function. At the same time, his pragmaticist semiotics transformed the world into an unlimited network of interpretants that showed how all orders are at least potentially intelligible. His transformation of semiotic anthropology dislocated the ego and made the group mind, as well as the collective unconscious, central to a transfigured sense of the human process.

In our conclusion, we will explore and radicalize four interconnected themes suggested by these innovations that promise to open up new prospects for pragmaticism. They are: interpretive musement, the archetypes (in the context of developmental Platonism), panpsychism, and the depth dimension of a self-transfiguring nature.

The culmination of Peirce's reconstruction of method is his analysis of abduction. The earlier concern with hypothesis became transformed into his concept of abduction (retroduction) proper. As noted, abduction takes a creative leap beyond the given example or case. This leap is akin to a Kantian transcendental argument in that it posits a rule for explaining what is observed. Unlike a Kantian structure, however, an abductive leap can be tested in the long run of experience. The rule created by the pragmaticist gives a causal explanation for the observed case. If deduction merely explicates what is contained in the antecedent, and induction merely gathers up class-specific features from samples, abduction transforms the very nature of thought so that novel and forceful categories can emerge that ground and support the edifice of knowledge. At the extreme edge of abduction is interpretive musement, a method that seems to be antimethodic in that it does not posit general rules or follow some kind of communal or scientific procedure.

The ultimate goal of musement is bringing the self into communion with God. There is a connection between interpretive musement and the argument from design, in that the muser comes to see the wonder and aesthetic power of the semiotic universe. God is fully semiotic and the signs of the divine are to be found throughout the innumerable orders of nature. Interpretive musement represents the fulfillment of the human process because it brings the human mind into contact with the divine mind. Michael Raposa has coined the term "theosemiotic" to denote this process by and through which the self becomes attuned to the traces of the divine sign maker in the world. Theosemiotic lies at the heart of Peirce's general semiotic theory. For Raposa:

> Universal semiosis is the mechanics, the dynamics of objective mind. In religious terms, then, it is the means by which God relates to and communicates with lesser minds. Moreover, given the fact of continuity, in one sense, semiotic is always already theosemiotic. If all of reality is continuous, then everything is potentially a sign of God's presence.[1]

It must be remembered that Peirce's God is somewhat vague in structure (at least from the standpoint of human knowledge). The "objective mind" is more delimited than God, and has direct semiotic manifestations. We have indicated that Peirce has two fundamental conceptions of God. On the one hand is the vague God of critical common sense, while on the other is the Absolute or objective Mind that seems to be more basic than God. Put in more traditional terms, we can distinguish between the God manifest more directly to the human process (God, or *der Gott*, in the language of Meister Eckhart), and the depth dimension of God (*die Gottheit*). This depth dimension is itself rooted in the greater nothingness that represents the abyss of God.

Theosemiotic lies at the heart of all forms of semiosis. Interpretive musement is the method by which we let go of more predictable abductions and hypotheses, so that we can enter into a deeper rhythm of semiosis. Abduction becomes transfigured into musement (and hence, theosemiosis) when the power of the divine is allowed to enter into the 'space' between and among signs. Peirce placed so much emphasis on thirdness and conceptual mediation that it is easy to overlook his implied commitment to an exploration of the empty spaces between signs. His concept of "ground," which we examined in chapter 3, points toward the depth structure of theosemiotics. This depth structure emerges whenever signs are allowed to point toward their whence in God's creative power and their whither in the hoped-for cosmic transfiguration.

Signs thus become open at both ends. In addition to their correlation with objects and interpretants, signs represent the body of God in nature. The universe of signs is also the universe of divine action and growth. Insofar as God is evolving, signs will participate in this evolutionary travail. Theosemiotic is the culmination of semiotics precisely because of the spiritual core at the heart of each sign.[2] At their 'bottom' signs become open to the creative origin of the world, while at their 'top' they become open to the agapastic forces of evolution. Insofar as God struggles within and against the other evolutionary orders of nature, signs will reflect this larger cosmic struggle.

Raposa acknowledges the radicality at the heart of Peirce's conception of God: ". . . God is a real continuum actually dimensionless, perfectly free and indeterminate, the primordial No-thing."[3] This dimension of God (*die Gottheit*, or greater nothingness) is not an attained body of signs, but lives as a kind of primal betweenness structure, keeping signs open and alert to the more manifest and finite dimensions of God. Signs contain and manifest traces of the greater nothingness (nature's potencies). Theosemiotics is a discipline that honors and nurtures these traces so that they may add their 'respects' to the life of signs and interpretants. Primal betweenness is a kind of nongrounded ground relation that does not add specific semiotic elements to the world so much as clear away impediments to a theonomous understanding of reality.

I have argued that Peirce was deeply religious throughout his career and that he struggled to find ways of showing the presence of the divine within the world. His nascent philosophical theology is tragically incomplete, yet its very incompletion has the kind of shock value that can pry reflection free from the grooved and obvious. Interpretive musement and theosemiotics represent Peirce's most mature response to the divine presence. There is a strong incarnational core to Peirce's semiotic theory. Not only do the three categories hunger to find a place in the realm of signs, but the divine hungers to leave its traces between and among signs. Some of these traces can be seen within given signs, while the deeper traces, those rooted in the greater nothingness, must appear in the between. Betweenness is not the same as thirdness. There is a strong sense of the irrational in Peirce's conception of God. If the manifest God of evolution is the locus of thirdness and concrete reasonableness, the depth dimension of God is located in the irrational self-othering ground (*urgrund*) of nothingness. I am persuaded that Peirce peered into this depth and came away with a transfigured understanding of the nature of the divine life. Had he sharpened his insights and let go of some of his more triumphalist elements, he might have shed further light on the depth dimension of the divine. His early commitment to the view that there is nothing that is not cognizable, hindered his efforts to gain access to the abyss of God.

Where do we go from here? There is a great "unthought" in Peirce's theosemiotic method. This unthought pertains to the tensions between the finite and evolving dimension of God and the depth dimensions rooted in the greater nothingness. God is unique among all of the realities in nature in being located on both sides of this great divide. Heidegger expresses this divide in terms of what he calls the "ontological difference." This difference is unlike other quantitative or qualitative differences within the world. It is a difference that can only be approached by a leap—since there are no analogical bridges connecting the 'halves' of this difference. For Heidegger, the terms used to denote the difference are "Being" (*das Sein*) and "beings" (*das Seiende*). In the context of a reworking of Peirce's pragmaticism, the terms to be employed are "nature naturing" (*natura naturans*) and "nature natured" (*natura naturata*). The former term refers to the elusive potencies of nature, potencies 'located' in the greater nothingness. The latter term refers to the manifest orders of the world. Heidegger's "Being" becomes "nature naturing," while his concept of "beings" becomes "nature natured."

Peirce had a preliminary grasp of the ontological difference insofar as he allowed God to have two fundamental dimensions. His failure to work out the full ontology of the divine stems, at least in part, from his overemphasis on rationality. This stress on thirdness made it difficult for him to probe into the irrational depths of nature naturing, even though he had a growing sense that these depths were lying at the heart of his cosmology. In radicalizing the Peircean legacy, we must let the shock of the ontological difference enter into the divine life.

Theosemiotic, as the core method lying at the heart of Peirce's semiotic theory, must itself enter into the momentums of the ontological difference. How does it make this transition from the seeming comforts of musement to the shock of nature naturing? The answer is already prefigured in Peirce. Insofar as musement wishes to enter into the rhythms of an aesthetically dense world, it becomes open to the semiotic structures of nature natured (the world's orders). The shock of the difference enters into theosemiotics whenever it lets go of its intraworldly participation in sign systems and feels the pull of the greater nothingness. On the other side of vagueness is a different kind of openness that flickers on the edges of critical common sense. Nature naturing enters into the movement of theosemiotics precisely at that point when musement veers away from attained signs toward the self-othering seed bed of all forms of semiosis. The greater nothingness (the Godhead/*die Gottheit*) overturns attained signs and fills them with mystery.

All of this is to say that Peirce's implied philosophical theology can be deepened and strengthened through the very method of theosemiotics that operates within interpretive musement. The method provides the way toward the proper understanding of the ontological difference. Once this occurs, several insights follow. The first is that God must be understood as having two *fundamental* dimensions. The first is the finite side correlated with the orders of the world (nature natured). This side is the side of developmental thirdness moving toward an ideal consummation in the *summum bonum*. The second is the infinite depth dimension of God correlated with nature naturing (the potencies prior to all efficacious possibility). God obtains in both dimensions. The second basic insight is that God must be both rational and irrational, but in different respects. The rational side is the easier to examine, and Peirce devoted his better energies to this task. The irrational dimension is extremely elusive precisely because it lies beyond all structures of intelligibility. Put in stronger terms, there is no thirdness in the depth dimension of the divine. The third basic insight is that God must itself be part of the tychistic structure of the world. That is, God must experience the presence of novelty and chance within its *own* nature. Divine growth is only possible where there is chance. This follows from Peirce's more general evolutionary principles where tychism works with and against synechism.

Moving to our second theme, we can ask: what is actually 'contained' in the mind of God? We have noted Peirce's developmental Platonism in which the forms are not preexistent but emergent from cosmic evolution. This is combined with an Augustinian sense that the forms are located within the mind of God. In moving Peirce's metaphysics forward, we must ask about how the forms or archetypes can be rethought along pragmaticist lines. Can the archetypes enter into a different configuration that honors the power of the not yet (would be) in Peirce's conception of inquiry?

The archetypes (a term not generally used by Peirce in this context) are located within the depth structure of the self. At the same time, they are manifest throughout the orders of the world and point to the ubiquity of thirdness. Consequently, it follows that the archetypes are especially intense manifestations of thirdness. They bring to a new level of intensity the continua of reason. In this sense they are like Hegel's concrete universals. They are general and fully incarnational. They represent centers of power and momentum that reach down into nature in its naturing. An archetype thus lives out of the power of nature's potencies while inhabiting the attained orders of the world. Yet there is a dimension of the archetype that Peirce understood far better than many contemporary thinkers. If Jung locates the archetypes in the phylogenetic past, Peirce makes the more daring move, consistent with his developmental Platonism, to locate them in the not yet of an open future.

The archetypes are thus groaning toward a transfiguration in the would be. This might seem like a strange implication to draw, but it is fully consistent with Peirce's metaphysics. If the forms exist at all, as concrescences of thirdness, then they must have a history. This history is manifest in the various stages of cosmic evolution, which has moved from the state of pure indeterminacy toward the state of manifest thirdness (the perfect crystal). If the archetypes/forms have a history, it should not be too difficult to see that they have a future. Thirds are cosmic habits. Habits are broken up and reconfigured by chance and novelty. Whenever a cosmic habit is broken open by chance, a new and more generic habit can take its place. This new habit gathers up the 'achievements' of the previous habit and transforms them to fit in with the new situation. Consequently, the new habit represents a creative advance beyond its antecedent one. We cannot predict what cosmic habits will eventually be manifest in the infinite long run. The archetypes of the self and of nature will develop along lines dictated by unforeseen circumstances.

In this sense, then, the forms are open to the power of the not yet that contains its own secrets. The archetypes are open in a radical way to possible transformations that lie beyond our available knowledge. If these developmental forms are located in the mind of God, and if God must itself evolve, can God have perfect foreknowledge? The answer seems clear. God cannot know the future of its own internal mental life because real chance can change the structures of the cosmic habits that currently prevail. Was Peirce ready to draw this implication? My suspicion is that his emphasis on the utter vagueness of ideas such as that of omniscience, was his way of acknowledging limits to divine knowledge. Is there a sense in which his tilt toward panpsychism is a way of trying to outflank some of his growing suspicions about the irrational depths of evolution and God?

Moving to our third theme, his commitment to panpsychism (the doctrine that "matter is effete mind") gave Peirce a means to establish the priority of feeling and mentality in his theory of relations. The connection between any two items in the universe is one of feeling, a feeling that has some minimal degree of mentality. Matter, when bereft of any mental aspect, only interacts through bare external causality. This externality breaks any continuum that might come to obtain in the world. Consequently, there is an intimate connection between Peirce's panpsychism and his belief in continuity. To examine the future transformations available to the panpsychist viewpoint, it is necessary to rework the parallel concept of continuity.

It is clear that Peirce linked the theory of continuity to that of panpsychism, largely because he wanted to preserve a sense of nature's vastness and its monistic structure. Rejecting all forms of Cartesian dualism, whether in epistemology, philosophical anthropology, or metaphysics, Peirce developed a conception of the world as a vast intertwined network of signs and generals, punctuated by chance. This growing and internally connected universe moves from the bare continuity of potentiality and possibility to the attained continuity of innumerable sign systems. These continua are not necessarily linked into one great chain of chains (or, more correctly, cable of cables), but seem to have their own internal branchings and subgroupings. Yet there is a strong tendency for any sign system, as the concrescence of feeling, to blend into its surrounding systems so that much more generic lines of connection can be established.

The image here is not so much that of discrete meaning packets bumping into each other, so much as it is that of a growing vine that entwines itself around any organism in its vicinity. Peirce's commitment to plenitude, which remains in a hidden dialectical tension with his sense of nothingness, compelled him to see signs as promiscuous centers of growth and intersection. Each sign system is like a climbing vine that hooks up with as much living semiotic matter as possible. The anthropocentric and anthropomorphic bias of his metaphysics, not to mention his theories of method, drove Peirce to overextend the metaphors of mentality so that he could secure a sense of the intelligibility of semiosis in the prehuman orders. But he paid too high a price for this maneuver and, against his own intent, drove pragmaticism away from the very nature that he wished to explore.

My account of Peirce has attempted to move interpretation of his work away from the currently fashionable neopragmatism that emphasizes contextual and arbitrary semiotic structures. The neopragmatic account would pry interpretants loose from their imbeddedness in nature and locate them within arbitrary and shifting cultural codes (read diachronically). Peirce's actual semiotic intent moves in the opposite direction; namely, to see nature itself as a vast semiotic network that shapes interpretants through a kind of primal secondness and thirdness (working through the built-in vector directionalities of the dynamic object). As we will see shortly, the best way to understand the depth commitments of Peirce's semiotic metaphysics is in terms of ecstatic naturalism, a perspective that he foreshadowed and helped to originate. The tension comes in precisely where his privileging of mentality threatens to undermine the naturalism lying at the heart of his vision.

Peirce made the panpsychist move because he was impressed with the ubiquity of forms of continuity in the world. He could not explain this continuity through a metaphysics of materialism or through an emphasis on efficient causality. The most important structures of continuity are purposive, hence exhibiting developmental teleological features. Purpose cannot exist without some kind of mentality. His strange neo-Lamarckian evolutionary theory resurrects purpose, but sheds no light on how purposes get integrated into the actual mechanisms of biological inheritance. The question before us is: how do we preserve the utter sovereignty of nature without moving into panpsychism and its concomitant privileging of purpose?

The shift to a developmental teleology moves us partway down the road by admitting that all purposes belong to fragmented and shifting conditions. Purposes are not preexistent entelechies merely awaiting the right conditions for their appearance. Where purposes appear at all, they must honor the forces of efficient causality and chance that surround them. But this innovation needs to be radicalized further. Peirce was far too eager to write purpose on the face of the world. In a reconstruction of his perspective it is crucial that the status of purpose be sharply limited in scope so that it is more properly seen in its semiotic role within those orders that do manifest a high degree of mentality. Very few of the known orders of the world manifest purpose, whether developmental or otherwise. Purposes do, of course, exist, and they can be fundamental to a number of the orders that we encounter. Yet their role in evolution remains deeply problematic.

Nature itself does not have an overarching purpose. We must be cautious about following Peirce in his sense of the whither of the universe. By the same token, our sense of the whence of the world must acknowledge the mystery of the greater nothingness. Nature is not a purpose of purposes, but an encompassing momentum that can tolerate the existence of some purposive semiotic systems, while providing no space for others. The same logic holds for feeling. There are relational structures in the world that are sustained by feeling, but most orders interact without this connecting bridge. Is nature the 'place' where agape is manifest? If we are prepared to acknowledge a kind of terrible grace in organic evolution, then we can use the language of agape in the context of cosmology. But there seems little warrant for doing so. Put in the strongest terms, nature is not some kind of ultimate 'something' that can bear specific traits, be they human or prehuman. Nature is the continual availability of traits, nothing more.

Panpsychism, in its desire to overcome Cartesian mind/body dualisms, says far too much about nature. Mind is as much a product of an indifferent nature as is matter. Mind is located within orders that are premental. To elevate mind to a generic category is to violate the basic insight that nature has no whatness. Innumerable 'whats' emerge from nature, and many more that we do not foresee will obviously continue to do so. But there is no reason to assume that nature is a vast pool of mind that links every 'what' together into a network of internal relations. Peirce's fascination with mathematical and logical models of continuity, and the concomitant notion of infinitesimals, blinded him to the deeper breaks within the world as a whole.

The breaks between continua are often profound, not to mention the tears within given continua. On a more basic level, there is the ultimate break separating the realms of nature natured from nature naturing. The radical reading of infinitesimals, suggested in the previous chapter, makes it possible to see how given continua emerge from infinitesimals that are not orders of relation or specific orders of relevance. There is a kind of self-fissuring within infinitesimals that breaks them open to the derived worlds of phenomena. Peirce was more concerned with the connecting power of thirdness than with the depth rhythms of the infinitesimals. Again, he turned away from the irrationalism lying within his cosmology and philosophical theology. This flight from his own most basic insights blunted his revolutionary power. If he had rejected panpsychism, he might have let the deeper logic of continuity emerge into some clarity. This logic would appear in the form of an acknowledgment of the supremacy of the potencies of nature naturing. Panpsychism would give way before the premental and prerelational mysteries of nature, mysteries that point to the maternal.

The infinitesimals thus belong in the realm where nature naturing gives way to nature natured. There is a sense in which nature naturing, as the domain of the potencies, hungers to manifest itself as the orders of creation. Taking our clues from Hausman's reconstruction of the infinitesimal, we have seen that the momentum of infinitesimals is from a nondeterminate to a determinate state. Thus it follows that the realm of infinitesimals is the locus of creation. I am persuaded that Peirce held the infinitesimals to be more basic than God in the sense that God, as a manifest order within the world, is also a product of the infinitesimals. Yet God has the unique status of reaching back down into the domain of the potencies. Consequently, both God and the infinitesimals occupy the cleft where the ontological difference manifests itself.

We do not know how or why an infinitesimal gives birth to a manifest order of relevance. Peirce was uncomfortable with the concept/ experience of mystery, and its relation to the presemiotic and maternal. We explored some of the psychological reasons for this in the introduction. Philosophically, his daring sideward glance at the ultimate fissure of the ontological difference brought him into the region where a transfigured conception of nature began to emerge. Most commentators have missed the radicality of his naturalism, preferring to see him in the shopworn categories of earlier versions of naturalism.

In his excellent study of Peirce, Christopher Hookway defines Peirce's naturalism in terms of the ". . . use in logic of facts about the constitution of the human mind and human inquiry."[4] Hookway understands naturalism to be part of the categorial structure of the working sciences. In this sense of the term, it represents an effort to describe the self and its world through broadly defined empirical categories. Hookway is clear that the term "naturalism" can only be applied to Peirce in a loose way, and that it becomes more tenuous when applied to the post-1880s writings. It is precisely this more descriptive sense of naturalism that Peirce challenges in his mature metaphysics when he sees that the heart of nature is the greater nothingness, rather than the domain of facticity. The earlier attempts to locate Peirce within the history of naturalism simply failed to see that he opened a new chapter in the history of the self-understanding of naturalism. As the title of this book indicates, Peirce, almost in spite of himself, provided the first systematic glimpse of what can best be described as an ecstatic naturalism.

Our fourth theme, then, is the depth dimension of a self-transfiguring nature. It is this theme that underlies Peirce's entire categorial structure and that lives as the great unsaid within pragmaticism and the classical American tradition. Peirce's struggles with evolutionary theory took the form that they did because he had only an incomplete glimpse of the scope and inner logic of the new naturalism. His overly generous sense of the role of purpose in the world represents a failed attempt to probe into the mystery of a self-transfiguring nature that continues to spawn semiotic orders of relevance while remaining hidden from the purview of human forms of inquiry.

Peirce wanted to see nature as somehow 'larger' than the domain articulated by the sciences. His analysis of firstness made it possible for him to peel off the cover protecting the preempirical dimension of the world. His attempts to find purpose in the world represented an effort to keep the future open to novel transformations. His rejection of necessitarianism and all mechanistic theories of evolution, cataclysmic or otherwise, points to his awareness that the orders of nature can and do transform themselves in ways that cannot be foreseen. Why does purpose become so important? It is clear that Peirce remains deeply concerned with the role of self-control in the self and in nature at large. The role of self-control is to bring human purposes into some kind of harmony with those of developmental thirds outside of the self. Without purpose, or so it would seem, the self would have no reason for the exercise of self-control. Peirce's stress on purpose thus has its roots in his value theory. We have noted that thirdness, already, as cosmic habit, manifests self-control and reasonableness. Thirdness is thus moral per se. Secondness and firstness are morally neutral, even though they can have strong moral implications when manifest. Thirdness, purpose, self-control, and evolution all belong together. To let go of the ubiquity of purpose is to let go of the good and to lose control over the direction of evolution.

The issue in the transition from descriptive to ecstatic naturalism is that of going beyond the dialectic of efficient and final cause to a deeper sense of the prepurposive potencies emergent from nature naturing. Descriptive naturalism fails to understand the ontological

difference (between *natura naturans* and *natura naturata*). This failure compels it to rely on a series of heroic, but ultimately futile, ma-
neuvers designed to rescue a larger sense of natural growth. The key
here is that growth is not to be located in some kind of panpsychist
purpose, but in the abyss of nature naturing from which the unpre-
dictable potencies continue, via the infinitesimals, to spawn the innumerable orders of the world. When Peirce went beyond earlier theories of the infinitesimals, he provided a means, and there are others,
for coming into the vicinity of the potencies of nature.

By failing to understand the differences between descriptive and
ecstatic forms of naturalism, earlier commentators (notably Buchler
and Goudge) were sometimes driven to see two Peirces, i.e., the naturalistic and the transcendental. This confusion makes sense if one does
not understand the role of the infinitesimals and the greater nothingness in the mature Peirce. The so-called "transcendental" Peirce is
actually the ecstatic naturalist who probed into the ontological difference (not named as such by Peirce) so that he could understand something deeper than purpose and developmental teleology. It is under-
standable that he retained his belief in panpsychism because he had
not yet fathomed the inner momentum of his own categorial structures.

Is this to say that we have some kind of privileged perspective, a
form of *besser verstehen* (better understanding) in which we can claim
to know more about an author's framework than the author could? Or
is this reading a kind of deconstructive inversion of a categorial structure in which the absent dialogue partner is forced into a kind of re-
luctant appearance? The understanding invoked here is more akin to
an emancipatory reenactment in which a vast unthought insight is given
the space within which to find its true measure. The ontological difference was operative in Peirce in a fragmented and ambiguous way,
thus manifesting itself through a kind of transmutation in the guise of
panpsychism and a privileged sense of purpose. Once the unthought
is freed from its broken appearance, it can assume a new clarity and
power that in turn reverberates back through the entire perspective.

Ecstatic naturalism, unlike its more prosaic descriptive cousin,
enters into the momentums of nature naturing and understands that
these presemiotic rhythms are the true grounds for all forms of semiosis
within the manifest orders of the world. At the same time, it listens to
the emergence of the various betweenness structures that obtain within
and around signs and their systems. Signs are what they are because
they move away from the potencies (operative via the infinitesimals)
that spawn them. The representamen, as the original sign in the onto-

logical triad (sign/object/interpretant), leaves the potencies behind so that it can assume its own autonomy. This process is further transformed when the interpretant makes yet further moves away from the powers of origin. Semiotic structures flee from the potencies and develop a kind of inertial momentum that moves them outward into intraworldy involvements.

The ecstasy of nature is not some kind of quasi-human emotion, but lives in the ejective and sign generating power of nature in its naturing. Nature becomes self-transfigured, not through an agapastic movement toward an ideal consummation in the *summum bonum*, but in the opposite directionality, in which infinitesimals make all orders possible. The potencies of nature naturing (the greater nothingness) make it possible for the possibilities of the lesser nothingness to obtain and goad actualities into existence. Nature is always more than the 'sum' of thirds, seconds, and firsts. It is always more than the three universes of firstness, secondness, and thirdness. And it is always more than the God that struggles within the heart of the ontological difference to bring some harmony to the recalcitrant domain of secondness. Peirce grasped the edges of the ontological difference and cleared the way for a radicalization of naturalism. In this radicalization, his own pragmaticism can be reconfigured to better correspond to the abyss within nature, an abyss that comes to meet thought in an ecstatic naturalism that lets go of the panrationalism that blocks the path of piety.

Notes

1. Michael Raposa, *Peirce's Philosophy of Religion* (Bloomington: Indiana University Press, 1989), p. 146.

2. I have examined the logic of signs in three works: *The Community of Interpreters* (Macon, GA: Mercer University Press, 1987), *Nature and Spirit: An Essay in Ecstatic Naturalism* (New York: Fordham University Press, 1992), and *Ecstatic Naturalism: Signs of the World* (Bloomington: Indiana University Press, forthcoming 1994).

3. Raposa, *Peirce's Philosophy of Religion*, p. 150.

4. Christopher Hookway, *Peirce*, in the series *Arguments of the Philosophers*, ed. by Ted Honderich (London: Routledge & Kegan Paul, 1985), p. 52. Hookway's book is one of the best on Peirce. It provides what I would call a middle-of-the-road reading in the sense that it balances the competing aspects of Peirce's perspective while shying away from the more radical dimensions in Peirce's metaphysics.

Annotated Bibliography

Students of Peirce will want to start with *A Comprehensive Bibliography of the Published Works of Charles Sanders Peirce with a Bibliography of Secondary Studies, Second Edition, Revised*, ed. Kenneth Laine Ketner, with the assistance of Arthur Franklin Stewart and Claude V. Bridges (Bowling Green, Ohio: Philosophy Documentation Center, 1986). For secondary literature after 1986, students are directed to the *Transactions of the Charles S. Peirce Society*, a quarterly journal in American philosophy.

There are a number of excellent full-length studies of Peirce. The following list is not meant to be exhaustive, but does give an indication of the scope and richness of Peirce studies since the 1930s. The books are presented in the order of their publication.

Charles Peirce's Empiricism, by Justus Buchler (New York: Columbia University Press, 1939). Reprinted by Octagon Books in 1980. This book represents Buchler's Columbia University Ph.D. dissertation and presents Peirce from the standpoint of his critical commonsensism, his pragmatism, his theory of the sciences, and his empiricism.

The Thought of C. S. Peirce, by Thomas A. Goudge (Toronto: University of Toronto Press, 1950). Reprinted by Dover in 1969. Goudge develops the thesis, foreshadowed in Buchler, that there are two Peirces, the sturdy empirical pragmatist and the questionable transcendentalist. His book is an excellent study of all aspects of Peirce's thought and is especially helpful on Peirce's philosophy of mathematics.

Peirce and Pragmatism, by W. B. Gallie (London: Penguin, 1952). Reprinted by Dover in 1966. This is a brief but highly readable introductory text and still represents one of the best entrance points for the beginning student.

The Pragmatic Philosophy of C. S. Peirce, by Manley Thompson (Chicago: University of Chicago Press, 1953). A solid overall introduction to Peirce's conception of method, the sciences, and the later cosmology. Thompson stresses the pragmatic and empirico-scientific elements in Peirce and locates his enterprise against the history of science.

The Development of Peirce's Philosophy, by Murray Murphey (Cambridge, Mass.: Harvard University Press, 1961). This is still regarded by many as the best text on Peirce and presents his thought from the standpoint of distinct stages of growth. Murphey is equally home in the logic, mathematics, metaphysics, and theory of method.

Charles Peirce and Scholastic Realism: A Study of Peirce's Relation to John Duns Scotus, by John F. Boler (Seattle: University of Washington Press, 1963). Must reading for anyone concerned with the metaphysical foundations of Peirce's conception of realism. This is more than a study in the history of ideas and probes into the philosophical aspects of Peirce's analysis of universals.

Charles Peirce, by Thomas S. Knight, The *Great American Thinkers* Series (New York: Twayne, 1965). A more basic general introduction that has a helpful account of the semiotic theory.

Peirce's Theory of Signs as Foundation for Pragmatism, by John J. Fitzgerald (The Hague: Mouton, 1966). One of the first systematic studies of Peirce's semiotics, with particular attention paid to the nature of the dynamical interpretant. This work is also a fine introduction to Peirce's overall perspective.

Charles S. Peirce: On Norms and Ideals, by Vincent O. Potter, S.J. (Amherst: University of Massachusetts Press, 1967). An important study that correlates the normative sciences with the human process and with the universe as a whole. Self-control and the growth of concrete reasonableness are central concepts in Potter's analysis.

Charles Peirce's Theory of Scientific Method, by Francis E. Reilly, S.J. (New York: Fordham University Press, 1970). A developmental study of internal aspects of Peirce's broader conception of science, with particular focus on what Reilly calls Peirce's "moderate fallibilism."

Peirce's Concept of Sign, by Douglas Greenlee (The Hague: Mouton, 1973). A slightly dated but still useful introduction to Peirce's semiotic theory.

Evolutionary Metaphysics: The Development of Peirce's Theory of Categories, by Joseph L. Esposito (Athens: Ohio University Press, 1980). A rich analysis of the evolution of Peirce's three primal categories that pays attention to the Kantian and post-Kantian traditions with which Peirce was in dialogue. The book concludes with a useful visual diagram of the various permutations of Peirce's categorial structure.

The Philosophy of Charles S. Peirce: A Critical Introduction, by Robert Almeder (Totowa, N.J.: Rowman and Littlefield, 1980). An analysis of Peirce's epistemology in the context of some more recent theories, e.g., Quine, Rescher, Kneale, and Kuhn. While this work is too focused for beginning students, it is a valuable guide to some of the more technical implications emergent from Peirce's theory of science and epistemology.

Charles S. Peirce: From Pragmatism to Pragmaticism, by Karl-Otto Apel, translated by John Michael Krois (Amherst: University of Massachusetts Press, 1981). This is an excellent and thoughtful guide to Peirce by one of Germany's leading semioticians and philosophers. Apel locates Peirce within and against Kant and places a great deal of emphasis on his normative conception of community.

Peirce's Conception of God: A Developmental Study, by Donna M. Orange (Lubbock, Tex.: Institute for Studies in Pragmaticism, 1984). This was the first detailed study of Peirce's philosophical theology in the context of his philosophical development. Orange contrasts Peirce and Royce in an interesting manner.

Peirce, by Christopher Hookway (London: Routledge and Kegan Paul, 1985). This is an excellent book for more advanced students, focusing on Peirce's argumentative strategies with a particular focus on his epistemology. Hookway adopts a middle-of-the-road strategy in the sense that he tries to show the coherence and consistency of Peirce's perspective, while downplaying the radicality of the late cosmology.

Creativity and the Philosophy of C. S. Peirce, by Douglas Anderson (Dordrecht: Martinus Nijhoff, 1987). A well-written and thorough account of the various forms of creativity in Peirce, from his theory of method to his later cosmology.

Peirce's Approach to the Self: A Semiotic Perspective on Human Subjectivity, by Vincent M. Colapietro (Albany: SUNY Press, 1989). This is a rich and evocative analysis of Peirce's conception of the semiotic self that focuses on the role of purpose and the inner semiotic life. There are interesting analyses of the relation between Peirce and such figures as Umberto Eco.

Peirce's Philosophy of Religion, by Michael L. Raposa (Bloomington: Indiana University Press, 1989). This is a very thorough analysis of all aspects of Peirce's conception of religious experience and its object. Raposa's conception of "theosemiotic" has become the center of much discussion and has proven to be a fruitful one for semiotic theory in general.

Charles S. Peirce: An Intellectual Biography, by Gérard Deledalle, translated by Susan Petrilli, Introduction by Susan Petrilli (Amsterdam: John Benjamins, 1990). A brief and crisp introduction by a leading French philosopher and historian. Deledalle focuses on the logic and semiotics as they pertain to Peirce's system of the sciences.

Charles S. Peirce's Evolutionary Philosophy, by Carl R. Hausman (Cambridge: Cambridge University Press, 1993). Hausman's book stands in the same league with Murphey's. It is a detailed and thorough analysis of Peirce's realism and advances into new territory with its rethinking of the concepts of infinitesimals and continuity. It places a great deal of emphasis on the semiotic (semeiotic) dimensions of objects and stresses the centrality of the ground and the dynamic object.

Index

223

About the Author

Robert S. Corrington is associate professor of philosophical theology in the Graduate and Theological Schools of Drew University. He has written forty articles in the areas of American philosophy, semiotics, theology, and metaphysics and has authored three book-length studies, *The Community of Interpreters* (Macon, Ga.: Mercer University Press, 1987), *Nature and Spirit: An Essay in Ecstatic Naturalism* (New York: Fordham University Press, 1992), and *Ecstatic Naturalism: Signs of the World* (Bloomington: Indiana University Press, forthcoming 1994). As co-editor he worked with *Pragmatism Considers Phenomenology* (Savage, Md.: The Center for Advanced Research in Phenomenology and University Press of America, 1987), Justus Buchler's *Metaphysics of Natural Complexes, Second Expanded Edition* (Albany: SUNY Press, 1990), and *Nature's Perspectives: Prospects for Ordinal Metaphysics* (Albany: SUNY Press, 1991). Past president of the Karl Jaspers Society of North America, he currently serves on the executive boards of the Semiotic Society of America and the Highlands Institute. Dr. Corrington is the recipient of the Church Divinity, Douglas Greenlee, and John William Miller prizes.